Sai Baba
AVATAR
A new journey into power and glory

Howard Murphet

Birth Day Publishing Company
San Diego, California, U.S.A.

DISTRIBUTED BY
SATHYA SAI BOOK CENTER
OF AMERICA
P.O. BOX 278
TUSTIN, CA 92681-0278, USA

This book may be obtained at your local bookstore or you may order it directly from Birth Day Publishing Company, at a cost of $3.60 for the paperback edition or $8.25 for the hardbound copy, plus 60¢ for postage and handling. Send check or money order to Birth Day Publishing Company, P. O. Box 7722, San Diego, California 92107.

Library of Congress Catalog Number: 77-83643

ISBN 0-9600958-2-9

Published by Birth Day Publishing Company
P. O. Box 7722, San Diego, California 92107, USA

This volume is respectfully dedicated to Bhagavan Sri Satya Sai Baba and his divine mission to rebuild for modern man the ancient road to the Truth of Being.

Acknowledgements

I wish to acknowledge my indebtedness to the many who have made this book possible and assisted in its production. Among these, my special thanks go to the following: the devotees who were willing to share their precious experiences with the world under their own true names; to my wife for her loving help and constant encouragement; to five karma yogins of the West who, with no motive save the joy of service to Sai Baba, have given most valuable assistance in their different ways — Dr. Samuel H. Sandweiss and Mr. Douglas Mahr of California, and Mrs. Lynette Penrose of Australia; to artist Larry Smith for providing the design element of the book, and to Lee Gerlach who did the final editing.

Finally, I would say to the many who, after reading my earlier work on Sai Baba, wrote requesting more information; thank you for your kind letters which helped to spur on my writing efforts, and I sincerely hope that each of you will find the answers to his questions on the profound subject of Sai Baba and his Path in the following pages.

NOTE: The words — *Arathi*, *Prashanthi*, *Puttaparthi*, *Sathya* and *Shakthi*, spelled correctly here, appear throughout the book in the form — *Arati*, *Prashanti*, *Puttaparti*, *Satya* and *Shakti*. This is done as an aid to correct pronunciation, as the *th* in these words sounds like *t*.

CONTENTS

FOREWORD

For the sake of those readers who have not read my earlier book, or any others, on the life of Satya Sai Baba, I should give here the main facts about his background, birth and childhood.

About the year 1872 — or earlier — a young, itinerant fakir settled in the (then) Bombay State. He became known as *Sai Baba* — a term of respect. He performed astounding miracles and gave spiritual teachings to the devotees (Hindu, Muslim, and others) who gathered around him.

His fame spread slowly in those days of slow communication, but between the years 1910 and 1918 (when he passed away), there was a steady stream of visitors to Shirdi. Before leaving his body, Sai Baba told one of his devotees (Sri H. S. Dixit, then solicitor and member of the Legislative Council in Bombay) that he would return as a boy in eight years.

On November 23, 1926, eight years after the death of Sai Baba of Shirdi, a boy was born in the remote village of Puttaparti, Andhra Pradesh, and named Satyanarayana.

There were many remarkable things about the child Satya, as he was called. Reports state that he manifested supernormal powers, often materializing, among other things, sweets and fruits for his companions, and — for sick friends — fresh, healing herbs that grew only in the far Himalayas.

After elementary education in the district, he was sent to a high school where his elder brother was a teacher. The hope of the family was that little Satya, a born leader, would graduate qualified for a good position in government service.

But early in 1940, when the boy was thirteen, he went through a drastic psycho-physical experience that seemed like a mysterious illness, with periods of unconsciousness and great pain. It lasted some two months. At the end of it Satya's powers seemed to have increased, and included such things as quoting long passages of Sanskrit that he had never ostensibly learned and giving erudite discourses on Vedanta.

Puzzled and worried by such phenomena, his father, one day during May, 1940, asked the boy who and what he really was. The answer came: "I am Sai Baba." No one in the village knew what that meant, but Satya's father feared for a while that his son might be possessed by the spirit of a Muslim fakir.

Following the announcement of his identity, devotees began to gather around the young Teacher. Stories told me by early disciples, and diaries I have read, give a picture of a tremendous flow of amazing *leelas* (miracles) from the young Satya Sai Baba. And also, right from the start, he gave spiritual instruction to the people who came to spend time with him at his ashram.

It was in 1957 that Satya Sai Baba first began giving public discourses in larger centres of population, and thousands of people flocked to hear him. For years a journey to his ashram at Puttaparti, where no roads or railways went, involved some travel on foot or by bullock-cart, with, in some seasons, waist-deep streams to cross. One's interest had to be strong to face the rugged journey. Even in 1964 the Indian theosophist, who first mentioned Baba's name to me, though he wanted to visit Puttaparti, thought the trip a bit too arduous. In fact, however, by that time there was a road of sorts to the ashram, and when we first met Baba, early in 1965, a number of keen western seekers had already found their way to him.

..:   ...   .

I have written this second book about Satya Sai Baba for several reasons. For one, a constant flow of letters from appreciative people of many countries, who have read *Sai Baba, Man of Miracles*, shows a genuine hunger for more information about the living God-Man of India. But perhaps my main reason for writing was that, after a period of rumination and contemplation on the subject, followed by a return journey into the realm of Divine Power, Love and Glory, I felt a strong need to say more, to make one more attempt to express that which is ultimately inexpressible.

I could at least add to the record some further uplifting experiences, and try to give a more understanding picture of the Avatar, and the world-redeeming Truths he stands for. I hoped that, if I could take the reader a little deeper into the significance of the mysterious God-Man, I might help him find new insights into the Man-God, which is himself.

If those aims are achieved for even a few people, I will be satisfied. Whatever the harvest, credit is due to the helpers who gave me their stories, with permission to use their names. Above all, it is due to the inspiration and grace of Satya Sai Baba, himself. For me the writing of the book has been a *sadhana,* and its own greatest reward.

1

STORIES AND SEQUELS

Thou hast given me seats in homes not my own.
Thou hast brought the distance near and made a brother
of a stranger.

—RABINDRANATH TAGORE.

Suddenly the coast of India lay below us, like a scene from an old dream: a palm tree dotted here and there on the parched earth, shimmering waves of heat, a long yellow beach, white lines of surf on the edge of the Bay of Bengal, house-tops of Madras. It seemed a hundred years since we had been a part of India's life, but it was not quite four.

In June 1970, we had said goodbye to Satya Sai Baba, and now in April 1974, with excitement and a little anxiety in our hearts, we were heading back towards him. There had been reports that the crowds around him had grown tremendously, and that he had become busier than ever with a great educational program.

"Perhaps he will not even see us," Iris said, as we circled above the airport.

I was more hopeful than that, but I had the uneasy feeling that things would not be the same as they had been in the far-off golden 'sixties. We had often comforted ourselves in our exile with memories of those years with Baba, some of which I recorded in my book, *Sai Baba, Man of Miracles.*

We remembered how, when he gave us his farewell blessings at Whitefield in 1970, he was truly the Divine Mother, and we were his children, setting off on a journey of necessity. But we would return, he assured us. Among the gifts he had materialized at parting was a small metal container, full of fragrant *vibhuti,* holy ash.

"Use some every day. It will never be empty," he had said.

Often during our four years away, the container had been almost empty, and we had felt downhearted about our apparent lack of faith. But then, miraculously, each time a little more vibhuti would appear in the bottom of the container, and we would be delighted. Though our faith seemed small and wavering, Baba's compassion was large. The container had never become quite empty.

Now we carried it with us, hopefully. There was still a little in the bottom, and we hoped that Baba would fill it to the brim before our eyes, as a symbol of his overflowing grace and love.

Sai Baba had been very much in our thoughts during the years between our departure and return. His image had not shrunk at all in the hard clear light of the scientific, materialistic West. In fact, the long view and much reflection had made us even surer of certain realities — the genuineness of his never-abating supernormal powers, the aura of divinity that clung about him.

We had some long stop-overs on the roundabout air journey from India to our ancestral home in Australia. The first was a three months stay in England where we attended as often as possible the weekly meetings at the Sai Centre in the home of Mr. S. Sitaram of Pinner, Middlesex.

Incidentally, something happened in England that recalled to our minds an event that took place in India in 1968, when we were staying with Baba and a small party in Hyderabad.

Iris and I, with Markell and Bob Raymer, wanted to see the museum. Baba asked one of his devotees in Hyderabad, Doctor Hemchand, to drive us there. The doctor had a large practice and was very busy that day. He respectfully pleaded that someone else might find it more convenient to take us. But Baba preferred instead to change the day of our visit so that the doctor himself could drive us there. Afterwards we saw the reason for this.

It was extremely hot weather in Hyderabad at the time, and on the return journey the doctor invited us to call at his home to see his wife and have a cool drink. His wife, he said, was just recovering from a heart attack. We had almost reached his house when I was suddenly overcome by pain and a terrible weakness that made me perspire profusely. The doctor and Bob Raymer, one on each side, practically carried me into the house and stretched me out on a couch.

Dr. Hemchand thought the symptoms suggested a heart attack, and said I must lie still until the heart specialist, who was attending his wife, arrived; he was expected within the hour and could do a proper diagnosis. Then the doctor telephoned to let Baba know what had happened.

When the phone rang in E. Krishnamurti's house, where he was staying, Baba was sitting talking to a group. Quite contrary to his custom, he went and answered the phone himself. "I'll come now," he told the doctor.

Within a short time Baba's car pulled up outside Doctor Hemchand's house. As he walked towards the front door, Bob Raymer was standing in the garden, thinking — he told me afterwards — "I wonder what's wrong with Howard's heart."

Baba must have picked up the thought for he stopped in front of Bob, pointed his finger, and said firmly: "There is *nothing* wrong with his heart."

Inside, he patted me and spoke like a sweet mother; then with a look of great power in his eyes he waved his hand and produced vibhuti to rub on my chest. "The heat," he said, "you've had a heat stroke."

But the heart specialist, after all the modern tests were made, decided that I had suffered a mild heart attack. Stretched out in Swami's long station wagon, I was taken to E. Krishnamurti's house and put to bed for two months. My wife, who is a qualified nurse, looked after me. Dr. Hemchand came every day, the specialist several times a week. Baba, for the few days he remained in Hyderabad, came to see me often. I gathered the impression that he thought the rest in bed would do me no harm, and the experience in that house would be good *sadhana*. It proved to be so.

Assuring me that there was nothing whatever wrong with my heart, and that he would be back, Baba went off to make a previously arranged visit to Africa. The Raymers went with him.

The treatment for a heart attack went on. But it was pleasant in that air-conditioned bedroom, with so many interesting visitors dropping in. K. Satyamurti, son of E. Krishnamurti, often sat by the bed, his face glowing with light while he told us the wonderful story of how he came to Baba. Other Hyderabad devotees came and regaled us with tales of their Sai experiences. I could not have had better therapy for mind and body.

The closest members of our own family could not have treated us with more consideration and generosity than this hospitable family in Hyderabad. Baba erases all caste prejudice among his devotees, thus, though the Brahmin cook was a little touchy about Iris going into his kitchen to prepare special dishes for us, the Sai link made us completely at one with Krishnamurti, Satyamurti and the ladies of their household, who were Brahmins in the true sense.

Baba returned from Africa and word went around that he was coming to Hyderabad. I had flu symptoms and was given heavy doses of antibiotics to cure me before Swami arrived. The result was that, the day he arrived, I was feeling horribly weak.

That night Baba slept in a room on the floor above, almost directly over me. Mentally, I asked him to give me strength. I even visualized an etheric tube running from my chest up to Baba, and prayed him to pour *shakti* (strength and vitality) through the tube into my body.

A great change came over me during the night, and in the morning I felt quite well and strong again. Baba came in before breakfast and asked how I felt.

"Thank you, Swami, for sending me that strength in the night," I said.

He smiled. "I put it right in there." He touched my chest at the point where I had visualized the tube entering.

Baba kindly arranged for us to go for a few weeks to his house, "Brindavan" at Whitefield, saying that Madras was still too hot for us to return to our residence there. He, himself, was going to Prasanti Nilayam, which was also too hot for my convalescence.

We were presented with airline tickets to Bangalore and at the airport there found Sai devotees waiting in a car to take us to Whitefield. In the house at "Brindavan" beds had been erected in the side room that Swami mostly uses for interviews. In another room electrical equipment for cooking had been installed. We found that Baba, with his usual care and meticulous attention to detail, had written to his caretaker there, Mr. Ramabrahma, and other devotees in the area, arranging everything for our comfort, including a car and driver to take us into Bangalore whenever we needed to go.

It was strangely empty at "Brindavan" without Baba, but we did have the pleasure of many long talks and walks with the late Mr. M. Dixit, a Sai devotee since the Shirdi days, and one evening we had an incredible experience with a cobra.

We were about to go to bed in the interview room when we saw a large white cobra through the open doorway. He was less than two metres away from the door at the edge of the concrete floor of the little verandah. It was dark outside but we could see him dimly by the light shining from the door and windows of our room.

There was an electric light in the ceiling of the verandah so we switched that on in order to get a better view and stood in the doorway watching. When the bright light fell on him, the cobra did not show any alarm or hostility. He remained quite still, body raised some three feet above the ground, unswaying but with his hood spread. On the back of the hood, facing us, was the outline of a human face — like one painted on a mask. The eyes seemed to be looking back at us as we stood staring at its weird beauty. From our level on the doorstep, we could see the cobra's real eyes facing towards the dark of the garden. He could also see us, of course.

As the cobra was somewhat to the left of the door we moved, after a time, to the open window on the same side, and had an even closer view of the strange markings on the white hood. It seemed amazing that the snake did not move when we were so near, but remained obligingly upright and statue still, while we studied him for some ten minutes. Then we put off the lights, closed the door, and went to bed.

The cobra is a sacred symbol of Shiva and Sai Baba is considered an Incarnation of Shiva; so some of our Indian friends maintained that we had been blessed with a darshan this way.*

In the cool, clear air of Whitefield I soon recuperated from the debility left by my malady, whatever it was. But I was constantly reminded by friends to take great care of my heart. All seemed to tacitly agree that Baba, who is always right, must have been wrong this time.

Nearly two years later in England I decided to find out what the heart specialists there thought of the situation. Their verdict after X-rays, electrocardiograms and all the blood tests had been taken, was an echo of Swami's voice in the garden: "There is nothing wrong with your heart." The specialist added: "I find it hard to believe that you had a real heart attack that time in India; you are not the coronary type."

Coronary type or not, I thought I was having a heavy heart attack about a year later in America. The same ache in the left arm as I had felt in Hyderabad, but this time there was also a murderous pain that set me vibrating like a dynamo from head to foot.

At the hospital where I was taken quickly by ambulance the doctors were told of my experience in India, and shown the medical documents from there, and also from England. They decided that this time the condition of my heart would be settled beyond question.

They put me in an intensive care ward, where for twenty-four hours the action of my heart was shown on a television screen, and recorded on graphs spread around the walls of the ward. Other tests were made and I was never out of sight of the nurse in charge. At the end of it all, the doctor in charge of my case said: "Whatever caused your violent attack it was certainly not your heart; there is *nothing* wrong with that. To diagnose the cause I will have to do more tests on other internal organs."

As the weekend in hospital had already proved alarmingly expensive,

I begged leave to have the further tests done after I returned to Australia. All symptoms having by then disappeared, the doctor agreed.

California eased the shock of the contrast between timeless India and the West; it is a kind of half-way house between the two. One feels there a reaching out towards new horizons of consciousness. This is an intangible thing in the mental sphere of the place, and a tangible thing in the many groups intent on the spiritual search — most groups born of the Eastern culture.

It was almost as if the aura of India still shone around us during the months we spent there, attending meetings at the Sai Baba Centres that were springing up in ever-increasing numbers, visiting, or going on outings with our many Sai Family friends, some of whom we had first met in India.

We spent time as guests of the well-known devotees, Walter and Elsie Cowan in Orange County, and while there visited Elsie's sister and her husband, Floy and Carl Anderson. Carl is a keen coin collector, so I took along the American gold coin that Swami had taken out of the air in 1967 when we were in the Horsley Hills with him.

Readers of *Sai Baba, Man of Miracles* will recall that Baba had asked me the year of my birth, and when I told him, remarked that he would get me an American coin minted that same year, but now out of circulation. Sitting there in a room in the Circuit House on the peak of the hills, he had circled his hand in front of us, and produced a gold ten-dollar coin with the date "1906" stamped on it. It looked quite new. Yet he had said he would "get" it, not "make" it. So it must have been old. I had never seen such a coin and did not know if it was really genuine, made-in-America, or not. Now from this expert coin collector I hoped to find out.

Carl pushed the spoiled cat Charlie off his knee unceremoniously, and eagerly examined the coin.

"These ten-dollar pieces are rare; I have never managed to get one, though I have a 'twenty'," he said. He pointed to the thirteen stars around the head of the figure of Liberty, remarking that there were only thirteen states when the United States was founded. Then he took his magnifying glass and inspected the coin for some time.

"Look," he said, handing me the glass. "See the tiny 's' beneath the feet of the eagle?"

I found it, though I would not have done so with the naked eye. "That means," he went on, "the coin was minted in San Francisco." Going through his catalogues, he told me how many were minted that year (1906) and their present quoted price — a great deal more than their face value. "But they are seldom up for sale," he concluded, cocking a questioning eye at me. "Neither is this one for sale, Carl. Sorry."

Though, unlike his wife, Carl was not a Sai devotee, he understood my feelings.

2
A TALE
FROM DOWN UNDER

One can taste devotion and love of God only through his Incarnation.

SRI RAMAKRISHNA.

During our year in America, my first book on Sai Baba was brought out by its London publishers. Copies of it were appearing in the Sai centres of California just before we left. The last state we visited was luminous Hawaii, where the Theosophical Lodge asked me to give a talk, and I spoke to them about Sai Baba. Then we flew to Fiji, the final stop before Australia.

Staying at the home of Mr. S. B. Desai in Suva, we found ourselves at the center of a whirlpool of Sai Baba activity. Many Indians there had already been to Puttaparti, and there were hundreds of devotees on the island. As my book had preceded us, there were thousands more who wanted to hear about Baba. So at the public gatherings it was like being back in India, with the rhythmic drums, the chanting of the bhajans, the eager faces drinking in every word spoken from the platform about the "Living God in India," as the press of Fiji calls him.

Apart from the public meetings, groups came every day to the house of Mr. Desai to talk to us about the one subject that seemed to matter to them — Sai Baba, his teachings, his miracles and their hope that he might one day come to Fiji. Then, after a few days of that perfumed Fiji hospitality, we at last turned our faces towards home, with perhaps more misgivings than Ulysses felt when he finally sighted the shores of Ithaca.

It was over eleven years since we had left Australia. Part of that time was spent in England and other European countries but almost six years of it in India. Now we felt that our home was everywhere, yet in a sense nowhere. If there were any roots that pulled on us at all, they were spiritual ones in India.

Australia soon confirmed our fears. Though the citizens are a friendly, open-hearted people, the country as a whole seems to know no other God but Mammon. The few earnest spiritual searchers we had known back in the far-off 'fifties had been scattered by the winds of time. No one had heard of Sai Baba, and we felt that no one wanted to. My book on Swami, which had raised such a stir in Fiji, fell on barren soil in my homeland.

In the Blue Mountains, some fifty miles from Sydney, Iris became the matron of a nursing home, and I settled down, temporarily, to write a biography of Madame H. P. Blavatsky. Our physical isolation from people of the same main interest as ourselves was relieved only by a very occasional visit from Arthur Poolman, a Sai devotee who lived in Melbourne.

But whenever we began to wonder if we had ever really lived that other-dimensional life with Sai Baba, a letter would arrive from an appreciative reader, showing that my book had struck a spark in some far corner of the world or, better still, we would get a clear sign that we were not forgotten, that our Sadguru was taking good care of both our temporal and spiritual needs.

The sudden appearance of a hernia put me in hospital, and led to a continuation of the medical search interrupted in America. The surgeon, when he heard the story and looked at the reports I had brought from America and India, decided to have further tests done on my heart, and to investigate the condition of any other internal organs that could have caused the trouble. Not until that was done would he operate on my hernia. But he could find nothing wrong anywhere. Echoing Baba, and the specialists of two other continents, he said "Your heart is quite sound. You have, it appears, at some time in the past had a mild heart attack. It *could* have been at the time you thought, in India. But such an attack often happens while people are asleep, and they know nothing about it until it shows up some time later on an E. C. G."

About my violent and expensive pain in America, he said: "I have a suspicion about that, but can only test it during the operation."

Afterwards I asked him if he had solved the mystery. "Yes," he replied, "some marks on the intestine confirm my suspicion that you were suffering a strangulated hernia. You could not see the hernia on the outside at the time, but the intestine was coming through an opening, and was pinched by the walls. This causes agonizing pain."

He went on to say that such strangulation usually needs prompt treatment to prevent gangrene setting in. In fact, he said, I was very lucky that the muscular vise had let go itself, and relaxed the hernia.

I remembered then how my wife and I had called on the name of Sai Baba when the pain was at its height, and how it had suddenly stopped. Mentally I thanked Baba again.

But does the Divine Hand stretch out to help only the devotees of the Lord, or others too? And what are the necessary qualifications for receiving such help?

Elfin-faced Rhoda May drove her sporty car too fast, smoked too much, read too little, thought that money grew on trees, and that God, like Santa Claus, was a nice fairy tale that belonged to time gone by. But all this was a facade to cover up an inner emptiness, a need for love and for a meaning to life.

"When I first saw your wife," she told me later, "I felt as if all the burdens had been lifted from my shoulders. It was — as if I had known her always."

One day, soon after they met, she said to Iris: "You have some special knowledge that I would like to have. Will you teach me?"

Iris knew what she meant and tried gently, in small doses, to give her some ideas about Vedanta, Bhakti and Baba. The latter seemed to have immediate appeal, but how deep? we wondered.

Soon after this she revealed to Iris that she had discovered a lump in one of her breasts. Being herself a trained nurse of long experience, Rhoda feared the worst because the lump seemed to be anchored, and it hurt when she tried to manipulate it. Iris examined the swelling and thought, too, that it was cancerous. "You must see a doctor at once," she said.

A senior doctor at the hospital where Rhoda worked examined her and confirmed that the growth was malignant. She should, he told her, have immediate surgery, but unfortunately he, himself, was leaving the next day on several weeks holiday. This gave Rhoda a good excuse for delay.

"Leave it till you come back," she said.

"Well, all right, but remind me as soon as I return."

Rhoda was about forty, and the mother of a young family. She knew well enough that the only cure for breast cancer was surgery, and that this would mean not only the removal of the breast, but also part of the pectoral muscle that supports the breast, and the lymph nodes under the arm. Such radical mastectomy was, she knew, the standard and only safe treatment. It is a disfiguring and usually traumatic operation.

Her mind rebelled against it. Yet the only alternative was death. She had read some statistics soon after the discovery of the lump and was alarmed to find that, for women of her age group, breast cancer was the leading cause of death — not only from the actual malignant growth in the breast, but from its rapid spread to other parts of the body, notably the lungs, liver, skeleton and brain.

She said nothing to her husband about her condition while she fought the inner battle between her horror of an operation, and her fear of death which was certain if she did not have the operation — and that soon.

She decided not to have the operation, and told my wife so. Iris was startled. "But surely — the alternative is worse...you want to live, don't you?"

"Yes — but *you* are going to cure me."

Iris was more startled. Miraculous healing was not one of her lines. After considering the statement for a while she said: "*I* can't cure you, but Sai Baba can. Perhaps he *will* — we must try."

Iris took the little gold cross that Rhoda posessed but would never wear because she was hostile to church religion. We put this on one of Swami's pictures and asked him to bless it; then gave it back to her and told her to wear it. In the meantime Iris had given her a packet of Baba's vibhuti with instruction to rub some on the affected breast daily. Above all, she must pray fervently and with all the faith she could muster. We, too, prayed to Swami every day for a cure, and that this lost and lonely soul might be brought to the acceptance of Divine Reality.

Before the doctor returned from his holiday the lump seemed to Rhoda to be getting smaller. So, feeling sure that a cure was taking place, she was careful not to remind him about the operation.

But a couple of weeks later, when he was visiting the hospital, he remembered, himself, and decided to give her another examination before arranging the surgery.

"That's strange," he said, "the growth seems to have vanished. But it must be there." He examined the breast slowly and carefully. "No", he concluded, "I can find no trace of it. Inexplicable!"

Rhoda, happy beyond telling, thought it would be no use trying to explain the nature of the cure, so she let him indulge in the usual cliches about the unexpected about-turns Nature sometimes makes. Anyway, he was very pleased about the cure for her sake.

Iris and I looked forward to hearing, someday, what Swami had to say about the event — if he said anything at all. Sometimes he speaks; sometimes he remains silent on these matters. Meantime Rhoda, herself, began to change noticeably, becoming a little calmer, a little more self-confident as life's deeper meaning began to dawn in her soul.

As the years passed among the lights and shades of our homeland, we realised the truth of Narada's bhakti teaching, that Divine Love does not diminish when the pupil is separated from the physical presence of the Master, that, in fact, it becomes more intense and deeper in its understanding. Yet we discovered, too, that — for us at any rate — the tangible presence, the close proximity, the sight of the beloved face, the sound of the sweet voice can give something that no amount of meditation and inner visualization of the Sadguru can give. We knew, without being able to explain it, the inestimable value of having a Sadguru alive in the world. And our longing for another sojourn near Sai Baba's physical form increased with the progress of the suns.

Economic and other considerations held this possibility beyond our reach for a time, but then the cogs of circumstance slipped into place, and we found ourselves aboard a ship bound for Singapore. Ships, with their relaxing, out-of-time atmosphere, have always been our favourite means of travel. But from Singapore we planned to fly across to India.

Among the items we bought at Singapore, that sparkling Mecca of shoppers, was a new style electric torch that gave a white light and a red light. It had an attractive design, and we began to discuss if we should get one for Swami, too. Though we knew that he did not usually accept presents, we wanted very much to take him some little thing as a sign of our love. But was this the right little thing? Well, it was a new design, and was unlikely to be in the shops of India, where imports were severely restricted. It was very light-weight, an advantage in air travel. But was it good enough? Would he like it? Would he accept it, or for that matter, anything? We would be offering it as an outer token of our feelings, and we knew from experience that when one offers flowers with devotion, he accepts them. After long debate, we decided to take this rather poor little gift to the one who commands the world's treasures. If there was no ego behind our action, he might not reject the gift.

And now, at last, the turbulent Bay of Bengal lay curling against the sandy beaches below us. The country looked brown and burned-up by the sun as we turned to land at Madras airport.

3
WONDERS
AT ADYAR

And I will speak to thee of that wisdom and vision which, when known, there is nothing else for thee to know.

BHAGAVAD GITA

The long, polished table in the dining room of Leadbeater Chambers, on the Theosophical Estate of Adyar, was nearly full that night for dinner. Being there was like another echo from a dream. Some of the Indian servants, gliding silently behind the chairs, were the same individuals we had known when we lived here in the 'sixties. But only two from the old group were among the diners at the table, and there was a difference of atmosphere.

Talk was free and open, and we quickly learned that two of the diners — a woman from Persia and a New Zealander — were Sai Baba devotees. One of the men, who introduced himself as Sigvaldi Hjalmansson of Iceland, told me that a publisher in his country was bringing out an Icelandic edition of my book on Baba, and that he had been asked to translate it. "I hope you will help me to meet the subject — Sai Baba," he said.

I knew that he edited the Journal of the Theosophical group in Iceland, and this was considered by many to be the best of the Theosophical magazines. I was pleased with his news.

In the old days a mention of Sai Baba's name would have brought a disapproving silence at this table. Why, I never quite knew. But I had heard some of the old hands say there was no need to go searching beyond the perimeter of the Estate for spiritual knowledge, that it was all here in the books of the great Theosophical leaders. I was aware, too, that they had a phobia about what they called "phenomena," stemming back, no doubt, to the 1880's when the early Theosophical Society, and Madame H. P. Blavatsky, herself, suffered hostile public reaction to her displays of wonder-working powers.

But, having done long research here in the Archives at the International Headquarters to write biographies of the two great founders, Madame H. P. Blavatsky and Colonel H. S. Olcott, I felt sure that those two, at least, would not agree to such a restricted outlook. Both had demonstrated in their lives that spiritual gold is where you find it. In their travels throughout India and the world, both had sought outstanding teachers, yogis and wonder-workers. One of the stated objects of their Society, indeed its earliest object, was the investigation of the latent powers in man and nature — those yogic and divine powers of which the ancient Rishis spoke, and which were now being abundantly demonstrated by Sai Baba.

Evidently during the four years we had been away some radical change had come about. Now practically the only subject at the dinner table was Sai Baba. Coralie Leyland, the New Zealander, mentioned that she had heard he would be visiting Madras in the next few days. This was great news to many at the table, not excluding us. As we had to stay in Madras for a couple of weeks to attend to some private business, including discussions with my Indian publishers, we were delighted with the thought that we might see Swami before going to his place at Whitefield, near Bangalore. But then we remembered that many rumors about Baba's movements were without foundation.

As soon as dinner was over, one of the two old-timers got up quickly and left the table. He had not joined in the conversation, and I sensed that he did not approve of all the talk about Sai Baba. The other one of the two, Charles Shores, eighty-four-year old Theosophist, and Bishop of the Liberal Catholic Church, was sitting beside me. He had joined in the conversation. Now he lingered and said to me: "I know it's difficult, but I would be grateful if you could arrange for me to meet Sai Baba."

I was pleased to hear this from our old friend, even if it simply meant he wished a cure for his stricken legs. (He now went about in a wheelchair.)

I warned him: "Baba does not cure everyone, Charles."

"Oh, it's not that, though I would like him to tell me what's wrong with my legs. But I just want to be in his presence, and feel his Divine Radiance."

Another pleasant surprise — not to say shock — came when I called on my publishers. As soon as the manager had greeted me and seated me in his office, he telephoned to all his top executives. Within a few minutes his office was full of them. Work stopped for the morning while they questioned me about Sai Baba. I discovered, to my surprise and joy, that through publishing my book, they had practically all, in various degrees, become devotees of Baba. It was all bhakti and no business that morning.

They insisted on providing a car to drive me back to Adyar, some eight miles, and offered to send another car to bring me next day for business discussions. As buses were overcrowded and taxis had become expensive, following the big rise in the price of Arab oil, I appreciated this kind of gesture. And, remembering the hard-boiled publishing world of the West, the morning's bhakti in a business office put me firmly back in the Indian scene.

The harsh realities of life must, I felt, have been just a little too much for plump, brown-eyed Coralie Leyland, even before the tragedy struck her. She was a professional orchestral violinist with the Australian Broadcasting Commission, stationed in Hobart, Tasmania, when a massive stroke paralysed one side of her body. She was at the time the President of the Theosophical Lodge in Hobart, and had read of Sai Baba. She believed that he would cure her.

As soon as she could manage to walk a little, she came to Adyar Theosophical Headquarters, with the express purpose of seeing Baba personally, as soon as possible. When we met her, she had already been to Puttaparti. Now she was walking quite well, though with a slight limp. But one arm still looked as if it would never play the violin again.

Yet Baba had had some profound effect on Coralie for she talked of his greatness and love to all who would listen on the Theosophical Estate. She was the apostolic proselytizing type, acting as if everyone should be brought immediately to the Sai light. At a party she held in her flat, she had a large picture of Baba, with incense sticks burning in front of it, in a kind of sanctuary at the end of the room.

In the corner of the crowded room I heard one Society official who had recently returned from overseas, ask, cynically: "What has he done for her?" Another official responded feelingly: "If you had seen her before she went to him, you would not ask that question. She could do nothing but cry all the time. She was in a terrible state, and look at her now!"

Several of the Headquarters' people expressed the opinion that Sai Baba had wrought a remarkable inner change in Coralie. And her energy was certainly tremendous. In the scorching sun of this unusually hot April most people stayed indoors during the worst hours of the days. Only mad dogs and Coralie ventured out in the midday sun. She could be seen, with an upturned basket on her head for a hat, limping hurriedly along the road to some place or another.

One blazing afternoon, soon after we arrived, she walked the five furlongs from her place to Leadbeater Chambers, and climbed the steep outside stairs to our flat on the top floor. She wanted to talk about Baba, and we were interested to hear about her exposure to him.

Baba had given her a room to herself the day she arrived at Prasanti Nilayam. "Where," she said, "I had the most beautiful night of my life. Such peace! I'd never known anything like it before."

At the private interview he granted her, Baba did not say he would cure her, but told her to stop worrying, think constantly of God and be happy.

After several weeks at the ashram, she said she was able to walk; "three or four times as well as before. And my arm is getting better." She raised it above her head to demonstrate.

"But it's not much use to a violinist yet, Coralie. I hope Baba will cure it completely."

"If he doesn't, it's better to be happy with one arm than miserable with two, as I was. For years I was plagued by unspeakable loneliness. Now that's all gone. Baba has brought me peace and joy."

"Have you any plans?"

"Only to spend more time with Swami. I'll return to the ashram as soon as I can."

The rumour that Baba was coming persisted among the Madras devotees, and interested the few at Theosophical Headquarters who wanted to meet him. Some said he should be invited to speak under the banyan tree. This noble tree, considered the largest (or second largest) from a single central trunk in the whole of India, has some special associations for me, personally. I have heard elevating spiritual discourses there from world lecturers, particularly from the late President, N. Sri Ram. And it was under this tree, with its sand floor, leafy roof and filtered, cathedral light, that the Lord Maitreya, He whom Theosophists call the World Teacher, first spoke through J. Krishnamurti. It was a spine-tingling experience for those present on that 28th of December, 1925. Annie Besant, and many others there, had no doubts, and Krishnamurti showed by the words he spoke afterwards that he was sure the World Teacher had spoken through him.

"The memory of the 28th should be to you as if you were guarding some precious jewel . . . I am sure He will come again very soon . . . A new life, a new storm has swept the world. It is like a tremendous gale that blows and cleans everything, all the particles of dust from the trees, the cobwebs from our minds and from our emotions, and has left us perfectly clean."*

And one morning, sitting there among the "pillars" under the green arches, while a few people moved about quietly preparing for some occasion, I had an ineffable Timeless Moment, myself. Suddenly I was enveloped in a white glory of Light that made the brilliant Indian sun seem like a candle by comparison, and objects seen by the outer eye faded into a dim background. At the same time the Light was suffused with a sweetness and bliss almost unbearable. It lasted only a moment, as man reckons time, but it does not belong in time. It was a glimpse of the Eternal, the Real, that lies beyond the transient unreality of this world. Yes, I thought, it would be a suitable setting for the Godman to speak to the followers of Theosophy — the "scientists of God," as the great philosopher Professor T. M. P. Mahadevan once defined us. But I felt a doubt. Was the time ripe? Only Baba, himself, would know that.

When J. Krishnamurti severed his connection with the Theosophical Society, at about the time of Annie Besant's passing, he gave his talks for many years outside the gates in a garden not far away. When we were in India during the 'sixties, he had been talking in that garden, several weeks a year, for over thirty years. Practically all the people at the Society Headquarters, including President N. Sri Ram, used to go to those evening talks.

To me he was the voice of Siva, breaking up the old dead thought forms. Whether coming from the Lord Maitreya or from his own Self, the gale that began under the banyan tree in 1925 had been blowing for forty years, cleaning away the cobwebs from minds and emotions. In his quiet, intellectual way, Sri Ram carried these cleansing Krishnamurti winds into the Theosophical organization where thought forms that had once carried vital spiritual life, were in some ways becoming corroded and clogged — as inevitably happens with the passage of time.

It seemed to me that the new President, John Coats, was sweeping away more of the outmoded traditional attitudes, freeing the channels for new thought, welcoming the young generation of searchers, whatever their attitude to the Time-honored images and concepts. Some day the organization might again become what it once was: an instrument designed and polished by the trans-Himalayan Mahatmas to search out and disseminate the Divine Truths that would turn the intellectual crest wave of the world towards spiritual shores.

But it was not that yet. It was still dragging too much dead weight from the sacred past. Three decades earlier its rigid conceptual structure could not have borne cyclonic Krishnamurti within its framework. How would it react now to Sai Baba, if he came?

But Sai Baba did not even come to Madras. The rumour died, and we heard that he had changed his plans and would not be coming this month — probably not for many months. So we must go to him as soon as possible.

We discovered that now the business of getting train tickets was even more troublesome than it used to be. One had to stand in a long queue, moving slowly through the hot, breathless hours towards the ticket window. To save us this ordeal a young Indian offered to do the job for us. We would not have to join the long queue, he said; he would meet a friend at the station who had a cousin working in the ticket office. There would be pay for him, of course, and *baksheesh* for his friend and his friend's cousin, but all of it amounted to very little

He obtained for us two precious tickets for an express train to Bangalore leaving in seven days. This was good work, the usual wait was ten days or more. Seven days would give us ample time to finish all our business in Madras, as well as visit some old friends there.

Two days before we were due to depart, the railway men went on strike, so no trains were running to Bangalore. The unofficial grapevine forecast a long strike. Officially, according to press and radio, there was no strike, or if there had been, it was already over. This must have been just the government's propaganda line, for, going to the station with all our luggage to catch our train, we found there was no train, nor likely to be any for — well, only the gods knew for how long. We quickly discovered, too, that because of the strike, all the road buses and air flights to Bangalore were fully booked for weeks ahead.

So we were securely trapped in hot Madras. It hardly seemed possible that, after travelling thousands of miles to see Baba, we were now unable to take the last short, 200-mile step to him.

Back at our quarters on the top floor of three-story Leadbeater Chambers we discussed the situation. It seemed quite hopeless; all we could do was sit here in the heat of an unbearable April that had mistaken itself for July — always the worst month of the Madras summer. Sit and wait while our available time in India was slipping away!

A slight breeze came off the shimmering Bay of Bengal and managed to reach us across the tree-tops that lay below our wide balcony. It helped a little, but we knew it would cease when darkness came, or soon after.

"Baba did not come to Madras, and now we cannot get to him. How long must we stew here?" Iris sounded as depressed as I felt.

"If only he would give us a sign that he wants to see us," I said. "Who knows, he may not even talk to us when we get there."

"Perhaps not. I guess we have done many wrong things," Iris agreed, unhappily.

A gloom had settled over my mind and heart by the time the heavy darkness fell. The slight breeze off the sea had died and clouds of mosquitoes drove us for protection into our beds under mosquito nets. The beds, too, we had placed out on the balcony to catch whatever freshness and relative coolness the night might bring off the sea.

I was the first in, diving under the mosquito net that was attached to a rectangular wooden frame above the bed. Before going to her own bed, Iris went around and made sure that the end of my net was tucked securely under my mattress. We knew from experience that if there was the smallest opening, some voracious little mosquito would get in, and make the night a misery.

I slept soundly and awoke next morning as the fingers of dawn drew scarlet patterns on the Bay of Bengal. Grey light was filtering in through my net. I was already feeling warm, so I threw off the light sheet, the only covering necessary on those April nights.

I was startled to see all around me what looked like little black chips. I picked up several and found they were, in fact, leaves, and, as the light increased, I saw that they were of many different shades of green, of different shapes and sizes. They seemed as if they had just been picked — so very fresh and green. Then I noticed another strange thing, a pleasant, delicate perfume was coming from them. It was not their own natural perfume for, though obviously from different plants, the leaves all had the same fragrance.

Lying there in this bed of leaves — there were scores of them all around me on the lower sheet — I tried to figure out how they could possibly have come there. It would have required a powerful wind, blowing upward, to bring them from the plantation below up to our balcony, but the night had been quite still. Even if they had managed to get up here, how could they get in through the net that did not have an opening large enough to admit a determined mosquito? And, how did they crawl under my top sheet, and acquire this haunting fragrance, redolent of the perfume inside a Hindu temple?

I could hear signs that Iris was now awake in the nearby bed. I told her about the strange discovery and she came quickly. The sun had popped up and was sitting on the rim of the ocean. In the bright, golden light we hoisted my mosquito net above its wooden frame and examined the leaves together. Many of them had specks of colored paste and powder on them.

"Turmeric, kum-kum and sandal paste," Iris commented; "the leaves may be from someone's morning puja. But however did they come here, and get in through the net? It must be one of Baba's miracles!"

The only other person living on the top floor was Kanta Devi from Honolulu. Half Hawaiian by blood, she was a deep student of Hindu spiritual philosophy and the related Hawaiian religious lore. Seeing her moving about on the balcony in front of her room, we called to her. She came towards us in her long white robe, with the stately glide of a temple priestess. When we told her the story and showed her the leaves, her face and eyes shone.

"That's certainly Sai Baba's *leela*. You are greatly blessed!"

As Iris prepared breakfast, I gathered the perfumed leaves carefully and put them on a shelf near a photograph of Swami. All my depression of the night before had evaporated, giving place to joy. Is all our gloom, I wondered just the shade of His outstretched, caressing hand, as the poet says? It would be great if we could always see it that way, anyhow.

That afternoon we had a visit from an old friend: Leela Mudalia who has known Baba since she was a child. She was one of the small party that enjoyed the miraculous Sai days in the Horsley Hills in 1967, as described in my first book on Sai Baba. She was a college professor of botany in Madras, and priestess at the Sai Baba Guindy temple, built by her father.

Hearing that we were at Adyar, she had come to tell us she had only recently been with Swami at "Brindavan," and that he had said he was expecting us soon. We showed her the leaves, now dried by the heat of the day, and asked her what plants they were from.

"Many different plants."

"From the estate?"

"Not all of them — no. Why?"

We told her the story of how we had found them that morning. Leela held some of the leaves in her palm thoughtfully. On her face was a far-away expression, on her lips a quiet happy smile.

"They certainly came as Swami's grace," she said. "It won't be long before he shows you a way to go to him."

Where there is a desire for mental tranquility, I hurry to grant tranquility. Where there is dispiritedness, I hasten to raise the drooping heart. Where there is no mental trust, I rush to restore trust. I am ever on the move to fulfill the mission for which I have come.

SATYA SAI BABA

4
REUNION

Has the time come at last when I may go in and see thy Face?

RABINDRANATH TAGORE.

The crowded bus bounced along over indifferent roads. In country towns it passed by some knots of waiting people, but stopped for others, packing them in where there seemed no space left. We wondered if the driver or conductor liked some faces better than others, or if — more likely — *baksheesh* was involved.

In Madras we had been told that this was an express bus and would reach Bangalore in six hours. We had already been eight hours on the road, including one sitting outside a small town garage while repairs were made to our engine. And judging by rare mile-posts glimpsed in the fading daylight, our destination was still several hours away.

Still, we did have seats, albeit getting harder every hour, and we were on our way to Baba. That in itself seemed miraculous under the circumstances. But in India, since we had met Baba, whenever we were in some difficult situation, a good angel always turned up to help us. On this occasion the angel was a Theosophist who held a high position in a government department. Though every bus seat to Bangalore was booked far ahead in time, and crowds waited at the bus depots to grab violently any unclaimed seats at the moment of departure, this kind Indian official had managed to obtain two seats for us. In addition, he sent two stalwarts from his staff to protect us in the departure scrimmage.

So on a hot high noon, a few days after our night of the leaves, we shook the dust of Madras from our bus tires and rolled inland. But when we finally crept wearily into Bangalore, church clocks agreed that it was either midnight, or close to it.

The place where we had booked rooms — a religious organization — was dark and seemed deserted. But persistent shouting aroused a watchman, sleeping on a verandah. He showed us to our quarters, carried our bags from the taxi, and shocked us by refusing a tip, with the words: "No, Sir, this is my *job*." There was no kitchen and no meals were provided, but we were too tired to eat anyway.

Next morning we found a restaurant that served an Indian breakfast which, though somewhat spicy, was very welcome. Then, after unpacking, and figuratively licking our wounds from the bus ride, we took an auto-rickshaw to an Indian home where we had been hospitably invited to take our meals, "whenever we wished."

After lunch the master of the house generously made his car available to take us out to Whitefield, and one of the ladies, who was very anxious to see Baba, offered to drive it.

So at last we found ourselves moving through the familiar streets and bazaars, and then out among the the fresh fields that lead to "Brindavan" where Baba spends most of the summer months.

As we drew near, I felt more and more like a Prodigal Son returning home — full of anticipatory excitement, but wondering anxiously what my reception would be. We drove past "Brindavan's" high brick wall and turned in at the gate, through souvenir vendors, beggars and others — a sure sign that Swami was there. In the grounds a big crowd was waiting — no doubt for Baba's *darshan.*

We parked the car near the house where the late M. Dixit's widow still lived, and walked up the curved, tree-lined road to the gate that leads into Swami's garden and residence. There was a guard on this gate, and we remembered that no one enters without an invitation from Sai Baba, himself. In the old days we had, over long periods, an open invitation to go in, and indeed we had at times lived there. Even so, when visiting, we had never presumed to walk straight in without Swami's previous invitation. So now the correct thing would probably be to wait with the crowd outside until he came out for *darshan.* Then if he wished, he would invite us in.

But suddenly I had an overwhelming desire to see him. We had waited so long; we had come so far; and now he was only a step away, on the other side of a gate. Must I wait for perhaps another hour? The look on the guard's face told me that I must wait. My reason told me to wait, but something beyond my reason told me to plunge in.

At the side of the gate where a path led down to the Satya Sai College of Science and Arts (the temporary building) there was a gap — unguarded. We moved around to that. We knew it would not be auspicious to take our lady driver friend in uninvited, so, for courtesy's sake, Iris stayed behind with her while I slipped through the gap, and walked boldly up the drive towards the portico. My ears were deaf to the loud protests from the guard behind me.

The first person I saw at the half-open front door was Indra Devi. She gave me a surprised and affectionate greeting.

"Where is Baba?" I asked.

"Around the side, there. But he is very busy — they are building the pandal for the Summer Course."

I was walking in the direction she had indicated before she finished speaking. An Indian, who had been talking to her, chased after me.

"Excuse me — but it's not really a very propitious moment — it would not be wise to go to him now..."

I looked at his face and did not recognize it. "I've waited nearly four years to see him; that's long enough," I said, and walked on.

At the side of the house Sai Gita, Swami's elephant, was chained to a tree. Near the tree the great pandal began and stretched to some new houses at the far end of the garden. It was the biggest pandal I had seen, yet it looked so light with its slim bamboo poles and thatched roof. The two ends had walls of plaited straw, but the sides were still open. In the midst of a group of men towards the middle of the pandal I caught sight of the shining red robe and dome of black, crinkly hair.

Swami certainly looked very busy. There were some men up under the high roof, placing colored bunting and streamers. He was directing them from below. I walked across the soft sand floor of the pandal towards him, then stopped, about ten yards away — and waited. He continued to direct his workmen up in the roof.

Talking to the men around him, and obviously very concentrated on the job in hand, his eyes passed over me, once unseeingly, then came back to rest on me; sudden recognition came over his face and shone in his soft, dark eyes. Ejaculating my name, he left the group, and came over to me.

As I stood looking at my beloved Sadguru again, the people, the pandal, everything around vanished, and there were only the two of us in the whole world. He patted my shoulder affectionately, rubbed my back, and uttered wonderful words of welcome. I went down on my knees before him. Helping me to my feet, he asked: "Where's your wife?"

"Waiting outside, Swamiji."

"Bring her in!"

After Iris had received her own warm welcome, and our lady driver was greeted with a charm that made her face glow, Swami left the pandal and took us into the long front room of his house. As always, there were people sitting on the carpet there, waiting to see him.

After a time he invited my wife and me into an inner room for a private interview. Diffidently, we offered the gift bought for him in Singapore. It was wrapped in brown paper; we hoped he would feel our love wrapped around it, too, as he held the parcel in his hand and went on talking. He showed that he was fully aware of many things we had been doing while away from him.

During a pause, Iris said: "Thank you for helping our friend Rhoda, Swami."

He smiled. "I cured her of breast cancer, but now she has cancer of the lungs."

This was startling news. We knew her lungs were not good and that she coughed a great deal, but — this was terrible!

"She must stop smoking," Swami spoke very seriously.

"I thought she *had* stopped, Swami." When we were leaving Australia, Rhoda had promised Iris to give up cigarettes, which seemed to be irritating her lungs.

"Only just!" he replied. "But don't worry. If she does not smoke any more, I will cure the lung cancer, too. She has great faith."

"Thank you, Swamiji."

As he seemed never to be going to open his parcel, I asked if I should open it for him.

"Why? I know what's in it. Torch — red and white light."

He laughed at our startled expressions. "I was there. I saw it when you bought it...'Will Swami like this? Is it the right thing to give him?' " He went on to tell us, laughingly, more about the discussion and debate we had had in Singapore.

Then to make us happy, he opened the parcel, flicked the red and white lights on a few times, and tossed the torch on to an armchair. He had accepted it, which, to us, was the most important thing.

I asked him if we could stay near him for about six months, wherever he might be during that time, and if I could gather material to write another book about him. He agreed to both requests. Then, with two words and a question mark in my voice, I probed for what he might have to say about the miracle of the mosquito net.

"Leaves, Swami?" I said.

He gave me a questioning look for a moment and then smiled. "Yes, I sent you the leaves." He mentioned some of the details of the episode on the high balcony at Adyar. To my wife, he said: "You see — he was depressed."

"Yes, Swamiji. And what a difference you made. You turned depression to joy — for both of us."

I was about to ask him why he used *leaves*, in particular, to send us his blessings and lift our hearts, when he said: "Some other time I will tell you about the meaning of leaves. We will have other talks — many."

Swami often gives you something to look forward to when he ends an interview.

Now he made a move towards the door: "Where is your baggage? I don't mean *mental* baggage — travelling baggage!" He laughed.

I told him it was still in Bangalore, as we did not know if we would be permitted to live at "Brindavan".

He smiled and patted me again. "I have a house — part of a house — waiting for you."

"Come — I will show it to you."

5
THE
RAINBOW MAN

*Nothing is a miracle to Holy Understanding, Which
is, O monks, the only miracle.*

"MIRDAD"

Sai Gita's bell rang rhythmically as she walked under the front portico. Swami called her name. She stopped and turned towards him as he
came through the door. He patted her trunk and spoke gently to her while
we waited, observing how much she had developed in our absence. But
she was still not a fully-grown elephant.

Leaving her to follow her keeper, Swami took us along the flower-
covered walk that ran beside the pandal towards a line of bungalows at the
far end of the grounds. These houses had not existed when we left in
1970, but now there were four of them and a building that housed a print-
ing press. He led us to the first bungalow, one side of which faced into the
pandal.

A very blonde child rushed towards Swami from the front doorway.
Her bright, blue eyes looked adoringly at him while he patted her head.
Then she bent down swiftly and touched his feet. Her parents, an American couple, stood by the door, eagerly awaiting Baba's arrival. They
proved to be Joel and Diana Riordan who occupied part of the house. We
discovered later that Madonna-faced Diana was the daughter of a Sai devotee we had known in America. This was Analise, the second wife of D.
Rajagopal, who for years had been chief organizer of J. Krishnamurti's
business affairs. Diana's father, now divorced from her mother, was a
wealthy industrialist of Italy.

After a few words with them, Swami led us into a room with windows opening onto the pandal. "This is for you," he said, while the room
breathed a warm welcome. The cupboards and built-in furniture were of

brown timber, and low to the floor in Japanese style. The general effect was intimate, pleasant, restful. We learned later that this interior decoration had been carried out by former occupiers, Steve and Irene Au of Honolulu. Steve was an architect.

While we were making exclamations of delight, Swami led us to the other two rooms that completed the apartment — a kitchen and a shower-room. Luxury, indeed, for ashram life!

"Thank you, Swami," we said. "It's beautiful!"

Baba is very human at such times. "Oh, it's nothing special," he protested. But we could see that he was pleased we liked the place so much.

Soon after that we moved our baggage to "Brindavan," leaving behind, we hoped, as much of our "mental baggage" as possible, for we were starting on a new, important chapter of our lives, and needed open, unconditioned minds. A few students were already beginning to arrive for the Summer Course, soon to begin. We looked forward to being part of this month-long unique program of spiritual education.

Meantime we got to know our neighbors in the rooms across the foyer. It was soon obvious that Diana was a one hundred-per-cent, unqualified devotee of Sai Baba. She often made remarks that seemed to Joel grossly exaggerated.

She told me in his presence: "Joel and I were quarrelling one day about Swami's omniscience. I said that he knew everything — even about the debate we were then having. Joel scoffed that I was talking utter rubbish. Next day I was standing in line when Swami walked passed. He paused in front of me and said quietly: 'I know everything.' "

"There are lots of things he doesn't know," Joel renewed the argument.

I tried to pour oil on the troubled waters: "Ramana Maharshi of Arunachala was once told by a follower that he could not be omniscient because he did not know when a certain man was arriving at the ashram. Maharshi replied, 'I know everything I need to know.' "

This did not satisfy either of the Riordans.

"Another thing," Joel went on, "Diana believes Swami is God."

"What do you say about that, yourself?"

"I don't know what God is, so how can I say anything! I only know that Baba is my best friend."

"So, if he's not God, what about the rainbow?" Diana queried.

I looked puzzled and she laughed. "They call Joel the 'Rainbow man.' Tell him about it, Joel."

Her husband made some rude remark and left the room. "He will tell you sometime," Diana said, and went off herself to feed the pack of lean and hungry dogs that somehow found a way in through the wall from the nearby village, to exploit her soft heart.

One afternoon, when Joel and I were sitting on a sand ridge at the rear of the pandal, watching electricians erect a loud speaker near our windows, he did mellow enough to tell me the story of the "Rainbow man."

I had gathered from some of his earlier conversational remarks, such as: "I once said to Clark Gable," and, "I had a call from my friend Mickey Rooney," that Joel had been connected with the motion picture industry. Now he told me that he had been a movie director in Hollywood. At another period he had been a car dealer in Los Angeles. He was for years, it appeared, deeply immersed in a life that knew only two gods – money and fame.

Diana was his second wife, he told me, the first, from whom he was divorced, being a well-known professional skater.

He said: "Diana had been over to India a couple of times with her mother, Analise, and both of them used to talk about Sai Baba's miracles. I thought they must both be mad, or going mad. I seriously considered divorcing Diana. But there was my daughter Chrissie to think of. Anyway, I finally decided that, before doing anything drastic, I would go over and see this character, Sai Baba, for myself. My parents had been show people and I was just about brought up in a circus. Like old Orson Wells, I was keenly interested in conjuring, and had seen what went on behind all the stage tricks. I figured that even if this character in India was a second Houdini, I would be able to expose him as a conjuror, and not a holy man miracle worker, as people claimed.

"Just before I left Hollywood, I was having lunch with an important guy and – to give him a laugh – told him what I was planning to do. He seemed to have heard of Sai Baba, or read about him – maybe in Schulman's book, or yours – anyway, he said, 'What are you going to ask him for, Joel?' Then the idea came to me; I answered: 'They say this character is God – so I'll ask him for something only God can make – a rainbow.'

"He laughed, and we talked about other matters, but I decided that was what I would ask for."

"Did your luncheon friend know any of the Sai Baba devotees in California, Joel?"

He grinned. "I checked on that later – for the same reason as you ask. No, he did not. He lived in a different world from them. No chance that anyone carried the story to Swami.

"Anyway, a few days after that I flew to India, bringing Diana and

Chrissie with me. It was early afternoon when we arrived in Puttaparti, and an hour or so later we went for a walk up that hill behind the hospital. It was a hot, dry day, and we went up for a breath of air. We sat on some rocks and looked out over the country. Grim, it looked, and parched — made me feel dehydrated just to see it.

"Then in the western sky a bright rainbow appeared. Odd, I thought, how can you have a rainbow without a drop of moisture in the air? Something else struck me, too, as peculiar. Instead of being curved in the usual way, the rainbow stood straight up in the sky like a column. I felt a bit spooky about it. Had this character heard my words right across in America, and caused this phenomenon?

"Then the colors started to fade out from the bottom up. I felt I needed a drink. But of course there's no alcohol at Puttaparti, and even the water was warm in that season." He stopped speaking, to watch Swami's two young camels go past, grabbing mouthfuls of hedge as they went.

"Did Diana see the rainbow, and did she know you had threatened to ask Swami for one?" I said.

"Yeah, I mentioned it to her on the way over on the plane. She saw the rainbow all right — ask her, yourself."

"So, what then?"

"We came down from the hill, and there was a message that Swami wanted to see us. Diana got more excited about that than she did the rainbow, but as we had come a long way, it seemed natural enough to me that he would see us on the first day.

"When we walked into the interview room, Swami's first words knocked me out: 'Well, character, how did you like your rainbow?'

"I was too dumbfounded to answer. He knew my name for him, and what I was going to ask for, and had put that odd rainbow in the sky! It all blew my mind.

"Well, I sat with the others on the floor, hardly hearing, and not understanding, what he was talking about. In fact, my mind was racing about like a rat in a trap, trying to find a way back to the common-sense world I knew. O.K., granted he was a mind-reader; telepathy does exist between people — it's been proved scientifically. But the rainbow must have been an hallucination — or I had been hypnotized.

"I'll give him another test, I thought to myself; I will ask him to produce some fresh fruit — out-of-season fruit — right here in this room, without warning.

"A few minutes after I'd had this thought, Swami stopped talking and waved his hand in his usual way. When he turned it up I saw a fresh fig sitting on his palm. He handed it to me without a word.

"I ate it later. It was as fresh as if just picked. Yet figs were out of season, and – I learned later – none grow in that area, anyway."

Joel's sharp blue eyes looked at me as if to say: "Now what about that for a script, and all absolutely true!"

"So, when you found he was not a fake, you left Hollywood and came to live near him?" I remarked.

"Well, I was tired of the American rat-race, and Swami gave me this house to live in. Anyway, we're on the edge of the biggest depression ever. Why wait there for the collapse of democracy?"

It was getting towards evening and we saw Swami's bright figure at the other end of the pandal, moving among some building workers. At the sight of him Joel suddenly looked guilty. "I had better go and see if the painters are still at it," he said. "If you turn your back, they stop work, or go home!"

I knew he had been given the job of superintending the painting of a wall of Swami's house. He liked to keep busy, helping in preparations for the Summer Course in whatever way Baba directed. We stood up.

"At first," he said, pointing, "they put a wall right across this rear end of the pandal. I was real upset because I had been thinking that Diana and I would be able to hear Swami's evening discourses through the open windows. You see, we can't leave Chrissie alone in the house at night. Well, the day after I was feeling put out about the wall blocking our view of the interior of the pandal, he told the workers to remove it – just as if he had read my thoughts again. Then," Joel added ruefully, "he put you two in there for the grandstand view."

"Our being there will make no difference," I assured him. "You have a standing invitation to come in and sit at the open window to hear Swami whenever you wish."

We strolled across the sand in the general direction of Swami, hoping we might score a smile, or even a word, from him. Then a short distance away we stood and watched him. He left the group of workers and came towards us. Joel was immediately erect and alert, like a soldier when the sergeant-major approaches. Swami smiled at him and clapped him on the back.

"Military!" he said. "I want those big gateposts painted today. Make sure the painters do it before they leave."

"Yes, Swami." I thought Joel was going to salute, but he put his palms together in the Indian gesture, and hurried away to locate his painters.

Swami spoke to me: "What do you think of the pandal?"

"So big, and yet such a feeling of lightness, airiness, Swami. Will it be filled with students?"

"There will be about 600 students this year. In the evenings when the public comes, the pandal will be full — overflowing."

He caught sight of some visitors arriving and left me. I walked on to watch Gita eating her large meal of leaves.

Next morning when I went for my pre-breakfast walk in the garden, I noticed that the posts of the big gate to the outer grounds were bright with new paint. They were broad, tall, decorative gateposts, and had been painted in various colors, so it had been quite a job to start so late in the day. I wondered how many painters Joel had employed on it.

Towards lunchtime Diana came into our apartment to indulge in her favorite occupation — talking about Baba. After a while I asked her where Joel was, as I had not seen him all the morning.

"Oh, he's not up yet."

"Heavens! Was he out late?"

"Very late. He spent half the night painting the gateposts. The men had gone home so he did the job himself. If Swami says do something, Joel does it — at all costs. Did he tell you about the rainbow?"

"Yes, what a story!"

"Did you see the rainbow yourself, Diana?" Iris asked her.

"Oh, yes. You couldn't miss it. All the colors — but straight, like a pillar. I think Swami did that to show it was special."

"Special for the sceptic."

"Yes. Joel told a lot of people, and he became known as the 'rainbow man.' Even so, I can't make him understand that Swami is an Avatar."

When I saw the "rainbow man" after lunch, his eyes were blood-shot and his face blotchy.

"You see," he explained, "I had to hold a torch in one hand and paint with the other. I put a net over my head, but it was impossible to keep it in place while I worked, so the mosquitoes got to my face, and drove me mad. Took me most of the night to get the job done. Now I'm scared to see how it looks, and hear what Swami says about it. The painters left early, while I was talking to you."

"It looked fine to me," I told him. "A tough job — dedicated to the Lord. You must be a karma yogi, Joel."

"Me — I'm just a mug."

6
EDUCATION FOR THE NEW AGE

The only proof of His existence is union with Him. The world disappears in Him. He is the peaceful, the good, the one without a second.
—From the MANDOOKYA UPANISHAD

We awoke to the sweet sound of distant singing. It grew in volume, as it passed near our wall, then faded as it moved away. We knew this was *Nagar sankeerthan* in which the students walk in groups through the village near "Brindavan," singing bhajans, the sacred songs of India. It was the first day of the "Course on Indian Culture and Spirituality," and every morning for a month here *Nagar Sankeerthan* would greet the break of day.

About an hour later, while we were having breakfast, we heard sounds in the pandal and, looking through the windows, saw a group of male students being taught yogasanas. This was also to be a regular morning parade. In another pandal, erected as a dining-room for the students, Indra Devi was teaching girl students, who, incidentally, performed their yogasanas in their saris. The teacher beneath our windows was a visiting Indian from London, named Mukunda Shah.

"I came out to Whitefield for Swami's darshan one day," he told me, "and while I was in the crowd I had my pocket picked. Lost a roll of a thousand rupees. Swami must have heard about it, because he invited me to live here for the Course and teach yogasanas — which, incidentally, I've been practicing all my life."

"What had your plans been before you were robbed?" I asked.

"I would have stayed in Bangalore a little longer, and perhaps come out for some more darshans. But when my Indian spending was stolen, I decided to fly straight back to England. Instead, well, here I am!"

I had never seen anyone so pleased at having his pocket picked.

Following yogasanas there was meditation and breakfast. Then by nine o'clock the students had to be ready for the first lecture.

This course, taking place during the summer holidays, was a remarkable thing. It had begun in 1972, and now, two summers later, the demand from university students all over India was so great that Swami had instituted an entrance examination. This was conducted by suitable devotees living in the various centres. Judge G. K. Damodar Row, for example, had been conducting one in Madras when we were there. In this way it was hoped to select the serious students from among those who merely wanted a trip, or were idly curious.

Despite rail strikes and semi-strikes, about five hundred had managed to reach "Brindavan" at the start — some from the other side of India, a thousand miles and more away. A group of American students were there, too, and individuals from several countries.

Before we went out to the pandal for the opening address, Kanta Devi came in waving the printed program of the course. Her eyes were shining. "What a spiritual banquet!" She really was delighted to be there, one of the few foreign adult observers permitted to stay at "Brindavan," and attend the lectures.

I could see what she meant when I looked through the names of the lecturers and the titles of their lectures. Some I had wanted very much to meet and hear, such as Mr. R. R. Diwakar, author, scholar, statesman, Minister for Information and Broadcasting in Nehru's cabinet and later Governor of Bihar. This well-known leader was to give a series of lectures on: "The States of Consciousness" — the subject of one of his published works.

Listed to lecture on "Advaita Vedanta" and "The Gita" was Dr. T. M. P. Mahadevan who was Director of the Centre of Advanced Study in Philosophy at the Madras University. I had heard him give some fine talks, and once, years before, was present in a room in Madras when Swami materialized a gold lingam in the form of a pendant for Dr. Mahadevan. It was on the eve of his departure to attend a Philosophy Convention in Greece.

One person I had heard give short addresses at some of Swami's meetings, and now looked forward to hearing at length on the "Culture of East and West," was Dr. V. K. Gokak, Director of the Summer Course.

When I first met Dr. Gokak he was Vice-Chancellor of Bangalore University. Soon after retiring from that post, he came to help in Sai Baba's burgeoning educational work. Apart from being a distinguished educationist, Gokak was a well-known poet and writer in India, and had spent many years as a spiritual searcher before he met Baba. Having received part of his university education at Oxford England, he would be an interesting speaker on the comparative culture of East and West. I knew his spiritual philosophy was strongly colored by the philosophic concepts of Sri Aurobindo which appealed to me, also.

There were many other professors and doctors of laws, literature, philosophy and science on the program — some distinguished men of affairs, too, such as General K. M. Cariappa who was the first Commander-in-Chief of the Army of free India, then Indian High Commissioner in Australia and New Zealand, and, for some years President of the All India Council of Sports.

All the speakers were followers, or admirers, of Sai Baba, and were giving their time and talents free to help in this advanced work Swami was initiating in the field of education.

"And to think we did not really want to come to the course!" I said. "The fewer people around Swami the better we like it. But it's not the first time Swami has known what we *should* do — and would enjoy doing — better than we know ourselves."

"How did he work it — this time?" Kanta Devi asked.

"He told Gokak to write and tell me I would be expected to give three lectures on some appropriate subjects during the course. I did not know then what distinguished company I would be in. Now I feel rather appalled at the thought."

For inscrutable reasons of his own, Baba seemed fond of springing these alarming jobs on me. The first time was when, soon after I met him, he sent word that he wanted me to speak the very next evening on his platform in Madras. The couriers who brought the startling message informed me that I was expected to deliver one of two preliminary talks before Swami's main discourse. The other curtain-raiser was Dr. T. M. P. Mahadevan. An audience of about 20,000 was expected.

I had lectured to small groups of a few score people at the Theosophical Society Headquarters, where I was living at the time, but the thought of 20,000 expectant faces in front of me just about paralyzed my power of thought.

But Swami was beside me on the platform, so all went well, and he taught me, once and for all, that a big crowd is no more difficult than a few people; both become a single unit — especially is this so in India.

There were numerous subsequent occasions when speaking jobs — spontaneous or nearly so — were handed to me casually by Baba. Whatever my feelings, I never never thought of refusing. Someone within me — wiser than my little everyday self — was happy and proud to serve in any way Sai Baba directed.

All my reference books were back in Australia when Swami's request for three lectures at the Summer Course had arrived in Madras. Fortunately, I had with me copies of two essays I had written, on "Divine Incarnations" and "Bhakti Yoga." I could base two of the talks on these. For the other, I decided to speak about the place of Theosophy in the Indian renaissance of last century. It was a subject I knew, and I felt that the Indian students should learn something about it, as a point where East and West, the "twain," met and merged with understanding.

Kanta Devi left with Iris, and I made my way to the male section of the pandal. The students, men in white on one side, women in bright saris on the other, sat expectantly in their chairs — the right arms of which were wide and flat, to serve as desks.

Outside Sai Gita's bell tinkled sleepily. A light breeze whispered through the trees, bringing subtle odors in from the garden. On the platform sat Sai Baba, looking innocently happy like a child, Dr. Gokak, calm and serious, and a Minister of the State Government who was there to make the inaugural address, opening the course.

Dr. Gokak gave a short speech introducing the Minister who spoke at considerable length. Then Swami stood up. From where I sat at the side of the platform, I could see the faces of the students brighten with eagerness at that moment. These students, I thought, will listen politely to us lecturers whatever our qualifications may, or may not, be, but the one they have really come to see and hear is Baba. He has that vital freshness, that authenticity, with a complete lack of pretentiousness, that rings the bell with the younger generation.

Now he lit the sacred lamp, sang a short Bhajan, and explained the object of the course, which was to take them beyond the confines of ordinary education, opening the doors to the rich wisdom found in India's ancient texts. This was their heritage, their right, and it was being denied to them in the modern schools which, following the West, laid too much stress on worldly knowledge, on the means of making a living. Man must also learn how to live. This, the spiritual culture of India teaches by showing him his true identity and the object of his life here.

The cure for the disease that is creeping over India from the western world, the disease of atheistic materialism, lies only in such an understanding. It must begin with the young people of India and spread from here around the world.

With so many students staying on the small college campus of "Brindavan," some rules and regulations were necessary. All must obey these, and not chafe against them. Such discipline was a good training for life, itself, where pleasure and pain alternate. So, real brotherhood must be put into practice on the campus. Remembering the Divine Principle animating all people, "Your eyes and ears will refuse to note the differences that cause conflict; your hands will refuse to engage in wrong activities; your tongue will not tarnish itself with low talk. Be determined to practice purity in thought, word and deed—for this is the central message of the Indian culture. That immortal culture will be explained to you in its many facets by the lecturers who have responded to the invitation of the organizers." (Tuition, board and lodging were, incidentally, being provided free of charge.)

The inauguration ceremony ended with Swami's address; then there was a break for morning tea, and the first lecture of the course was given: "An Introduction to the Yoga of Patanjali's *Yoga Sutras*." It was delivered by Professor N. A. Nikan, a Cambridge graduate in Philosophy who had held the post of Professor of Philosophy in Mysore University, and was later Vice-Chancellor of that University.

A clear and interesting speaker, Professor Nikan gave a series of lectures on Patanjali during the course, and another series on the Upanishads. His lecture and discussion on the opening day lasted till the noon luncheon break.

In the afternoon there were two lectures on the Vedas and the ancient Indian culture, bringing us to five o'clock and tea. At 5:30 the students gathered in the pandal again, and bhajans were sung by representatives from each Indian State. Following that, the chairs were placed along the sides of the pandal, leaving the whole middle free for packing people in as only the Indians know how.

The people to be so packed were soon streaming in from the main gate, along the garden paths, and into the pandal. They were people of all ages who had come out by car and bus from Bangalore. The seats were filled quickly, and then others sat cross-legged, close together, on the sand floor behind the students who were already seated there. When every inch of space was taken, the late-comers stood along the open side of the pandal behind the chairs, and at the end, by our house.

At 6:30, or thereabouts, a student selected from the males and another from among the women, stood up and gave summaries of the day's lectures. Towards the end of this event, I saw Swami coming from the side of his house. First he went towards the tree where Sai Gita waited with upraised trunk holding a garland. There was the usual ritual, Swami being garlanded by the elephant, and then feeding and patting her a little. This pleased Sai Gita and the people watching, especially those with cameras. Then Swami moved quietly inside the pandal, and onto the platform.

As the mosquitoes were beginning to bite, and I had not put on any repellent, this was my cue to go inside our house and sit behind mosquito screens at the open window. We had two windows looking into the pandal, so there was plenty of room for Joel, Diana and Chrissie, as well as ourselves.

Baba stood up and waited while the microphone was adjusted to his height. Standing near him, with note-book in hand and a taller microphone before him, was the eminent scientist, Dr. S. Bhagavantam who would act as translator. When Baba gives a long discourse to a large audience, he speaks, usually, in his own native Telegu.

Incidentally, most of the lectures of the course were given in English, and if any pandit spoke, like Baba, in his native tongue, it was always translated into English, which is understood by educated people in all parts of India.

With its fourteen main languages and hundreds of dialects, India as a nation suffers the same handicaps of linguistic intercommunication as, say, the continent of Europe. The legacy of the English language was one boon left by the British. There has been propaganda against its continued use by narrow ultra-nationalistic groups, but it has real practical value as a link language – as illustrated at this course.

Baba began, as usual, with a sweet song that gave the motif of his coming discourse, and then spoke on an aspect of the Vedas, explaining the deeper meanings, and their application to life, through the use of parables and analogies. This constant use of little stories to throw light on great truths is in the tradition of some other great World-Teachers, such as the Buddha, Jesus and Ramakrishna. Swami's evening talks at the Summer Course (he gave seven a week for the four weeks) are published each year in book form under the title of *Summer Showers*.

Inside the room little Chrissie stopped her playing and chattering and listened quietly to Swami's voice, though she had no idea of what it was all about. After a while she went to sleep. The complete silence and stillness in the pandal below us was broken only by gusts of laughter when Swami made a joke.

At about 8:30 the discourse ended with Baba breaking into a bhajan. For ten minutes he led the crowd in singing, and then during *Arati* (light-waving) left the stage and went to his house. When Arati ended the crowd dispersed, and the students went to their supper. It had been a long day of activities, from before daylight until 8:30 in the evening.

The next day would be as long, and the days after — six days a week for four weeks. Sundays would be a little easier, with some social service in the mornings and elocution practice — leading to oratory competitions — in the afternoons.

We, fortunately, were able to do the course in a little easier style. If we did not feel like going into the pandal, we could hear a lecture while sitting or lying on our beds. Even while cooling off from the heat of the day under a cold shower, one was regaled by the voice of professor or pundit, rolling in through the open window, bearing us the wisdom of ancient Aryavartha. It was a unique inwardly-transforming experience.

The aim of higher education in the West is to train the student for a vocation — doctor, engineer, scientist, teacher, and so forth. It scarcely ever gives him more than a taste of his own literature, art and history. It makes little or no attempt to teach him about the true purpose of life, about how to live and how to die.

Unfortunately, this kind of secular education has been imported to India. The technology it offers is good for raising the Indian standard of life, but the materialistic philosophy it brings is something that must be countered. Otherwise the tragic spiritual vacuum of the West will suck dry the last stronghold of faith and hope.

For reasons known only to God, Himself, India has always been the world's spiritual Mother. Within her ancient wisdom are found all the seeds of mankind's religious thought and practice. Yet, hypnotized by material progress and prosperity, many of India's sons are worshipping the western god of Mammon, unmindful of the ultimate, sad emptiness this inevitably brings.

It is to stem the dark stream of Godless philosophy that Sai Baba is taking appropriate action. The spiritual life of India must be rejuvenated and renewed, he says; India must again become the guru of the world; only thus can the world be saved from itself.

The Summer Courses at Whitefield are only small samples of the great things Baba plans to do, and is already doing. He began by establishing a university college for women at Anantapur, a few miles from his ashram in the State of Andhra Pradesh. His second college was for men at Whitefield in the State of Karnataka. These two were launched before we left India in 1970. When we returned we found that several more of his colleges had sprung up in different parts of India, and his plan remained firm — to have at least two Sai Baba university colleges in every State of India.

In these colleges the students will not only be trained for their chosen vocations in the world, they will also be instructed in the spiritual meaning of life as expounded in their own ancient Sanskrit culture – the *Vedas*, the *Upanishads*, the *Bhagavad Gita*, the *Brahma Sutras*, the great epics and puranas, and the many works on yoga philosophy and practice.

The ancient wisdom contained in these works, "The Perennial Philosophy," as Aldous Huxley calls it, has been taught by the great Teachers of all time, and lies at the base of all religions. The spiritual instruction given in the Sai Baba colleges is not, therefore, of the narrow, denominational kind. It is broad-based and deep, giving the student a better understanding of his own traditional religion, whatever that may be, giving him an understanding of those basic questions of the human heart – why are we here, how should we live, what is the purpose of life and the meaning of death?

The numbers going out into the world from the Sai Baba colleges are few compared with those from the secular colleges. But like the leaven in the loaf, the few have the power to raise the many. As Jesus said: "The kingdom of heaven is like unto leaven which a woman took and hid in three measures of meal, till the whole was leavened."

And the few will multiply like compound interest, or like a snowball rolling downhill. Some of the best students in his existing colleges, Swami says, will become teachers, professors, principals in his new colleges as these arise, until the Sai citizens are a power in the land – in the professions, in commerce, in politics, in all walks of life.

Baba's final plan envisages more women's colleges than men's. One reason for this is that he sees women as a more powerful leaven than men in raising the generations ahead to new high levels. Mothers, he says, are the child's first guru, and they have a tremendous influence on the future. "They are the makers of the nation's fortune or misfortune, for they shape the sinews of the soul. If you want to know how advanced a nation is, study the mothers. Are they free from fear and anxiety, are they full of love towards all, are they trained in fortitude and virtue? As the mother so the progress of the nation; as the mother, so the sweetness of the culture."

With this educational program, added to his other constant work of teaching crowds and instructing individuals, how long will it take Baba to carry out the first part of his life's work – the changing of India? I asked him this question on one occasion.

"Not so long," he answered, surprisingly. "The beginning is always the hardest – laying the foundations. Now it starts to move."

"I know, Swami, that you are planning for India to be the guru of the world once again. But will you, yourself, go abroad and teach?"

"Yes, I will go when the time is right."

Revolutionaries and social reformers strive to change the world by working from the outside on the existing, faulty social systems. But, sooner or later, the newly-installed "ideal" social system founders on the same rock as did the old one — the selfishness of man, his lusts, greeds, fears and ignorance.

Baba works from the inside, striving to change the heart of man. When that has been changed sufficiently, social systems will take care of themselves.

Man is half-animal, half-god — somewhere between the two. By the slow process of evolution the animal part is being transformed towards the Divine. But in his present state of technical knowledge, can man afford to wait for the snail of evolutionary process to do its work? In one place or another place, men are guarding enough nuclear weapons to "destroy the world six times over." There is a grave risk that animal-man will trigger off the third world war — the nuclear holocaust. If that happens, as a leader in-the-know remarked, "the following war will be fought with bows and arrows." What, if anything, remains of mankind will be back to the primitive.

We are in desperate need of a God-man, an Avatar, with the alchemical formula to transmute the heavy, down-pulling lead of human nature into Divine gold. Part of that formula is the irresistible force of the Avatar's Love-Power, part of it is a new, revitalized statement of the Ancient Wisdom, the Perennial Philosophy. At this point in time, man has evolved far enough for this old-new Wisdom to be taught more directly to the man-in-the-street than ever before. What, then, is this Wisdom, this Philosophy, that is being heard again, with a new clarity, an undiluted emphasis, by a Voice with the ring of authority and power?

7
THE ESSENCE OF
THE ANCIENT WISDOM

But happily there is the Highest Common Factor
of all religions, the Perennial Philosophy which has
always and everywhere been the metaphysical system of
the prophets, saints and sages.

ALDOUS HUXLEY

Three concepts lie at the core of the Perennial Philosophy or Ancient Wisdom. They might be called doctrines in that they have been taught by saints, seers and sages from time immemorial. They can however be tested by each individual for himself in the proving-grounds of meditation and contemplation.

First: beyond, and at the same time interspersing, this ever-changing world of things, men, and even gods, is a changeless eternal Reality. In the *Secret Doctrine* H. P. Blavatsky calls it, "An Omnipresent, Eternal, Boundless and Immutable Principle on which all speculation is impossible since it transcends the power of human conception . . ." Philosophers call it "The Absolute"; the Hindus call it "That" or "Brahman." It has been called the "Pure Light of the Void," the "Abyss of Godhead," the "Divine Ground," the "Formless Divinity," "Absolute Consciousness," and other names.

Like the circumference of a circle — which is in fact used as its symbol — Brahman (to use the Hindu name) has no beginning and no end. It has always been and will ever be. Like the screen on which the moving pictures play out their drama, Brahman is a changeless background of a constantly changing universe.

But it is more than that. Without this Eternal Divine Principle, the worlds we know through our senses and minds would not exist. All, from mineral to man to the highest Gods, have emanated from It. All are, therefore, part of the One which has, in Its Becoming Mode, taken on the

appearance of the Many. All are One, for within the many separate individuals is the one eternal Essence, which is the true Reality. Was it Omar
Khayyam who said:

> When all is One, there is no room for sorrow,
> Nor for this gaudy myth of you-and-me.
> These that we call yestreen-today-tomorrow
> Merge in the moment of Eternity.

In the fullness of the aeons all the many separate forms will merge
again with the Divine Ground from which they came. Then begins the
Night of Brahman when there is no universe, no "becoming" — only
"being." Of the nature of that "being" within Brahman we have no idea
for our human consciousness is now fully occupied with the "becoming
mode" in which we find ourselves.

But — teaches the Ancient Wisdom — eventually another Day of
Brahman dawns and another phenomenal universe emerges. Like day and
night, like the ebb and flow of the tides, the "becoming mode" — when
the One appears as the Many — recurs with rhythmic periodicity. Then in
that mode you and I forget our Spiritual Home and wander through the
worlds lost in our own selfhood. Yet we need not wait through aeons till
the Night of Brahman before returning to the bliss of the One Self, to
"the land that is nowhere, that is the true Home."

Second concept: Man's Spirit, called by the Hindus the "Atman" or
the "Self" (with a capital 'S') is identical with Brahman. This truth was
expressed often and in many ways by mankind's earliest known spiritual
teachings — the *Upanishads* of the *Vedas*. "The inner Self sits ever in the
heart of all that's born," they say. "Smaller than small, yet greater than
great, in the heart of this creature the Self doth repose."

The same Truth has been taught also by the great World-Teachers,
and can therefore be found in the scriptures of all major religions. The *Old
Testament* of the Hebrews states that God made man in His own image,
and later it says in the *Psalms*: "Ye are Divine! All of you are sons of the
Most High, notwithstanding that ye die like mortals," and, "I have said, ye
are gods." Jesus Christ echoed this, and emphasized man's divinity in the
words: "I am in the Father and you are in me, just as I am in you." In the
Koran of Islam, Allah, the Almighty, states: "I am in your souls! Why see
ye not?" And Lord Krishna, the Voice of the Supreme God, says in the
holy *Gita*: "But he who seeketh Me with heart resolved, he surely findeth
Me, his inmost Self."

The mystics of all religions, going deep within their own souls, have discovered the truth of this concept for themselves — as anyone can. Probing to the depths, and discerning the Real hidden in the Unreal, one Sufi mystic wrote: "There is naught within my robe but God, Himself."

But the mass of mankind has always found this concept hard to understand and accept. Looking at themselves and their lives, and comparing this with their ideal of God, they have, no doubt, found the idea too far-fetched to be true. They are like a man suffering from amnesia; he does not know his past, his true identity, and he does not really want to know for fear it may upset his present way of life. Perhaps, because of the nature of its incredibility, this most important truth of being is not taught by run-of-the-mill ministers and priests of the orthodox religion.

But Sai Baba puts more emphasis on this concept of the Ancient Wisdom than on any other. He is constantly telling his followers that they are not the body, but the Atman, and that the Atman is identical with the eternal Brahman.

"Are you God?" a man asked him, bluntly, once in my presence. "*You* are God!" he replied, and went on to explain that while he, himself, knew he was God, his questioner, who was also God, did not know it.

But there is knowing and knowing. So deluded are we men so buried in the depths of *Maya*, illusion, that it is not enough to be told this Truth, even by an Enlightened One. Indeed, if it could be proved to us by geometrical theorems, algebraic equations and all the other tools of the logical, rational mind, we still would not apprehend it in the real sense.

We have to know the truth without the intervention of the logical mind, as we know the fact that we exist, and that we are conscious. We do not need proof of these things. Such inner knowing is called unitive knowledge because it is known by union with, or identity with, the object or truth to be known.

It is possible for a human being, if he so desires, to reach this unitive knowledge, to identify himself with his Spirit, his Atman, and therefore with his Divine Ground of Being. How this can be done belongs to the third concept of the Perennial Philosophy.

Third concept: Man's life here on earth has one over-riding aim: to discover his true identity, that is, to reach the unitive knowledge of his oneness with God. He has of course to live his earthly life, engaging in his profession or business or trade, but that is not his main purpose; in fact, his work, itself, can be used as a means towards reaching his goal — the break-through from ignorance to knowledge, from darkness to Light, from the transient to the Eternal.

As we said, this break-through will not come from being told the great Truth about ourselves by a Teacher. Gautama, the Buddha, was once asked by one of his listeners: "What is the difference between a Buddha and a non-Buddha?" The Enlightened One replied: "The only difference is this: a Buddha knows that he is a Buddha, but the non-Buddha, who is in reality also a Buddha, does not know that he is a Buddha, and therefore does not act like one."

But those listening, even if they accepted this strange statement from the Great One, did not suddenly realize their Buddhahood, their true Selves.

The way to beat the aeons and realize your divine identity in this lifetime is to travel the road of yoga. This road, like a modern expressway, has a number of lanes. Though you must use all the lanes to some extent, there is one best suited to the particular psycho-physical vehicle in which you are now travelling. You should use that lane more than any of the others.

There is, for instance, the fast lane of the Jnana Yogi. The Perennial Philosophy is all he needs as a working hypothesis. He practices the metaphysical disciplines of discrimination between the Real and the apparent until he comes to a full realization of his divinity, of his identity with Brahman.

But few can travel this lane without a crash. To succeed one must have a particular kind of mental constitution, and must have travelled the yoga highway, using the other lanes, for a long period — perhaps for many lifetimes. Certainly *Jnana Yoga* is not for one who is on the preliminary stages of the spiritual life. "The Unmanifest is very difficult for embodied souls to realize," says Lord Krishna in the *Gita*. And that's what the Jnana Yogi is attempting.

Another traffic lane on the highway is the one known as *Karma Yoga* — or the way of desireless action. Doing "good works" is not enough if they are carried out with desire for renown, honors, money, or rewards of any kind. The every-day actions of doing your job *are* enough if you dedicate those actions to God, and eschew all attachment to the fruits of your work. You must have no anxiety or concern about success or failure, praise or blame, or any other result.

"Work is worship," Baba says. "Work for the love of God and leave the fruits of your labor to Him." But, of course, you must find the right occupation: one that will not harm, but will in some way benefit, your fellow men.

The *Bhagavad Gita* gives an inspiring chapter on *Karma Yoga*, pointing out how it purifies the heart and leads directly to man's goal of liberation from the thraldom of the flesh.

But it is difficult to make steady progress on this or any other lane of the yoga highway without a Divine inspiration. Such inspiration comes through the emergence, from time to time, of a Divine Incarnation in human form. Jesus, the Christ and Gautama, the Buddha are considered Incarnations of Divinity in Christian and Buddhist theology. But the most powerful statement of this aspect of the Ancient Wisdom is contained in the *Bhagavad Gita* where Krishna is shown as an Incarnation of the Supreme God.

Intense love and devotion, towards Christ, Krishna or any other Godman is called the *Bhakti Marga* or the yoga of Devotion. This loving worship of an Incarnation, and constant contemplation of His Attributes, offers the best and easiest lane-way for the majority of people. "Those whose minds are fixed on me in steadfast love, worshipping me with absolute faith, I consider them to have the greater understanding of yoga," said Krishna. His "me" refers of course to any form that the Supreme God had taken, or would ever take, on earth.

Constantly aware of Who he is, an Incarnation can most effectively remind his followers of what they have forgotten, and through his grace and love lead them surely towards their destination. But neither devotion alone nor works alone will suffice. Both together are essential. So *bhaktas* must spend time on the karma lane-way, and vice versa.

Another yoga lane on which all must spend some time is that known as *Raja Yoga*. In this there is much inward-looking and use of will-power to control mind and emotions, to concentrate the mind and go beyond it in meditation and contemplation. For a few this is the main way along the route. All must practice, to some extent, its disciplines of mind control, meditation, self-enquiry.

Whatever the main yoga lane-way selected for an individual by circumstance, Teacher and temperament, the important thing to remember is that man has a double nature, a false ego created by his desires, and an eternal Self. His yogic task is to irradiate the false ego with Divine Light and so merge it into his eternal Self. As this happens, his sense of separateness diminishes and his feeling of unity with his Divine Ground increases. Eventually he is completely identified with his eternal Self, and all action, all motivation comes from that high level.

But, like the Prodigal Son, man does not, for a long time, want to go back home, his memory of it is dim, coming, if at all, only in brief flashes. Even after he remembers, and desires to go back to where he truly belongs, the journey will not be a short one. Altogether, with his going out, his

wallowing forgetfully in the flesh-pots of the world, and his return along
the yoga highway, much time — as man knows time — has been or will be
spent. Indeed it requires many lifetimes on earth, and in other locales
between earth lives, say the Hindus, the Buddhists, and some sects of the
Christians and Moslems who believe in reincarnation.

There are, however, many people in the world who think we have
only one life on earth, and at death are liberated from our bondage. Indeed, at death, a chance *does* come for liberation, as *The Tibetan Book of
the Dead* teaches, and as people who have tottered on the borders of
death, and returned, have confirmed.

At the abrupt change in consciousness brought about by the transition called death, the Individual has a sudden clear vision of the Pure Light
of the Void (Brahman). If he can hold his gaze upon It and move steadily
towards It, he is saved, liberated; he achieves the bliss of union with the
Divine Ground.

But only those who have lived the yogic life, have striven towards
this goal, and whose thoughts are thus on the Divine at the moment of
death, are likely to take advantage of this avenue of escape.

The vast majority will turn away from the Light that is "like a thousand suns," and, led by desire of one kind or another, will move off into
the astral planes. Those who have lived good lives on earth will reach —
and perhaps dwell a long time in — one of the high heaven planes, but, the
Ancient Wisdom teaches, they, too, will eventually return to life on earth.
Heaven is not liberation; it is a joyful interlude between lives.

The Voice of Brahman, speaking through Lord Krishna in the *Gita*,
says emphatically: "At the hour of death, when a man leaves his body, he
must depart with his consciousness absorbed in me. Then he will be united
with me. Be certain of that. Whatever a man remembers at the last, when
he is leaving his body, will be realized by him in the hereafter; because that
will be what his mind has most commonly dwelt on during his life.... If
your mind and heart are set upon me constantly, you will come to me.
Never doubt that."

These, then, are the basic concepts of the Perennial Philosophy: the
eternal existence of a Divine Ground of Being; Man's identity with It, and
his capability of realizing this identity through conscious Union with the
Divine Ground. Such realization, which is the whole purpose of life on
earth, is achieved through the self-disciplines called Yoga. Great help is
given in this by the coming, from time to time, of Divine Incarnations,
through whose mediation and grace the Way to the Goal is made easier.

Lord Krishna taught these eternal verities in full several millenia ago;

Christ and others taught them in part. They are again being taught in full by Sai Baba. His life, his daily discourses, the Divine power shown in his miracles, are being used towards this end, being used to polish new facets of the ancient Diamond of Truth — to irradiate the dark storm clouds of modern skies.

Man is burdened with the delusion that the true is the false, that the temporary is eternal. Long identification has trained him so. He has to be re-educated into the right vision. The truest thing, that fact that persists unchanged, is the 'I' itself. All else is unreal, but appearing as real. You may ask, how is this so? I grow old; I change; I am healthy; I fall ill. But in and through all the growth and decay the 'I' persists. 'I slept well,' you say. But during sleep you were not aware of the body, the senses, the mind or the external world. Yet the 'I' persisted through the dream world, through deep sleep.

SATYA SAI BABA

8
THE
REPAIR SHOP

*Far, far away is He, and yet He is very near, resting
in the inmost chamber of the Heart.*
MUNDAKA UPANISHAD

During our first weeks at "Brindavan" Swami seemed to be treating us with the special consideration accorded to home-coming prodigals, or lost sheep, found again. He gave us a sweet smile, and often a word, whenever he saw us.

But the day came when that treatment stopped. No more smiles, not even a look of recognition! He simply gazed through us as if we were not there.

What had we done to deserve this, we wondered. "I have been talking to people in the outer grounds," Iris reflected, ruefully. "He does not approve of that when one is living inside. I guess it looks like parading one's privilege. I should not have done it, but they were old friends I wanted to see...."

Well, maybe, I thought, but how then have *I* sinned?

We had known others — Indians and one or two westerners — who had been put in the "repair shop," as some call it. I remember being surprised to find one young Indian, who had been close to Swami, waiting with the crowd beyond the gate.

"I'm not permitted inside," he told me.

"Are you being tested, or something?"

"I was tested long ago. I think I'm being polished." He smiled painfully, as if the abrasive hurt somewhat.

Then there was the young Australian, Peter Rae, who quickly discerned why he was "in for repairs." "One morning," he told me, "I was feeling frustrated because people around in the rooms kept spoiling my meditation. I got so frustrated and up-tight that I gave up the meditation, and went outside. Then, soon after, I went to the front of the Mandir to wait for Swami's darshan, but there more irritating things happened; it finished with an Indian pushing me aside and almost sitting on top of me.

"I blew my top; said something very rude to the Indian, grabbed my bag and went off in a rage. Later I found another place to sit in the circle. But when Baba came out, he completely ignored me. I was used to him giving me a warm smile and often saying something to me. Now, whenever he seemed to be coming towards me, he changed direction and went somewhere else. Or he looked through me, as if I was empty air.

"Suddenly I realized that I should not have lost my temper in either case. I should have kept my cool, and felt nothing but love whatever happened. Swami confirmed this in the way he often uses to teach me. Soon after the darshan I overheard two devotees talking; one of them was explaining to the other how he tries always to treat every person as if that person was Swami, himself.

"I went back to my room to think. Then I picked up a copy of the *Bhagavad Gita,* and opened it at random. This is another way Swami teaches me. My eyes immediately fell on the verse:

> He who sees the Lord within every creature,
> Deathlessly dwelling amidst the mortal,
> That man sees truly."

Peter had had his re-adjustment, and was out of the repair shop by the next darshan. And mighty happy he was to be out of it because some cold draughts blow through that shop.

But with some people it takes a long time, and a good deal of inward searching, before they diagnose the fault that must be corrected. Swami never seems to tell them directly — at least not in the cases I have known — though he may give them indirect, subtle guidance and instruction, as he did with Peter.

The treatment certainly makes you look within as objectively as possible. Careful inner scrutiny will inevitably reveal plenty of faults and failings. Then you have to decide which particular fault is in for treatment and repair. On the other hand, Swami may have quite another reason for ignoring you, for withdrawing the benign look and standing you in the corner of the schoolroom, to change the metaphor. There may be another kind of lesson you have to learn.

One day a letter arrived for me from a man who wanted to translate my book, *Sai Baba, Man of Miracles* into another Asian language. He asked me to request Baba's permission and blessings for the work — if, indeed, he should do it.

This meant, to seek his permission, I had somehow to breach the intangible wall around Swami, and risk a rebuff. Soon afterwards I saw him walking beside the pandal, and, with some trepidation, strode over and confronted him. Quickly, before he could turn away I told him about the letter and the request.

He smiled with a warmth that swept the painful, rejected feeling from my heart. "Yes," he replied. "Give him permission, and send him this." With a quick whirl of his hand, he took some vibhuti from the air and gave it to me. "He's a good man. He has my blessings," Baba concluded. I knew that he had never met the man, personally; but that, of course, is never necessary.

Immediately following this happy incident, Swami returned to the practice of looking through us as if we were a pair of uninteresting gateposts. We began to wonder if we would be permitted to go to the ashram at Puttaparti if Swami went there, as predicted, at the end of the Summer Course.

In the last few days there were several lectures on the subject of Sai Baba, himself. One was given by the eminent scientist, Dr. S. Bhagavantam who, since his retirement, has spent most of his time working for Baba — not only as a translator, but in the organizational work connected with Satya Sai educational and other activities.

Dr. Bhagavantam is a keen, accurate observer, and does not brush aside facts just because they do not fit into the current framework of science. He gave the audience some inexplicable facts in his lecture.

"Observing over a long period the amount of food that Swami eats, I worked out that it was equal to about 1000 calories a day. I, myself, would collapse on that amount, yet Swami uses up three or four times as much energy as an ordinary man like myself." Another fact: "It's common knowledge that Baba's formal schooling did not extend beyond the first grade of high school, yet with great acumen he advises the scientists, doctors, lawyers and business men who come to him for counsel on their practical affairs. Furthermore, though he never reads — never, indeed, has time to read — the Indian and world scriptures, he quotes from all of them." Another fact: "I am rather proud of my English, having spoken it for forty years, and used it for lecturing to scientific groups overseas. Baba often deflates this foolish pride when I am translating for him on the public platform. He will often supply the right English word when I am unable to bring it to mind, and correct any deviation I make in the translation. Yet he had very little formal schooling in English. "Knowledge and expertise in these, and many other matters, seem to have been born in Sai Baba."

Bhagavantam told an amazing story about his reactions in the early days he spent with Swami. "I saw him materialize on the public platform a large precious stone set in silver-colored metal. I felt no amazement about this because I had watched him perform many materializations. Next, Baba placed the stone, in its setting, against the forehead of the large silver statue of Shirdi Sai Baba on the same platform. It stayed there, and I was dumbfounded. Even if it contained a magnet, the metal setting and stone would not hold against the silver of the statue.

"I was so amazed that I discussed the matter with a group of colleagues at the ashram. No one could explain the phenomenon.

"Then I laughed at myself — after swallowing the camel I was rejecting the gnat. If Baba had the power to materialize, why should it be odd that he also had the power to make one metal adhere to another — the laws of physics notwithstanding!"

The great scientist has written: "Today I do not ask silly questions. I do not try to find out what natural law he is breaking, and how. When a scientist finds that something happens which cannot be explained or grasped by the laws known already, he just accepts that something; and that is a not-yet-explained phenomenon. This is how science has grown. So, since what I have seen (and what I am seeing and what I shall see hereafter) do not come under any known laws of science, I simply enunciate the law that Bhagavan Sri Satya Sai Baba transcends the laws of science; and that becomes a law of science."

Talking to various people about Swami's evening discourses — which we enjoyed so much through our open windows — we discovered that he was using them not only to teach the multitude, but, at the same time, to give pointed instruction to a few individuals in the audience. Listening to him, you would never know which individuals were getting the special, timely advice; but they themselves knew.

For instance, a married couple of our acquaintance had been quarrelling even more than usual one day. That evening, as they sat listening to Baba's discourse, they heard him suddenly take up the subject of quarrels among people whose personalities chafe against one another. He talked about the Divine Family of Shiva, his consort Parvati, and their two sons, the elephant-headed Ganesh and Subramanyam. What pointed differences there were between these unique individuals! One might expect plenty of conflict, misunderstandings, quarrels. Yet there was always harmony between them. Why? Because each saw beyond the outer personality differences to the inner Atman where all are One. Thus they were able to understand, tolerate, and even enjoy, the differences and diversity of their unique personalities.

Everyone, Baba said, should see the conflicting differences in personalities — the selfishness, intolerance, misunderstandings, prejudices — in others as only partial realities. They will all vanish with the passage of time. Be constantly aware of the Eternal Divine Self in all. This is the only way to live in harmony with relations, friends and neighbors, he told them.

He looked directly at the couple as he said these things, and, because they had experienced his omniscience before, they knew he had been aware of their bad quarrels, and that the lesson was specially for them. They must try to live his teachings.

On occasions during the course, various people whom I had known as close Sai devotees, in earlier days, came to "Brindavan," not to attend lectures, but just to see Swami. As had been their privileged custom in the past, they came directly into the long ante-room, and waited, hopefully, for a word or two with Baba.

"Things have changed," one of them told me, mournfully. "The crowds around Swami are far too big now. We old devotees used to enjoy wonderful, long talks with him on our personal problems. Now he does not have time for us. He passes us by with a fleeting smile, and sometimes not even that." The devotee's smile was bleak, his face as long as the room.

So, I thought, Iris and I are not the only ones feeling neglected. Perhaps, after all, there had not been anything specifically wrong in our conduct. Perhaps Swami was just testing us — and testing these other long-established devotees — to see if we are fit and ready to move up to a higher class in his school.

I recalled the gesture he often made in the old days when he would pat me on the chest, and say, sweetly: "I am there always; your heart is my house." I had seen him do, and say, the same thing to others, too.

Baba, who knows his identity with Brahman, speaks as Brahman when he says, "I am in your heart." Brahman, he teaches, as the Ancient Wisdom taught, is in the heart of all that's born, but there It is called the Atman. The Atman, Brahman, and Sai Baba are one.

We must understand that this presence of Baba in the spiritual heart is a *conscious* presence. Brahman is universal consciousness, present in all conscious beings. Through this universal consciousness, with which he is identified, Baba is plugged into our individual consciousness, which is only a part of the Whole. Whenever he wills it, he can know what we are thinking and feeling.

If we, on our part, can become continually aware of his conscious presence, our minds and hearts will be *en rapport* with him – with the Divine Mind, as it is expressed through the personality of our beloved Guru.

How wonderful it would be to have him always vividly and fully there with us, even though the seas divide! This surely is a lesson that he is trying to teach us. We must not stay forever in spiritual childhood, needing the Parent's physical presence all the time for assurance and comfort. We must grow to where he dwells with us forever, wherever we are. How long does one need in the repair shop to have that much extra spiritual power and capacity installed?

However long, it is a lesson doubly worth learning – not only for our own progress, but also for our heart's peace. The crowds around Baba are increasing, and will increase still more. His chronological time is limted, on the physical plane, to the twenty-four hours a day allotted to human beings. If we don't want our hearts to ache and our eyes to weep because our ration of that chronological time is too small or non-existent, we must find the timeless Lord within ourselves. He is there waiting to be recognized.

So, during the Summer Course we experienced the practical beginnings of a great lesson. Later it was to be demonstrated, and beautifully illustrated, by a special disciple of the Lord Sai.

The sugar cane should welcome the cutting, the hacking and the crushing, the boiling and the straining to which it is subjected; without these ordeals the cane would dry up and make no tongue sweet. So, too, man must welcome trouble for that alone brings sweetness to the spirit within.

Some of you feel neglected by me when disappointment or trouble come upon you. But such obstacles alone can toughen your character and make your faith firm. When you hang a picture on the wall, you shake the nail and find out whether it is firm enough to bear the weight of the picture. So, too, in order to prevent the picture of God (His image in your mind and heart) from falling and being shattered to bits, the nail (i.e. God's Name) driven into the wall of the heart has to be shaken to ascertain whether it is firm and steady.

SATYA SAI BABA

9

THE
LORD'S LEGS

*I say to you there is not God and Man but only
God-Man or Man-God - only ONE.*

                                        MIRDAD

Among the old friends I often saw gathering at "Brindavan" for
Baba's evening discourses was Dr. Sunder Rao. I could pick him out in the
crowd streaming through the gardens by his shining dome of head and
large, gentle eyes. Greeting each other, we would stand talking briefly,
while Gita swung her trunk and feet expectantly, as she waited to garland
Swami. Inside and outside the pandal, there was the same air of expectancy until the red-orange robe emerged from the side door.

If Dr. Sunder Rao, who was a leading eye-specialist of Bangalore,
happened to arrive early, I would get a longer chat with him. He had some
interesting things to tell, especially as he had come closer and closer to
Baba during our absence. His son-in-law, Sri D. Narendra, had been
appointed Principal of the "Satya Sai College of Arts and Science" at
Whitefield, and all members of his family circle were ardent Sai devotees.

On one of these evenings he told me about a sudden sickness that
had temporarily crippled Sai Baba's body. This had, in fact, happened only
a couple of weeks before Iris and I arrived back in India in April, 1974.
The doctor suggested that I confirm the details of the case with Dr. V. K.
Gokak who was living in the same house as Swami during the illness.

But, as busy Director of Studies for the course, Gokak was not easy
to pin down. He bustled from point A to point B, head thrust forward,
heavy, horn-rimmed spectacles sliding down his nose, often — even on
warm days — a scarf around his neck. In his dark western clothes, contrast-
ing with the Indian white, he looked more like an absent minded dean of
his beloved Oxford than an educational leader of India. Eventually he

found, or made, the time to talk to me, and we sat together on a low stone wall in a quiet part of the garden. Readily, he answered my searching questions about the series of events that Dr. Sunder Rao had described. He was able to confirm, and fill out with more details, the doctor's account. Then later I talked to Joel Riordan who was an eye-witness to some of the scenes. Finally, before I left India, Swami, himself, gave me permission to write the facts of the story.

Here they are. One day, about the middle of March, 1974, Baba's close disciples observed that he was moving about with some difficulty. Questioned, he told them that he had some pain in his feet and ankles. The pain began to creep further up his legs, leaving paralysis in its wake. Soon the paralysis was half-way up his calves, then above the knees, and he could neither walk nor stand alone. To go to his bathroom, or anywhere else necessary, he had to crawl on his hands, dragging his useless legs behind him.

This all took place at "Brindavan," and the few men, who had the right of access to his private rooms there, became very alarmed. On several occasions Dr. Sunder Rao, the only medical man in the group, tested Baba's legs with a needle, and found that they were completely lacking in the normal reflex to sharp pricks. There seemed to be no sensation whatever in the legs.

The doctor begged Swami to let him call in a leading neurosurgeon of Bangalore. Swami refused, remarking that a medical man could do nothing. He would, he assured his disciples, cure himself at the right time.

But when? With the passing of the days the faith of those around him weakened, and their fears grew stronger. Tears ran down Joel's cheeks as he watched the suffering of his "great friend." One day he shouted to the others: "*Do* something. Get the best specialist you can, *now*. If you don't, *I* will."

"It's no use," they told him, quietly. "Swami has refused to see an outside doctor, and we can't force him to."

Out in the gardens, the crowds knew that something was amiss with Swami's health, and rumors ran riot. Knowing this, and wishing to allay fears, he sometimes sat near an open upstairs doorway, writing. The sight of him brought comfort to the crowd. He could not, of course, give his usual darshans, walking through the grounds, but to help ease the public tension, he would at times give a standing darshan through a partly open door. Unseen by the waiting crowd, there was a disciple on each side, supporting him as he swayed on paralyzed legs.

One thing that startled the group of the inner chambers was the cause of the illness. They all knew that Swami had been seriously ill before, and had cured himself in a trice when he had willed to do so. But on these occasions he had made it known that he had taken upon himself the disease of a devotee, who would have been unable to bear it. This had happened not only during his present Incarnation but also during his former life at Shirdi.

The disciples naturally assumed that the cause was the same this time. Swami, however, stated that this time someone had poisoned him. Just before he left Puttaparti, someone had sent up a food offering; it was poisoned. Oh, yes, he assured them, he had known the food was poisoned, known who the poisoner was, and was fully aware of his thought, which was: "If Sai Baba is God, let him prove it by overcoming the effects of this poison. If he fails to do so, he will die, or else be crippled for life."

So Baba had eaten the food because, he told his disciples, "If the man needs this to establish his faith, I will help him."

If Baba had countered the effects of the poison while eating it in his private rooms, or immediately afterwards, the poisoner would have thought that Swami had not eaten the food. There could have been several reasons for his refusing it — human reasons. It was necessary for Swami to suffer a while from the poison. The man who had made this attempt on his life would know why he was suffering, and would expect him to die or be permanently crippled thinking, "I've proved he is an ordinary man and an imposter." Then Baba would glorify the Divine Power by an instantaneous and complete cure.

But the disciples, full of fears, their faith shaken, wondered if Baba could really throw off this crippling thing that mounted upwards like the deadly hemlock Socrates had swallowed — except that its progress was slower.

Dr. Sunder Rao exemplified the conflict of doubt and faith in all minds when he issued an ultimatum, to Baba. "Swamiji, if you don't cure yourself by 6:00 p.m. tomorrow, I will bring in the specialists and go ahead with full medical tests to determine a treatment, and, hopefully, a cure."

Baba said nothing, and Sunder Rao knew that it was a hollow threat because he could not force the Lord to submit to his plan. But it made him feel better to release his feelings that way.

They all knew it was no use asking Baba to name the poisoner — aware as he would be of their feelings towards the man. How many of them could have practiced the Divine understanding contained in Baba's words: "The sun of God's love shines on good and evil alike. I shall not forsake even those who deny or deride me. Those who stay away, those who stray away, will at last be drawn near and saved. Do not doubt this!"

One might wonder why anyone in the world should want to harm the Man who feels nothing but Divine Love for all. One might, until one remembers what happened at Calvary to another Incarnation of Love and Truth. "It is more dangerous to teach Truth," wrote sage Tsiang Samdup, "than to enter a powder magazine with a lighted torch." Those who awake the sleepers from their false but pleasurable mortal dream with the sharp prongs of Light — are never without active enemies.

Some, in their foolish ignorance, crucify Sai Baba through the newspapers for the sake of a sensational story — and a fat check. Some attack him to gain publicity for their own money-making stunts, like the "wonder-working yogi" who, a few years ago, issued competitive challenges to Baba through the gutter press. Some turn against him, with various degrees of bitterness and spite, because he has not given them the miraculous worldly favors which they assumed were their right.

But it seems that his most vicious and deadly enemies are to be found among the magicians of the left-hand Path. I heard of one such yogi-of-the-left from some young people at Prasanti Nilayam. They had been to the magician once while Baba was away on tour. He was apparently a tantrist, teaching the lower sex tantrism — proclaiming it a speedy road to liberation. But it is a dangerous road, at best. The tantrist, seemed, to the casual observer, to have the benevolent expression of a Buddha, shining above his ochre robe, but beneath he was full of lust and hypocrisy. His yogic practices had deteriorated to sex orgies, aided by hypnotic power.

Certainly his hypnotic powers were tremendous. A good proportion of his pupils were from outside India. One of these, a young, attractive woman from the Far East, related how, when at the ashram he first called her to him, she felt a power, like invisible hands, pulling on her thighs, forcing her to walk towards him. Terrified, she remembered Sai Baba, and inwardly called on his name. The spell was broken; she turned aside, and soon after made her escape from the ashram.

A young Dutch woman, after spending a short time near Sai Baba, had heard that a number of people from the West were going to this particular magician. Unaware of the nature of his teachings, she decided, out of curiosity, to visit him. Soon after she arrived, the magician with the deceptively Buddha-like face told her to go into a certain room and take all her clothes off. A little apprehensive, she did as ordered and sat on a couch, thinking that perhaps a lady doctor would be coming to examine her.

Instead the yogi, himself, came in. He told her commandingly, to lie prone (in the *savasana* posture) on the couch as he wished to test her reflexes and relaxation capacity. After giving her some relaxation and breathing routines, he began to massage her body. The massage became gradually more erotic. But the woman's responses were only surprise, alarm and fear.

After a time the black magician exclaimed, "Your body is dead. Sai Baba has killed it. Get dressed!" He appeared to be full of a fierce anger as he left the room.

Presently an Indian woman came in, explained that she was one of the yogin's advanced pupils, and had been ordered by him to teach her some yogic exercises that would revive the flow of vital energy in her body, making her receptive to the teacher's special dynamic yoga. The Dutch woman found that the special exercises were a form of masturbation.

That night she found the yogin dominating her mind in dreams. She fought against the influence, calling on Baba's name repeatedly, and asking him for help. The black magician's power seemed to weaken and retreat. Next morning she jumped on the first bus that passed the ashram, not caring about where it was going.

A bearded young man from America, who was at the same ashram for a few weeks, told me that the yogin had stated he could dominate a pupil's mind and will absolutely – given time. A pupil so completely dominated could be sent out to murder anyone the tantrist desired out of the way. The American added it was known to several in the ashram that one pupil was being trained, conditioned and overshadowed by the tantrist for the purpose of killing Sai Baba. As the dark hates the light that overpowers it, the black magician hated Baba who frustrated many of his designs.

How many times must the Sai power have defeated the machinations not only of this particular magician, but of other dark forces! These struggles go on within the intangible zones, unperceived by ordinary men. Fortunately the powers of Light are always in the end stronger than those of Darkness.

Despite all the enmity and hate in certain areas, there may not, of course, have been a black magician behind the poison attempt, but simply some callous person, prepared to risk Baba's life for the sake of a test.

On the night following his ultimatum to Swami, Dr. Sunder Rao had a dream in which he was sprinkling water on Baba's injured legs. Some years earlier Swami had cured himself of paralysis of his left side by the sprinkling of water, so the doctor thought his dream may simply have been one of wish-fulfillment. On the other hand, it may be a sign that a cure was coming soon.

Next day, after the morning at his surgery, he went out to White-field. Swami seemed worse. Sunder Rao applied further tests, and found the paralysis had crept higher in the Lord's legs. The six o'clock deadline came and went. But the doctor, of course, made no move to carry out his threat. What would be the use unless Swami agreed!

Yet the whole group felt they could not bear to sit there any longer, watching the Lord suffer, and unable to do anything about it. When would he cure himself? *Could* he, in fact, do it this time?

Swami was away in his bathroom when one of them expressed this question, and this doubt. It seemed like a sad lack of faith, the doctor thought, but his own mind had been registering the same terrible questions. It had been reminding him that sometimes the powers of darkness seem to be given full reign for a period. This was the case with Jesus in his last days when he was taken and mocked, tortured and crucified, and cried out in agony from the cross: "My God, why hast thou forsaken me?" For all his Divine powers, Jesus had died at the hands of his enemies.

Swami re-entered from the bathroom, dragging himself across the floor. Sunder Rao, Gokak, and a young disciple named Muralli ran forward to help him into his chair. One of Swami's brothers placed a fresh glass of drinking water on the table beside him. Joel was not present, but most of those who had witnessed the progress of Baba's paralysis were there.

After a long silence, Swami drank some of the water. Then he said something like: "I've had enough of this. It must end!" A look of great power and authority came into his eyes. The disciples sat up, alert and expectant.

Swami dipped his fingers in the tumbler and sprinkled a few drops of water on his right leg. Then he kicked the leg forward, and swung it freely, to show it was normal again. Sighs of relief and exclamations of joy echoed through the room.

Before Swami could treat the left leg, Dr. Sunder Rao told him about the dream, and asked if it would be possible for him, Sunder Rao, to sprinkle water on the leg and cure it. "Yes, if I give you the power," Baba replied, and handed the tumbler to Sunder Rao.

The doctor dipped his fingers in the tumbler and shook a few drops on the Lord's left leg. The miracle took place. Swami kicked and swung the left leg freely, then stood up and walked across the room, as if nothing had ever been wrong.

Tears of joy shone in the eyes of all, as their hearts rose up with Baba, singing their silent thanksgiving.

Become aware of your reality and you will lose the sense of identification with the body. That will make you disease-free and you will have perfect 'ease.'

Be ever in the consciousness that you are but a shadow of God, His image. Then no harm can hamper you. God walks along the Royal Road of Truth. The shadow holding to Him by the Feet, falls on hollow and hill, fire and water, dirt and dust. But, holding to the Feet as the shadow, you will be unaffected by the ups and downs of life.

SATYA SAI BABA

10
ON A
WHITE HORSE

In the crystal of quiet I gaze and the gold is there.... In the silence what ancient promise again renewed!

–A. E.

"Come to Puttaparti in four or five days," Swami called to me as he walked past, leading a large group of students towards the buses that were to take them to Puttaparti. Swami was going, too. The students had stayed back after the Summer Course especially for this treat. Some, I was told, would be able to spend only a few days at the ashram at Puttaparti before returning to their homes.

So, I guessed that Baba meant there would be accommodation for us at the ashram after the first students had left there. He had given me a beaming smile, so maybe "repair shop" days were definitely in the past. Still, my greedy heart ached for the old days when he used often to take me — sometimes both of us — in the car with him on such journeys.

"You'll be seeing him again soon, Gita," I told her, wanting to console myself as well as the elephant. A monkey in the tree chattered, as if he, at least, could not care less who came or went.

Three days later we had a chance to share a taxi to Puttaparti with Doctor C. G. Patel and his wife. It was less than the "four or five days" mentioned by Swami, but taxis had become expensive, so we took the opportunity, hoping for the best. Dr. Patel had spent many years in Uganda, and had been one of Idi Amin's medical advisers before the great expulsion of Asians. Now the couple were living back in India. During the hundred plus miles to Puttaparti he told us some interesting things about his experiences in Uganda and Baba's prophecies and warnings concerning the expulsion.

During 1968, in which year Baba visited Uganda and met Idi Amin, he advised Patel, and other Sai devotees living there, to leave the country as soon as possible. In four years time, he warned, all Indians will be forced to leave, in a hurry, so it was better to get away earlier, when they would have the chance to bring their worldly goods with them. Neither Patel nor the other devotees acted on this prophecy; the idea that they would be thrown out of Uganda seemed rather fantastic to them, then.

Either Dr. Patel or his wife was able to visit India and see Sai Baba at least once a year, and at each visit, Baba repeated the warning, pointing out that the time was drawing closer when the Government of Uganda would expel all foreigners from the country. But still Patel took no action in the matter.

When Swami's last warning came, saying that there were now only three months left, signs in Uganda supported the prophecy. Patel then moved, but it was already too late to get all his assets out. Most of his money he was able to transfer abroad, by various means, he said, but much valuable property he was forced to leave in Uganda. In fact he felt it was only by the Grace of God that both he and his wife escaped with their lives. The doctor knew too much about Idi Amin for his own safety.

"If I had acted on Swami's warning the first time, or the second time, or even the third time, I could have sold my property, got the money out, and left the country without the terrible frightening experience we had at the end."

All of which goes to show that the Lord can see the road to wise action ahead, and point it out to his devotees, but he can't force them to take it. They are beings of free will and free choice. This applies to spiritual as well as worldly matters.

We were coming into the clean-swept landscape where bare hills, with weird, iron-stone backbones, lie like sacred dragons, guarding the way to the Place of Peace. Our road began to saunter through ancient villages, unchanged since our last visit, unchanged since the beginning of time. But over the last few miles the surface had changed somewhat; we could even stay in top-gear most of the time!

Suddenly we were there, an unfamiliar high wall on one side, a bazaar of stalls and flimsy shops on the other. Through a new entrance we turned into a new Prasanti Nilayam. Most of the low, terraced houses, that once lined one side of the white Mandir, like a row of kneeling people, were gone. In their place stood great, three-storied blocks of residential units. On other sides were more big blocks, some completed, some half-built, some with only foundations in evidence.

The Mandir, itself, had expanded outward, sprouted an attractive temple roof, and changed its color from white to various shades of warm grey, trimmed with delightful pinks and greens. Though not yet completed, it stirred the heart as only a divinely beautiful, living temple of God can.

A plump little man wearing glasses found us accommodations in a ground-floor unit that had a broad closed-in verandah, and contained two day-beds. He also supplied us with mattresses and other odds and ends that make life more pleasant. His name was Sri Chiranjeevi, which means the "ever-liver," and for his many kindnesses, while we were there, we hoped his name would prove correct.

Though outwardly the village-ashram of Prasanti Nilayam had greatly changed, the inner life-style remained much the same as of yore. The evening bhajan was beginning by the time we had unpacked our few things, so we set off for the Mandir. On the way we passed by the end of a grand auditorium situated impressively where open sleeping sheds had once stood. While Iris found a place in the ladies' area, I went to the men's side of the prayer hall, and squeezed myself into the crowd on the verandah there.

From where I sat I could see the door through which Swami was almost sure to come when he left the interview rooms or came down from his own quarters above. I was rather anxious about what kind of reception I would get, if any — especially as I was here earlier than invited.

After some time the door opened and the small red-robed figure began to move slowly along the verandah in my direction. He paused frequently to speak to individuals sitting on either side. Whatever his greeting might be to me, the very sight of him warmed my heart, as always.

When he finally saw me at the very end of the verandah, his face seemed to light up — with surprise, I thought. He stood in front of me and let me touch his feet. He asked me how we had come, where we were accommodated, and if we were quite comfortable — truly the loving Mother welcoming a son who had arrived unexpectedly early. No signs of disapproval!

Then he went outside among the people who were sitting on the sand at the front of the Mandir. Bhajans continued inside and outside. Suddenly the singing came alive inside the prayer hall, and I knew that Swami had gone in and taken his place on the platform. Through an open window I could now see him on his high chair, waving his hand to brighten the bhajans.

My mind then, for some reason, switched to a story told by a great devotee, named Hilda Charlton. She had spent about sixteen years in India, searching for spiritual light under the guidance of several great Teachers before she came to Sai Baba. After a time with Baba she had gone to New York and started there a center for spiritual instruction, meditation and healing. From time to time I heard about the wonderful work of this center from young people who came from there to spend time with Sai Baba. Later I witnessed its wonders for myself.

But I want to give here Hilda's account of a remarkable vision she had in this prayer hall as she watched Swami sitting in his high chair. She said: "As I sat in the bhajan hall at Prasanti Nilayam, listening to the joyous songs sung by the devotees, and looking at Sai Baba sitting in his chair on the dais, suddenly over Baba's head there appeared a figure of great beauty, riding a white horse. At this time I did not know the significance of this symbolic figure. I asked someone if there was in Hindu scriptures a person who rode a white horse. I was told that the Kalki Avatar rides a white horse, and Kalki is the Avatar for whom people are looking forward."

Hilda goes on to say that, later, an American student carried out for her some research into the Hindu classics on the subject of the Kalki Avatar. The results, she says, were startling in their description of Sai Baba* and the age in which we live — known in the Sanskrit classics as the Kali Age. It began at the time of Lord Krishna's death, some thousands of years ago.

One of the great epics, the *Mahabharata*, forecast that this Kali Age would be marked by: moral decline, the spread of intoxicants, political corruption and oppression, famines and wars, atheism, spiritual decline, dishonesty and crime, the collapse of family life and social order, bitter class competition, unemployment problems, migrations, promiscuity, decline in the practice of Vedic truths and the prevalence of falsehood.

No doubt many of these terrible characteristics have been in evidence in every century since the Kali Age began. But today they are *all* here, all rampant, all on a greater scale than ever before. Furthermore, with the advanced technology available to the Dark Forces, the very existence of humanity on this earth is threatened.

But, Hilda Charlton points out, her student's research showed that there is hope for us. Long, long ago while Krishna was still on earth, the great sage Markandeya told the Pandava brothers during their forest exile about a talk he had had with Lord Vishnu, one of the Trinity in the Godhead, whose concern is the preservation of the universe. In this talk, taking place a few years before the Kali Age began, Lord Vishnu told how Light would come to earth when the evils of the Age had reached a level that required the direct action of God. Lord Vishnu said to the sage Markandeya: "When evil is rampant upon this earth, I will take birth in the family of a virtuous man, and assume a human body to restore tranquility by the extermination of all evils; for the preservation of rectitude and morality, I will assume an inconceivable human form when the season for action comes. In the Kali Age of sin I will assume an Avatar form that is dark in color. I will be born in a family in south India. This Avatar will possess great energy, great intelligence and great powers. Material objects needed for this Avatar's mission will be at his disposal as soon as He will think of them. He will be victorious with the strength of virtue. He will restore order and peace in the world. This Avatar will inaugurate a new Era of Truth, and will be surrounded by spiritual people. He will roam over the earth adored by the spiritual people.

"The people of this earth will imitate this Avatar's conduct, and there will be prosperity and peace. Men will once more betake themselves to the practice of religious rites. Educational centers for the cultivation of Brahmic lore, and temples, will reappear again everywhere. Ashrams will be filled with men of Truth. Rulers of the earth will govern their kingdoms virtuously. The Avatar will have an illustrious reputation."

This prophecy concerning the Kalki Avatar, from the *Mahabharata*, is collaborated in the ancient classic, the *Vishnu Purana*, which also mentions that this Avatar will display great superhuman powers in establishing the new age of Truth. It adds that, "His parents will be devotees of Vishnu, and will reside in a village worshipping the cowherd form of Sri Krishna."

Sitting there that evening on the verandah of the prayer hall, watching Baba's beautiful, unique "inconceivable human form" I thought to what a remarkable degree he fits the description of the Kalki Avatar. He is dark in color. His family was devoted to Vishnu. In fact his mother and grandmother were performing rituals of worship to Satyanarayana, the immanent aspect of Vishnu, for months before Baba was born. Their intense prayers were for a son, and when he arrived he was called Satyanarayana. When in his early teens, he announced that he was Sai Baba, he became known as Satya Sai Baba.

The prophecy said that the village of the Kalki Avatar's birth would worship the cowherd form of Krishna. Puttaparti was called, in earlier years, "Gollapalli" which means the "Home of Cowherds." When the prosperous area became a multitude of ant-hills (legend says through a cobra's curse) the name of the village was changed to "Puttaparti." But to eliminate the effects of the curse, to bring back the early cowfarming prosperity, the cowherd form of Krishna, called Gopalaswami, was worshipped in the village. This was the situation at the time of Sai Baba's birth there, so that, in this respect also the prophecy was fulfilled.

In fact, the Gopalaswami temple in the village was built and endowed by the Raju family into which Baba was born. In addition, his grandfather, Kondama Raju, dedicated a temple in the village to the consort of Krishna, the goddess Satyabhama. Krishna was, therefore, doubly worshipped in the village.

Sai Baba, himself, when young, directed some villagers to wash the stone used as an idol of Krishna in the Gopalaswami temple at Puttaparti. When this was done all could see an outline picture of "the cowherd form of Krishna," leaning against a cow, his flute at his lips. Presumably, the villagers had not known, or had forgotten, that this image was buried under the grime of the years on the old stone.

Lord Vishnu, talking to sage Markandeya in the northern regions of the *Mahabharata* epic, stated that he would be born as the Kalki Avatar in southern India. Certainly the village of Puttaparti was in the far south to the people of those ancient northern kingdoms. A glance at a modern map will show that, lying near Anantapur, it is well in the southern half of India.

Great energy and great powers are striking characteristics of Sai Baba — and also the fact that material objects are at his disposal as soon as he requires them. These are not only the objects he brings with a wave of his hand, but also the wealth he needs to build colleges, and travel about the country, dealing with the many facets of his mission.

In a lecture at the Summer Course, Dr. Gokak made the point that in the modern world power lies in money. Most of this money power, he said, has been and *is* in the wrong hands. It must come into the right hands where it will be used for divine purposes. We see this happening with Sai Baba. For years now, through legacies and bequests, money has been flowing into the Satya Sai Central Trust. This is administered by some of his close and trusted disciples, and funds from it are used for Baba's work in the world — especially for the big educational program.

A very interesting feature of the ancient prophecy is the statement that "educational centers for the cultivation of Brahmic lore... will reappear." "Brahmic lore," knowledge of the Ways to Brahman — as revealed in the ancient Indian scriptures, and revitalized by modern spiritual Teachers — is what is being taught and cultivated in the Sai Colleges and Courses. No other Avatar has carried out this kind of educational program. It is for people who will live, not as monastics or hermits, but as householders conducting the affairs of the world.

Baba is already "adored by spiritual people" in India and other countries. He has not yet begun to "roam over the earth," but has often stated that when his first house, India, is in order, he will travel and teach abroad.

The white horse on which the Kalki Avatar rides is probably symbolic, for he could not travel the long distances required for his mission on a horse. Cars are the horses of today, and there is food for thought in the fact that all of Baba's cars are white. They have come to him, often from devotees living abroad, in different colors, but, before using them, he has always had the colors changed to white. Swami's modern "white horse" is well known to folk in the fields and villages through which he passes. I have seen them stop work in the fields to bow in a gesture of prayer to the "white horse" passing by, or run out from the houses in the villages to perform some act of worship.

The restoration of "order and peace in the world" and the inauguration of "a new Era of Truth" is Sai Baba's aim; he has made this clear many times. His achievement of this aim is our hope for the future. But we must not expect this "Kingdom of God" on earth to come quickly. That was the mistake some of the apostles of Jesus made two thousand years ago. Baba has given himself another lifetime, another immediate Incarnation for the work. He says that about a year after he passes away from this life, he will take rebirth — this time in Kerala in the deep south. In that Incarnation he will be known as Prema Sai.

The bhajans ended and during the Waving of Lights Swami left the room and went through the door at the end of the verandah. To the eye of the world he was just a man, though an extraordinary one. To many devotees who have "experienced" him, and to some living Indian saints of deep spiritual perception, he is a major Avatar.

Hilda Charlton writes: "We have come upon the earth at the right time... through just a little effort on our parts, we can achieve *Mukti* (liberation). All we need to do is to keep His love in our hearts, His name on our lips; He will do the rest. What splendor fills the mind and heart in remembrance of Him!"

I am new and ever ancient. I come always for the restoration of Dharma (righteousness), for tending the virtuous and ensuring them conditions congenial for progress, and for educating the "blind" who miss the way and wander into the wilderness. Some doubters might ask, "Can Paramatma assume human form? Well, man can derive joy only through the human form; he can receive instruction, inspiration, illumination only through human language and human communication.

—SATYA SAI BABA

11
LIGHT IN WESTERN WINDOWS

*And not by eastern windows only, when daylight
comes, comes in the light.*

—ARTHUR H. CLOUGH.

After breakfast at Prasanti Nilayam the crowd begins to gather, and a semi-circle forms in front of the Mandir, men on one side and women on the other. Sitting there in rows on the clean sand, they face the Yoga Pillar in the center of the circular lawn, but their attention is beyond that — on the door at the end of the verandah from which Swami is liable to emerge at any minute.

It is expected that his morning darshan will begin at nine o'clock. But there is no certainty; it may be earlier or it may be at any time during the morning. When at last his robed figure — a spot of vivid red against the blue-grey background — does appear, a hush goes over the crowd, like the hush of nature at sunrise.

Then he begins his slow progress around the semi-circle, here and there he stops, perhaps has a word with someone, perhaps circles his hand to take vibhuti from the *akasha*. Now and then he points to someone and makes a gesture towards the verandah. Knowing that this means an interview, the person concerned jumps up eagerly and hurries to the Mandir. By the time Baba has finished his round, the verandah is usually crowded with people, who, in smaller groups, will be taken into the interview room, until everyone has been seen.

After the door closes behind Swami, the circle outside breaks up. The darshan is over; the interviewees for the morning have been selected. By what criteria does he select them from the crowd? In my presence someone once asked Baba that question.

"I see into the mind and heart," he replied. "I see who has an urgent problem and needs the help of an interview."

There are, indeed, some who do not need a verbal interview to obtain real help from Baba. Not only the Indians know, from experience, that darshan alone can bring blessings, contentment and concrete assistance in life's problems. Light rises in the east but soon shines on western windows. I talked to a few young westerners on whom the rays of Light had shone.

There was, for instance, the stubby young American with a dark, wedge-shaped beard who told me: "I was mad, I think. I would hear voices in my head urging me to kill, to rape, to assault young girls. . . . I believed there were demons around me, or in me . . . it was terrible!

"I came to Prasanti Nilayam, and have waited many hours – sitting here in line day after day. Baba had never given me an interview. But all the time his invisible help was there. I know it! He has driven the voices away. I have been made clean inside; I am cured – permanently!"

Tall, blue-eyed David Anderson of New York had become disillusioned with the emptiness and insincerity of life while still a student. He had dropped out of college and tried to find fulfillment or escape through sex and drugs. The escape was temporary; the emptiness that followed was worse than before.

His first step towards the spiritual path came through meeting Ram Das (Dr. Richard Alpert, formerly a psychologist at Harvard University) who had tried all the escape mechanisms that David had tried – and more. Then through meeting his Indian guru, Richard Alpert had found the true way to the higher states of consciousness.

After a long talk with David, Ram Das sent him to Hilda Charlton's New York Center. There he heard inspiring talks, meditated and received the spiritual influence that led him to Baba. He stayed in India a year. Then he returned to America, worked, saved enough money to come again to Baba's ashram, and had been there another six months when I saw him in 1974.

During all his time there, David had had very little external contact with Swami – one group interview during which there was no individual exchange between him and Baba, he said, and a few words spoken to him directly by Swami during darshans. Nevertheless, he had become, in his own words, "Conscious of Baba's ability to be aware of my unspoken thoughts and plans. I gradually came to understand that the most important things that were happening to me were internal and spiritual in nature."

Even so, there were times when David felt angry and hurt because

Swami showed him so little outward attention, and he would make up his mind to leave. But something deep inside him knew that Baba's actions were correct, and that it would be spiritually weak to run away.

When I was talking to him, he had, through Baba's austere treatment, come to this conclusion: "The key to everything here is Love with a capital 'L'. If you feel that Love, then no matter if Baba never looks your way, you still have gained the only important thing. Without the Love, if you have had a million interviews, you will come away with nothing."

Wise words from a young man, I thought. Without any of the expected outward favors from Swami, he could still feel the embrace of the Divine Love that flowed to all.

"How much longer will you stay?" I asked.

"About a month. Then I will go back to the States and finish my college education."

Back to the life he had earlier thrown away in disgust, but now he would carry Baba in his heart and the old life would take on new meaning and depth.

Young Richard Bayer of the refined, intellectual face, was another who, at that time, had never had a personal interview, though he had spent much time at the ashram. He liked to put his thoughts on paper and wrote, among other things: "Baba has never taught me in ordinary terms any lessons in philosophy or religion; I was never initiated into any specific religious practices, or given a fixed set of rules to live by. Instead I learned by watching Him; I learned that the qualities of Compassion, Forgiveness, Truth, Righteousness and Peace come from an inner source, and that each individual must train himself to find these attributes within.

"Baba taught me by allowing me to watch him showering Love on mankind, and by giving me the inspiration and strength to turn my vision inward. I learned that Baba can lead you to your own Divine Center, but only you, yourself, can allow it to happen."

The same search for spiritual meanings, plus the power of vibhuti and faith, is the theme of the story told me by thirty-two-year-old Maurice Barrett-Mendoza. Known to his friends of the Mandir circle as "Mo," this tall, solemn-faced young man has a background of Latin American Catholicism. By profession he is a teacher.

He was living in New York in 1971 when his cousin, Rosa, returned from a visit to India, and announced radiantly: "I have seen the Teacher we are all looking for — Sai Baba!"

During the next two years Mo and Rosa read and talked a great deal about Sai Baba, and started going to Hilda Charlton's New York Center.

They found an American *sadhu* (holy man) who, people said, had been with Sai Baba. The sadhu did not say so himself; he said nothing for he was practicing complete silence, and was known as Mouni Gill. Among the young and old who often came to sit near the Mouni in West Central Park were Mo and Rosa. "When sitting near him one felt warmth and joy."

Eventually Mouni left the bench in the park, and with a group of some thirty followers set off, in a hired bus, going they knew not where nor why. Mo was part of the travelling group. Moving slowly southward, they finished up in Mexico. There Mo left the group, and continued on alone into South America.

In August 1973, after he had been in South America for some months, he received a cable to say his mother was extremely ill in hospital in New York. He had always felt very close to his mother, Doctor Ofelia Mendoza.

Returning quickly to New York, he found her in a very weak condition, being fed intravenously. She had, Mo was told, a cancer that was not amenable to surgical treatment. Indeed, her conditon was so critical that the doctors gave her only a short time to live. They were treating her with hormones to slow down the progress of the disease, and delay the end, but no cure was expected.

Rosa still had some of the vibhuti she had been given by Sai Baba. She and Mo brought some, along with a photo of Baba, to the bedside. Dr. Mendoza agreed to take some vibhuti regularly, as they requested. The three of them also spent much time praying to Sai Baba for a cure of the cancer.

Almost immediately after starting on the vibhuti, Dr. Mendoza's morale lifted, and her physical condition began to improve. After a month, she was released from hospital. But there was still much pain, and she was kept on the hormone treatment.

"If I get well enough to travel, I will go to India to see Sai Baba, the Divine Mother," she told her son. Her desire to do this seemed very great. She was, he said, a very spiritual woman who had lived a life of practical service to mankind.

On December 15, 1973, Mo, his mother and Rosa were on a non-stop flight from New York to Bombay. After a night's rest there, they caught a plane to Bangalore. As Baba was not at Whitefield, they hired a car and travelled to Puttaparti. At the ashram they were given a room where Dr. Mendoza rested, for she was still quite weak, and the long journey had been exhausting.

Mo felt quite inadequate to describe her meeting next day with Sai

Baba. "It was too moving to talk about," he said.

Faith and vibhuti had brought her so far, Swami told her, and now she was under his very special care. In several more interviews, and with more vibhuti, Swami built up her strength and fostered her recovery.

Some nine months later, when Mo told me the story at Prasanti Nilayam, his mother was back in New York, at work. "Yes, she is completely well, again," he said.

Another young man from Hilda Charlton's Center was Howard Levin, a Jew with intelligent, piercing eyes, pale face and black moustache. An engineering draftsman by profession, his life-style was to live frugally while in New York in order to save his money for long visits to Sai Baba.

After several talks in the magic circle in front of the Mandir, and in our rooms, I asked him to write an account of how his time with Baba first began, and developed. This is his story:

It was in the winter of 1970, after having read and studied the *Gita*, Vivekananda and several Buddhist texts, that I came to the definite conclusion that an Incarnation was due on earth. Perhaps, indeed, He had already come. I was actually in India when I came to this conclusion, and thought that this was the most likely country in which to find the Incarnation, if he had already come. My mental image of such a Man was a Buddha-like figure, sitting under a tree in padmasana, dispensing blessings and discourses. After a long search in many places, I began to feel a sense of complete failure, and started to pray for help. My prayer was: "Oh, Lord, if you have taken birth anywhere, let me please find you and stay with you."

About three months later I heard that some friends of mine were at Whitefield, near Bangalore and decided I should go there and see Satya Sai Baba, about whose miracles I had heard.

As I walked through the gate at "Brindavan," I had the feeling that it was a holy place. Twenty minutes later I saw, in a crush of people, a little hand waving goodbye from a car. A fleeting glance it was, but enough to make me wait for Baba's return!

I was among the westerners who were living on the campus at "Brindavan" when Swami returned. He came to inspect the rooms. As he walked past me, he remarked: "New man." A girl close by complained of a stomach ache. Baba rolled back his sleeve and produced vibhuti for her. This was the first miracle I saw, and it seemed to me so natural — no show at all.

Baba then told us that when the classes began at the College, there would be no space for us in these rooms. We were worried and everyone was hoping that he would let them stay in his own bungalow. I wondered if, as a "new man," I would be included, should he do so.

The next day Baba came and said he had made arrangements for us to stay inside his bungalow. "This is your mother's house," he said, "You are always welcome." I was included.

Every evening he sat and taught us bhajans. He would sing to us in his sweet melodious voice. Often he gave us fruit and sweets — clothes, too, sometimes, and even money if we ran short. We had long group interviews with him, often lasting for three hours. I remember him leaning forward from his chair on one occasion and asking softly: "What do you want?" Someone replied, "Your Grace, Swami." "Yes, yes, — but some worldly gift?" He held his hand forward as if ready to make something the moment we made a request, but we all remained silent. Then there was a chorus of voices saying: "We want only your grace, Swami."

He seemed very pleased with this response, and began to discourse on the longing of the individual soul to merge with God. He used many parables to illustrate his points.

At the end of each interview, he would materialize a big handful of sweets — usually ladus, Mysore pak or halvah. It was always warm, as if just out of an oven, there was always enough to go around. Once he said to me, "Swami loves you more than a thousand mothers."

During that first eighteen months with him, I saw many sides of his personality. At different times he would be our mother, our father, our best friend, our Lord and Master, a joking child, a stern disciplinarian. He became everything to us, and we soon began to feel that he was the very basis and focal point of our existence.

I witnessed so many miracles. Rings, jappamalas, pendants, lockets, sweets, vibhuti, all seemed to pour from his hand quite naturally whenever he wished. Very often, too, our experience showed that he knew our innermost thoughts and feelings. We were quite sure he knew our spiritual needs. Often he showed that he knew what we were doing and saying when we were out of his sight; this once caused a laugh on me.

It was in December, 1971, and we were in Madras with Swami. Christmas was drawing near; we asked him if we could sing some Christmas carols for him. He agreed, so on the afternoon of Christmas eve, we rehearsed a few carols on the roof of the building where we were staying. Someone in the group suggested that we practice the song Bing Crosby made famous — *White Christmas.* I said, "Don't be ridiculous! Swami would not appreciate *that*."

When evening came we went to Baba's gathering. As we were to sing the carols, we were put into the first two rows. When from the dais he gave us the signal, we sang three or four of the carols.

Then Swami said, quietly, with a side glance at me, "Sing *White Christmas.*" We gave the best rendering we could, spontaneously. I felt foolish, but Baba seemed to enjoy it.

When the time eventually came that Baba stopped showering his attention on me, I was quite upset. Many ideas went through my mind. Perhaps I had failed him. Perhaps he was angry with me for my sinful thoughts — of which there were enough and to spare. In fact, I began to feel sure that this must be it, because he often gave me angry looks that held me back from him.

But then he would come to me in dreams, and say, "I'm *not* angry with you."

So what was it? I felt desperate, hungry for the love I had once received. Then I began to look at myself more and more. Finally a little voice from the depth of my heart began speaking to me: "Is Swami just a body? Is he not inside you and everywhere, pouring out his love and sweetness?" So — through a long and very painful process — I began to establish a contact and dialogue with the inner Baba.

In this way I get guidance in my actions. But there is a danger in this, too; the voice of my own desires could pose as the voice of the inner Baba. So I try to make sure that I am not led against the teachings Swami has given us verbally.

I look at the situation this way. A mother breast-feeds her young, but then weans them to more solid food. Baba does the same with us. He nurtures and pampers us, keeping us near him, but teaches us that we must go beyond the limited form, and see God everywhere. The change from the milk to the solid food is painful at first, though.

The first time I returned to America after being with Swami I was still very much in the baby stage. I felt the separation from him so much that it was difficult to sleep at nights. But on my second return to New York, after another period with Baba, things were not quite so bad, because I felt his presence more with me. On my third trip home, after Swami had almost totally ignored me in India, I found that I did not miss his physical form. I felt him there in New York with me, guiding and watching my every action. And it seemed that everything happened so perfectly for me.

My contact with Sai Baba has given me a firm foundation of faith in God, and a belief that someday, somehow, the good within me, and the good in the world, will triumph over the evil. Wherever I go now I have a sense of His personal Presence, protecting me, guiding me, watching over me. He gives me signs, personal signs, which lets me know he is always there.

Yes, I believe He is the Incarnation I was looking for. I would say He is Krishna all over again, but that, of course, is an experience of the heart. I pray that by His grace I may always feel Him within me, wherever I may be.

A young American who had evolved his own formula for coping with Swami's "cold shoulder" treatment was Johnima, leader of the *Lite Storm*. This was a colorful troupe of four minstrels (two young married couples) who played and sang for Swami, usually songs of their own composition.

It was their third visit to Sai Baba when I saw them. During an earlier visit they had learned many Indian bhajans, and the music they were now composing was filled with the love of God. It was – like their pre-Sai music – modern, stormy, high-spirited, and rather alarming to some old Indian devotees. But it was unrestrainedly devotional, and Baba seemed to like it. In fact, he often sat on the stage with them when they were performing.

One of their many good memories was the night, with Swami on the stage with them, when he said: "New song. Sing a new song." Johnima told the story: "We all waited expectantly for the inspiration to come. Then we started a chord, and the words and music of a new song flowed through us. It was very beautiful, and when Swamiji started singing with us, we felt real bliss. Many people afterwards expressed wonder that Swami had joined in this new creation as it flowed from us, but, at the time, we felt it was quite a natural thing. After all *he* was really the creator and we were only his channel. We called the song: 'You are in my Heart.' "

Johnima and his wife Sui-San had a small daughter. Neither of them had wanted children but Swami had told them it was their duty to have one. The baby was born in a house near "Brindavan" just after the Summer Course in 1973, and two weeks later, at a naming ceremony, Swami called her "Sai Sangeet," which, Johnima informed me, means something like, "The form of music of Sai."

Seeing Sui-San nursing the baby one day, I asked her, "Are you glad, now, that you had it?"

"For Him – yes. But I don't really feel it's *mine*. I feel I'm baby-sitting for God."

In truth that is what all parents are doing, and it would be a fine thing, in every way, if they could realize and remember it.

Johnima said that he had had a lonely childhood, with no friends except Jesus, whom he had regarded as his brother and playmate. Many years later when he first saw a photo of Sai Baba at the home of Richard Bock in Hollywood, it seemed just as if his friend Jesus had changed into

Sai Baba.

During their visits to India the Lite Storm singers had for months basked in the sunshine of Swami's loving care and attention. But, Inevitably, as it must be for all, the time came when the pampering in the kindergarten was over. In fact, for much of the time I knew the Lite Storm at the ashram in 1974, the cold shoulder and stern look from Swami were in evidence. How the other three felt about it I don't know, but Johnima said,

"There is Love behind Swami's frown, as behind every single thing he does. So even if he scowls at me, or ignores me — which is even worse — I continue to smile at him."

All these young people, and others I met around Sai Baba, were to me a sign of the spiritual tide that is rising among the younger generation in the West. The spiritual understanding I found illustrated again the ancient verity that soul-wisdom does not depend on the chronological age of the body.

This profound truth is symbolized in the sacred scriptures of India by the image of Dakshinamurti — a young man sitting under a banyan tree with a semi-circle of old sages before him. He is the Teacher, they the pupils. The same truth is illustrated by other examples in yogic literature and occult experience. For instance, the highest in the Paramahansa Yogananda line of Gurus is Babaji, who appears as a young man of about sixteen. Again, in the hierarchy of Masters and Adepts of the Great White Brotherhood, the one above all, who is known as "The King of the World," has the appearance of a very young man.

Writing to Dr. Annie Besant of his first sight of this exalted One, J. Krishnamurti, who was then, himself, only fourteen years old, said, "I was taken to see the King, and that was the most wonderful experience of all for He is a boy not much older than I am, but the handsomest I have ever seen, all shining and glorious, and when He smiles, it is like sunlight."*

Scatter the seeds of Love in dreary desert hearts; then sprouts of Love will make the wastes green with joy, blossoms of Love will make the air fragrant, rivers of Love will murmur along the valleys, and every bird will beat, every child will sing the song of Love . . . .

The service of man by man can lead to the discovery by man of the God that is his own reality.

—*SATYA SAI BABA*

12
MYSTERIES
OF HEALING

If your heart is united with God, you will be set free from karma even in this life.

BHAGAVAD GITA

Walking around the semi-circle, giving his morning darshan, Swami stopped before a woman and her small son who were sitting in the front row. The little boy was a cripple, unable to walk or even stand alone.

We saw Swami wave his hand indicating that both should go to the Mandir. The mother stood up. Swami took the boy by both hands and raised him to his feet. Instead of collapsing when Baba let him go — as we expected — the boy remained standing, though in a bent position.

"Walk!" Swami commanded, giving him a firm pat on the back. The boy straightened and walked towards the verandah. A sound like a swish of wind went through the crowd. Then, in the hush that followed, all watched the little cripple walk unaided, and climb the step onto the verandah. Swami followed, and took the mother and child into the interview room.

The crowd dispersed, buzzing with talk of the miracle. I located some people who were acquainted with the boy's family, and a doctor who knew his condition. After discovering all I could from these people I left the unit where I had been asking questions and making notes.

As I came from the building into the sunshine, I saw a knot of people coming from the Mandir. In front was the little cripple boy, walking alone, his face shining with pleasure. Behind came the mother with some friends and well-wishers. I joined the group just before they reached their rooms. In high spirits the boy ran the last few yards, climbed the steps, and went inside to see his father.

Invited inside, I was able to talk to the father, mother and some of their friends. The family, I discovered, was from Assam in the far north-east. At the age of six the boy had contracted chicken-pox. This, the father said, was followed by a condition which the doctors called muscular dystrophy. The condition got steadily worse, and during the last year his son had not been able to walk or stand unaided. The boy was now twelve years old, and according to medical opinion, would get even worse, and die in a few years.

This was the gloomy situation, when Baba slapped him on the back and said, "Walk!" The mother could not tell me much of what went on inside the interview room; she was too overcome with emotion in the presence of the Lord. She knew that Swami had said, "Don't worry. He is under my care and everything will be all right." Special medicine and vibhuti had been materialized on the spot for the boy.

Some weeks later I saw the lad with his mother, waiting for Swami's darshan in the grounds at "Brindavan." The joy that had transfigured his face was still shining there, and I knew that he had gained some inward precious things along with the ability to move about on his two legs.

Of the thousands of sick who sit hopefully in the Mandir circle, or along the tree-lined drive at "Brindavan," a few are cured, many are not. "Why does Baba not cure everyone, and remove all suffering?" — some people ask. Certainly, like Jesus, he has the immense compassion to do so. But the question of healing the human body poses deep problems and a many-sided mystery.

For one thing there is the philosophical question of free will. Man, as an individual, is given a degree of free will, and, of course, the responsibility that goes with it.

"I will be free," said the ancestral Spirit of mankind as God held him by a shining cord. "Then shalt thou be suffering. Pride will seduce thee, and thou shalt bring forth death," said the Supreme Voice. "I needs must strive with death to conquer life," responded the newly-created one. Thereupon God loosened from his bosom the shining cord, and the Spirit of Man was free to go forth into the world, to make his mistakes, to suffer thereby, and to grow in strength, wisdom, and stature from his suffering.

Disease and suffering are brought about by the ignorance and errors of man. If God wiped out all disease and suffering, with a wave of His Hand, they would return through the same human channels of ignorance and error. That is why Jesus said to at least one of those he cured, "Go your way and sin no more," the implication being that only by refraining from his former mistakes could he remain whole.

For God, Himself, to remove all sin and disease — ignorance and error — He would need to take away the free will that He has given, and turn man into a puppet, to be manipulated by Divine strings. And man could not, in this way, learn the lessons he is here to learn, and develop along the intended path.

In Divine healing, as demonstrated by Jesus and Sai Baba, it seems that the state and attitude of the patient plays a vital part. There is the question of belief and faith, for instance, Jesus said, "If thou canst believe, all things are possible," and pointed out that even faith the size of a grain of mustard seed was sufficient to work great miracles.

What is faith or belief in Divine power? Some people who declare that they have it, and indeed seem on the surface to have it, evidently do not, for no cure comes in answer to their fervently-voiced faith and prayer. On the other hand, there are people who are miraculously cured despite what *appears* to be weak or nonexistent faith.

So faith and belief are evidently something below the surface of the mind. They are not the result of rational thinking, but of inner experience — or, perhaps, of slowly built-up knowledge that belongs to the unconscious areas of mind. The mustard grain of faith may be there without the rational mind being aware of it.

One who declared that she "invariably lost her faith," and was cured despite that, was a young anthropologist from America. She had been in India for three and a half years, mainly with Baba, searching for the Truth about life. During a long period of Job-like suffering she had, she believed, learned some important lessons on the spiritual path, and had named herself, "Om." Living in a cave near Puttaparti, when I knew her, Om wrote down her own testament of personal suffering, and the miraculous cures that Baba brought her. Here are extracts from it:

"I began a bout of amoebic dysentery. Baba told the other foreigners that I had died, and for a while I certainly did not experience my body. When I returned to body consciousness there was a change in my mental set-up. I had previously been fighting to get well, but now I did not care if I lived or died. I recovered."

In the following extracts, where she writes that Baba told her to do this or that, she means that she received the messages telepathically.

Baba told me, "No more doctors; I will be your doctor." A couple of weeks later I broke my foot and was hauled to my room for hours of agony and panic, the anthropologist in me knowing the plight of unset bones. But gradually I surrendered to the idea of being a life-long cripple. The pain was still intolerable, and I wept in front of Baba's picture, begging for help.

He responded immediately: "Physically give up, go limp, like the man in the cinema who is shot." My whole body was at high tension with fighting the pain. But I did it; I went limp; surrendered entirely to the pain. Then there was no pain. For ten days the foot remained broken, yet without pain. When Baba quietly healed it in a bhajan, I felt regret because with the body's recovery came the return of limited consciousness.

Then came hepatitis and the near-insanity that goes with it. I understood that I must surrender, but my mind quailed. Baba directed again, and after two weeks healed me. Then there was malaria. With inability to keep down even water, I had thirteen days of no food or water. This to me was Baba's most significant miracle. He kept me alive with the vibration of the sound "Om." Several times a day during the thirteen days I was drenched in that sound. Then came another instant healing.

Many lesser diseases followed, all meeting the same rapid demise. Then last spring I fractured my skull in a car crash. The police arrived and went to fetch an ambulance. My brain shrieked to Baba for help. He affirmed that he would cure me, but not say when.

Refusing to go to hospital, Om was, after a half-hour's debate, put on a bus, travelling to her place of destination. It was to be a very long journey.

"Baba instructed me to feel the slightest receding consciousness at the center of the pain. As long as I was right there at the center, I could bear it, but the least distraction was unbearable agony. Anyway after many, many hours on the bus, striving to follow Baba's directions, there was again instant healing. This, of course, brought major reactions from the passengers and the driver of the bus."

Sometime later she was cured of a stomach ulcer by Baba's vibhuti, and: "since then," she writes, "my sadhana has been to listen to the vibration of the 'Om' sound within, and not be ill. My experience during the long series of illnesses was that I lost faith invariably, and was entirely negative. Baba's message to me was 'give up, be willing for perpetual pain, or to recover, or to be an invalid, as God wills. But suspend all conclusions, thereby neutralizing the pressures.' "

But she did, in fact, have faith, as it was defined to her by Sai Baba: "Faith is that state of being beyond both certainty and doubt, unaffected by the alternation of opposites. It is the balance point of equilibrium wherein all sufferings cease."

She concluded with these words: "Sai Baba's love is boundless, unlimited, unconditional. In return he asks sincerity alone. If we need help, all we have to do is to ask, and often not even that." What is such an attitude if not "faith"?

In answer to a query from a New Yorker, Baba once said: "Do you think I would confront you with pain, were there not a reason for it? Open your heart to pain, as you do now for pleasure, for it is my will, wrought by me for your good. Welcome it as a challenge. Do not turn away from it. Turn within, and derive the strength to bear it and benefit by it."

Then there is the thorny question of *karma*. Some eastern religionists regard this as an all-powerful Law, bringing inevitable retribution for wrong actions in past lives. Most western religionists do not believe in it at all.

There are deep-lying tendencies in our characters some of which were part of our equipment at birth. Vedantic philosophy teaches us that these tendencies are the result of our actions and life-style in former incarnations. Even if some of them appear to be inherited from parents, they are probably still karmic, in the sense that the parents were chosen specially for the transmission of the tendencies that are inherent in the karma of the person coming to birth.

Karmic tendencies towards wrong actions can be eliminated in only two ways. One, by pain and suffering that teaches the lesson that must be learned, and only when that lesson is fully learned, will the person's character change and his bad karma be wiped out. Two, by complete and utter surrender to God, which brings redemption. Surrender to God means finding your own true Self, and brings a basic change of character that wipes out all evil tendencies. Or, to put it in Christian terms, sin and the tendency to sin are redeemed.

While the karmic tendencies towards wrong doing and wrong living persist, it is not of much avail to cure the physical disease, which is, in reality, only a symptom of the inner "disease" or disharmony.

For inscrutable reasons of his own, Baba did cure the husband of the Delhi woman whom Arnold Schulman calls "Asha."* Her husband was dying of inoperable cancer of the ears and throat. Asha came to Puttaparti to beseech Baba to cure him. She went through much austerity in this, and Baba finally cured the husband who went back to work in his office. But eighteen months later he was hospitalized with cancer of the lungs, from which he died within three months.

Generally, if a disease is karmic, and the inner change necessary to eliminate whatever is left of the karma, cannot be brought about, Baba does not cure the disease. That he did so on this occasion, and brought temporary relief, simply shows the kind-hearted compassion of the Divine Mother.

Sai Baba does not talk much of the karmic nature of sickness; perhaps because it has been somewhat over-emphasized in the past among Hindus and Buddhists. Nevertheless, he does at times point to the significance of this factor.

Dr. K. C. Pani, an Indian medical man working in Washington D. C., U. S. A., had been a devotee of the departed Shirdi Sai Baba for a quarter of a century when, in 1969, he heard of his reincarnation as Satya Sai Baba. Then he began praying to both Sai Forms for the relief of his wife's crippling arthritis. Seeing Satya Sai Baba in a dream, he thought it was only a "psychological dream," and prayed, "If it was really you, Baba, come again." Baba came in another dream that same night, and Pani believed.

He visited Prasanti Nilayam the same year, and Baba said, "When I first came to you in a dream, you did not believe it, I had to come a second time."

During their time in India Swami brought deep joy and renewed faith to both Dr. Pani and his crippled wife. About the wife, who is herself a medical doctor, Swami said to Pani, "She must go through some more karma; but she will improve and be able to function." Through the Sai Grace, the couple gained the inner strength to bear the suffering and sorrow.

Young Subrata Das, son of Banamali Das, ex-Advocate-General of West Bengal, was struck down with rheumatoid arthritis while studying law at Cambridge University, England. This was in 1962, and in the following years he was treated by doctors in both England and India, mainly with cortisone and gold injections. But he continued to hobble about painfully on crutches, and the consensus of medical opinion was that his condition was incurable.

In 1973 he was brought to Sai Baba at Prasanti Nilayam. At the first interview Baba overwhelmed him with so much Divine Mother Love that Subrata melted into tears. Unconscious of any pain, he walked from the interview room without his crutches, and the crowd waiting outside shouted for joy. But when Subrata returned to his home in Calcutta, his faith fell away, doubts tormented his mind, and his condition deteriorated.

"I am a doubting Thomas," he accused himself, sadly. It was 1974 when we talked, a year after his dramatic cure. He was still not using crutches, but painful traces of the disease were present. It was his karma, he felt, and he did not have the necessary faith to completely overcome it.

"So, you are not really cured," I said.

"No, but greatly improved. The doctors say I should be dead with the amount of cortisone I have taken, so Swami is looking after me. But the great miracle is my change of heart and mind. Thank God I had this disease to bring me to Sai Baba!"

Was it karma or a terrible Job-like test of faith that came to Mrs. Ira Ramakrishna of Terricherry, Kerala in April 1970? First of all her faith was built up through a number of Sai miracles that had happened to close members of her family, and she was very content, feeling joy and security in the sight of the Lord. Then the blow fell.

It was early morning and she was on her way by car to see Sai Baba. With her were her son, daughter and daughter-in-law. In the country on a lonely stretch of road they met with a major accident. In her written account she does not say what caused the accident, but simply states that when she regained consciousness, everyone else in the wreck was unconscious, either dead or badly hurt. The road was empty, not a soul in sight anywhere.

"I was like a mad woman. I screamed and screamed. Then I calmed down and began calling on Baba for help. In less than five minutes a bus, two police vans and three cars appeared in a procession, as if God had sent them."

When the bodies were extricated from the wreck, it was found that her son was dead, and her daughter and daughter-in-law had terrible injuries, and were near to death. In the vehicles that had come there was exactly enough room to convey them all in comfort to a hospital in Bangalore.

Both Mrs. Ramakrishna and her daughter spent several months in hospital. The daughter-in-law, who had been married only seven months, had a spinal fracture that paralyzed her whole body. The driver of the car had many fractures.

Like the friends of Job, who told him in the extremity of his afflictions to curse God, many of Mrs. Ramakrishna's friends advised her to stop worhipping Baba, especially as this terrible tragedy had happened while she was on her way to see him.

But, after three months in hospital, the ladies completed the interrupted journey to Whitefield, this time by ambulance, attended by nurses from the hospital; the daughter's leg was just out of plaster and the daughter-in-law was still paralyzed. Baba climbed into the ambulance and showered them with his love and blessings. He said that now all would be well, and that, after some years, the daughter-in-law would be able to walk again. (When Mrs. Ramakrishna gave me this account some four years later, her daughter-in-law was beginning to move about a little.)

After the accident Mrs. Ramakrishna's life-style changed. She became even more devoted to Baba, visiting Prasanti Nilayam frequently. She was content to live a quiet life, engrossed in her hobby of gardening, and practicing the Presence of God in all her activities. When crises came to her or her family (as they inevitably must in human life), she always had Divine help to see her through. Sometimes Baba appeared to her, giving her advice and encouragement, in dreams. Frequently the help she received had the touch of the miraculous.

A karmic blow can be, and often is, a test of faith. Like Job, Mrs. Ramakrishna had passed the test and been purified thereby. Though, sadly, she had lost her son, she had gained something very precious — a greater awareness of God's love and His constant presence in her life.

Once in a Sai interview, when only Iris and I and Dr. Gokak were present, I asked Swami directly why he healed some people and not others, hoping he may give me the master key to the mystery. His answer was profound and not easy to understand. Afterwards I talked it over with Dr. Gokak and, as far as my understanding reaches at present, here is a paraphrase of what Baba tried to convey to me.

The sun shines on everything; it may be blocked from you by clouds or walls or some other obstacle, but it is shining, nevertheless. In the same way Divine Love shines on everyone, though many hide behind the clouds and walls of their own mental conditioning, and do not allow themselves to receive it.

This Divine Love, coming through the Sai Avatars, is a positive force; in fact it is the great positive force of the universe. If it is able to reach to the negative pole of the sick person, there is a conjunction, a wholeness is created, and a cure results. If, on the other hand, the positive force is blocked by the walls of the ego, by some emotional or mental obstruction, there is no conjunction, and no cure. If the disease is a temporary one, Nature herself will cure it in her own way and time; but if it is chronic, karmic, persistent, only this opening to the positive force of Divine Love can remove it. That Love, fully received, will burn away lingering karma and karmic tendencies.

It behooves us, then, for we are all sick in some way, to search within ourselves for those walls of conditioning that insulate us from the rays of Divine Love. Just as the photographic negative receives the light, unresistingly, so we must open ourselves to the flow of Divine Light. To

Sai devotees, Baba is the great Holy Lens through which the Light and Love shine. Other searchers have found other Lenses; each to his needs and his temperament. In the end, however, each will discover that his own true, atmic, immortal Self is the Lens for healing Love to the little self — to the mortal mind and body. For, in this chrysalis called man, we are, each of us, two — the negative, temporary, lower ego, mostly disharmonious and ill-at-ease, and the positive, eternal Self. This is the lesson that Baba emphasizes.

You might say that the karma of previous births has to be consumed in this life, and that no amount of Grace can save you from that. Evidently, someone has taught you to believe so. But I assure you, you need not suffer from karma like that.

When a severe pain torments you, the doctor gives you a morphine injection, and you do not feel the pain, though it is there in the body. Grace is like the morphine; the pain is not felt though you go through it. Or the Lord can save a man completely from consequences, as was done by me for the bhakta whose paralytic stroke and heart attacks I took over in that Guru Pournima week.*

—*SATYA SAI BABA*

13
SAFARI
WITH SWAMI

*Is my gloom, after all, shade of His Hand, out-
stretched caressingly?*

—*FRANCIS THOMPSON*

One evening as I was walking past the end of the great auditorium at
Prasanti Nilayam, I heard Swami's voice call my name. Turning swiftly, I
met him coming out of the doorway. The man with him stood back as he
came up and spoke to me. He asked me what I thought of the new Prasanti
Nilayam, and told me how busy he was with construction problems — it
was almost as if he was giving reasons for ignoring us in recent days.

"Yes, I can see that Swami is busy," I agreed; "Too busy!"

His searching look changed quickly to one of kindness as he penetrated to my thoughts and feelings.

"No, not *too* busy," he said, moving closer. "Soon just a small party
of us will go away to the mountains. Then I will have time to answer all
your questions. But tell no one about this."

A few days later I was called to the interview room, and told that we
(Iris and I) must be ready next morning at daybreak to leave with him for
Whitefield. My wife would travel in a car with some other ladies; I was to
go with Swami. My heart leapt for joy.

The secret, early morning move was, I guessed, to avoid big crowds.
And, despite our excitement, we kept a tight hold on our lips, while
friends plied us with pointed questions. The air seemed charged with the
expectation of something about to happen.

Next morning in the first grey light I made my way to the meeting
place in front of the Mandir, and was astounded to find a crowd already
around the circle, and along the drive to the gate.

In the front seat of the waiting car, with Swami's driver, were Sri

Nakul Sen, ex-Governor of Goa, and his son. A man, who seemed to be the master of ceremonies, ushered me into the back seat, and I knew that I would be sitting with the Lord, himself. Had the good old days really returned? It was like a happy dream.

Presently Baba was sitting beside me, and we were driving away through the ranks of hungry eyes, praying hands and faces that seemed to beseech his early return.

On the trip, as of old, Baba talked, laughed, sang and led us in any bhajans we knew. When I had almost given up hope of breakfast, we turned into a wood of young eucalyptus trees and stopped in a glade known as Baba's favorite picnic spot. The car with the ladies had followed us in, and soon we were all enjoying an Indian picnic breakfast. Swami as usual ate little, but his presence made our meal seem like the food of the gods.

We were back in our rooms at "Brindavan" by mid-morning, but nothing further had been said about a journey to the mountains. So I wondered.

I was already in bed that evening, and Iris was about to retire, when one of the students arrived with a message from Swami. It was to the effect that we were to be ready to leave at dawn next morning, and should bring some warm clothes with us. We were going to the mountains.

The start was not as early as planned because we had to collect our warm clothes from Bangalore. Moreover, the party was not as small as I had hoped. Swami was taking about a dozen students from his college at "Brindavan," as well as ourselves, the Riordan family and several other people.

Our destination, we learned, was Ootacamund, queen of the Hill Stations in the Nilgiris, and close to their highest peak, the Dodabetta (8640 feet). The route passed through a Wild Life Sanctuary, and Swami intended to spend a night there at one of the forest lodges. My happy anticipation that this safari might bring us something like the Horsley Hills feast of miracles* was reinforced; it was in this same Wild Life Sanctuary that he had performed similar *leelas* — during the time we were away from India.

Mr. N. Kasturi was a witness and wrote an account of the event in the ashram magazine, *Sanatana Sarathi*, of April 1973. The gist of the story is that on Sivarathri Day that year Baba left the crowds that had gathered at "Brindavan," hoping to witness the usual miracle of the Lingam production from Swami's mouth. He led a small procession of devotees to the Wild Life Sanctuary in the Nilgiris. In addition to those travelling in Swami's car, there were two van loads of other devotees and a bus load of his college students. Several Westerners, including Mr. John Hislop and Miss Gerry Brent of California, were in the group.

In the jungle, near a stream that marks the boundary between the States of Karnataka and Tamil Nadu, the party stopped and found a patch of sand. Here they all sat down in a semi-circle facing Swami. A number of officers of the Sanctuary, trackers, mahouts and forest tribesmen had joined the crowd. A herd of wild elephants was not far away.

Bhajans were sung for a time. Then — just as I remember him doing at Horsley Hills — Baba smoothed the sand in front of him, and on it drew a design with his forefinger. Then he heaped some sand on the design, put his hand into the top of the heap and brought out a magnificent, translucent lingam. Holding it up for all to see, he said "From Kailas! The lingam worship is just over at that place. See, the sandal paste is still wet and the kumkum dot is still on the lingam." And so they were.

Following the same procedure, Baba produced from the identical spot on the sand, a small silver lingam, then a silver vessel full of fragrant "Amrit" (Nectar of the gods). While the crowd again sang bhajans, Swami went around the circle pouring a spoonful of the Nectar on the tongue of each person present. "When he sat down," Kasturi wrote, "We noticed that the vessel was as full as ever."

After that, Swami drew another design on the sand, piled sand on it, and took from the pile a silver image of Shirdi Sai, his former Incarnation. This he handed to Mr. Kagal, Inspector-General of Police of Karnataka State, for his domestic shrine.

The sand *leela* over, Baba took his group to the bungalow at Bandipur where bhajans were held until midnight. It was at this same bungalow that our party now stopped for the night on our way to Ootacamund. Swami was given a delighted and worshipful welcome from the manager and staff at the lodge.

The next day we all went for a ride through the forest in jungle buggies. The Wild Life Sanctuary Officer, who accompanied us, confirmed that tigers, cheetas, wild elephants and various kinds of deer roam the reserve. We sighted a herd of wild elephants and some spotted deer. One has to be very fortunate to see the big cats in the daytime.

At breakfast next day, still at the forest lodge, Swami gave a short lecture to one of his devotees. The man had bought some petrol for one of the vehicles in the safari convoy, and had refused the reimbursement offered by Swami's acting treasurer. Perhaps he had thought he was being liberal and generous in this way. If so, Baba soon disillusioned him. As near as I can recall, this is the important lesson Swami gave that morning.

"When Swami offers you money, you must take it because what belongs to the Father belongs also to the son. To refuse shows egotism and pride. All wealth, temporal as well as spiritual, belongs to the Father. Man's wealth is like a tank that will be emptied. The Father's wealth is like a well fed by an eternal spring. Whatever is taken from it, the well remains full."

The humbled, but puzzled, devotee asked: "But if I *want* to give something, will Swami never accept it?"

"Yes, if it is given without ego and with pure love. Swami will accept then, and return the gift a hundred-fold to the giver in some way. To give with true love in your heart is to give to God. But *your* gift was wrapped in ego and self-importance. That kind of selfish giving is really like selfish taking."

The lecture was given with love vibrant in Baba's voice, but, even so, the devotee looked very downcast when Swami left. At the table with us was Colonel S. P. Jogarao (retired) of Indian Army Engineers. He was a good companion and now showed his kind heart by remarking to the deflated devotee: "That lecture was meant for all of us." Indeed it was — for all and everyone!

We drove through the neat tea plantations around "snooty Ooty," as it was called in the days of the British Raj. Europeans first began to settle up here on the heights, as long ago as 1821, and, later in the century, it became the summer resort of the Governor and government officials of Madras Presidency.

Beyond the town we climbed a hill overlooking a fine panorama of slopes and valleys, marked with the green, geometrical designs of vast tea plantations. In a sheltered nook we stopped in front of a two-story house that looked like a small chateau. Known as "Walthamstow," it had been built for the British Governor as a summer residence over a hundred years earlier.

But I am sure that never such a crowd awaited the arrival of the Governor as now was waiting in the gardens to welcome Sai Baba. My heart sank at the sight. At Horsley Hills, I thought, we had him to ourselves for at least a few days — until people, like hounds, scented out his hiding place. But now all of Ooty seems to have known of his expected arrival, and most of Ooty must be here.

"Walthamstow" had been empty for some time because the man who owned it, along with its acres of tea plantation, lived elsewhere. It was his good fortune — in more ways than one as things turned out — that the Ooty Sai devotees had requested its use for Baba and his party.

In the big ballroom Swami did a few steps of the old-fashioned waltz, remarking, "English dance." It seemed as if he could see the dancers of long ago, photographed on the *akasha*. For a while he walked about the room, making the characteristic upward gesture of his open hand that he uses when raising the psychic atmosphere.

But whatever earthy vibrations were still lingering in the old ball-room, were soon erased when Swami turned it into a bhajan and prayer hall. In the mornings and evenings he would open the doors to the gardens, and the crowd would come streaming in, filling the hall, and overflowing into the adjacent rooms and corridors. Then, with either Baba, himself, or his enthusiastic college students leading the bhajans, the panelled walls and high ceiling would reverberate to the joyous music, praising the names of God for an hour or more.

Despite the demands of the crowd, Iris and I did, as promised, have a number of happy talks with Swami — personal ones, some of them in our room, impersonal ones also in his sitting-room, where he answered many questions on matters spiritual. Every day I was hoping that he would take us for a drive and give us the joy of yet another "miracle outing."

We *did* go out with him one day, not for creation *leelas*, but for something almost as striking and memorable. Not far from Ooty are the handsome Wellington Barracks, built, by the British, of warm brown stone in an emerald green setting. Could such a place as army barracks, however attractive, have any interest for Sai Baba?

One day I saw a Major-General in resplendent uniform, with several of his senior officers, waiting, hopefully, for an audience with Sai Baba. The man looked quite human for a general, so I ventured to go in and engage him in conversation.

"Lucky I'm here at this time," he told me. "I'm actually stationed up on the Tibetan frontier, but am down here for a conference. My regimental HQ is at Wellington Barracks." He smiled, white teeth gleaming in his dark handsome face. "I had Swami's darshan once before; now I'm hoping for an interview." I stayed until Swami came out and invited the military men into an inner room.

One result of this was that next day we found ourselves driving along the mountain roads towards the Wellington Barracks. Somewhere behind us, with the Major-General in his staff car, came Swami. He had agreed to address a parade of soldiers at the Barracks.

As an old British army man, myself, I felt there was something incongruous about this idea. The Indian army reflects the British army — by which it had been trained for so long — in its uniform, insignias of rank, system of discipline, methods of training and other ways. But there are differences.

When we arrived, I expected to see ranks of soldiers ready to salute the arrival of the General with his official guest. Instead, to my surprise, I saw lines of soldiers sitting cross-legged on the barrack square. And further on, outside the big hall, were rank upon rank of highly-polished army boots — minus their soldiers' feet. Where were the soldiers belonging to that army of empty boots? Some, no doubt, were those parading, at the squat, on the barrack square, but mostly I found, they were inside the hall, cross-legged, in sardine formation on the floor. What would the Duke of Wellington have said?

I found a small space by the side wall, and joined the army officers, N.C.O.'s and soldiers at the squat. Iris had gone off to do the same with a group of ladies on the other side of the hall.

Presently there was a stir near the front door, and along the aisle between all the khaki came the small robed figure of Swami, followed by the General and other top-ranking brass — all emblazoned with colored ribbons and insignia. If Swami looked out of place, he did not seem to feel it. While the officers marched, he moved along in his graceful, relaxed manner, smiling to the people on either side.

They proceeded to the stage and sat on the waiting chairs. The Major-General stood up and addressed the gathering. He told his soldiers how fortunate they were to have the darshan, and to receive a divine discourse, from Sri Satya Sai Baba.

What, I wondered, could Baba say to these men whose profession was the art of war, death, destruction? He stood easily on the stage a bright, red-gold figure in the sea of drab khaki. He spoke in Tamil, the language of the State in which this regiment was raised. The discourse was not translated into English, and I was not able to follow much of it. But later I was told the main points of his speech.

He extolled the fine positive qualities which the army inculcates, and on which it stands — self-discipline, courage, comradeship, patience, loyalty, steadfastness, and above all, self-sacrifice. The army is, indeed, a very good training ground for spiritual sadhana and advancement which requires these very same qualities.

In battle soldiers should remember that, as Lord Krishna said, nought but the body is slain. And what is the body but a garment to be cast off at some time? Then the immortal soul will put on another garment — another body. For, as Krishna assured Arjuna before the battle of Kurukshetra, "Never was there a time when I was not, nor you, nor these lords of men; nor will there ever be a time hereafter when we shall cease to be."

I recalled that the great World Teachers have never taught the doctrine of "peace at any price." Krishna told the warrior Arjuna to "go in and fight" at Kurukshetra, knowing that there would be great and terrible destruction, but even that was better than suffering the evil that existed. Rama led his army to destroy the incarnated demons in ancient Lanka. Jesus said: "I did not come to bring peace but a sword." He taught that we should return good for evil done to us, but not that we must let wrongs and injustices against others stand unchallenged. His violent expulsion of the cheating money-changers from the temple is surely a symbolic directive to right actions.

Disciples of Sri Aurobindo have told me that when World War II broke out, their Master said that, if the Nazis won, it would put back the Divine Plan for a thousand years. Then he proceeded to use certain of his great occult powers, such as out-of-the-body travel and dynamic telepathy, to influence the course of the war against the Nazis. I have met with other evidence of the truth of this statement.

Though I hate war, myself, when I volunteered for army service in 1939, I thought that, at whatever cost, the war against the spread of Nazism must be fought. I still think it had to be. There are values for which we must be prepared to lay down our little earth-lives — hug them to our hearts though we do.

Back in a sitting-room at "Walthamstow" the Major-General showed me a ring on his finger. "Swami materialized it for me in the car on the way back here — fits exactly." He was like a happy child that has just received from Santa Claus the gift he longed for.

Then in serious tones he said: "Now in battle the awareness of His constant Presence will be my armor. He has promised to take care of me."

Among the Sai devotees who came to "Walthamstow" was our old friend from Madras, Sri G. K. Damodar Row, retired Judge and practicing Advocate. Along with Colonel Jogarao, who was then Swami's chief executive for construction work, Damodar spent some hours in consultation with Baba, and both men wore a cloak of mystery. Just before we left Ooty we learned what the subject of consultation had been. The owner of "Walthamstow" wanted to sell the property, and Swami after discussions on all aspects of the matter, had finally decided that his Central Trust should buy it.

"Swami is not going to become a tea planter," Jogarao assured us, laughing. "The plantation will be rented back to the former owner. I think

Swami will use part of the house for a Sai school, and that he intends part of it as a summer holiday resort for Sai devotees. He may give some Summer Courses up here, too, and later have a University College built in the grounds."

So, I mused, the British Governor's old residence, the place of parties and the "English dance," is now to play a role in the Sai educational program for hastening the Hour of God.

On the return journey we stopped in the Wild Life Sanctuary for a picnic luncheon. My mind again turned towards the hope that this journey with Swami might, even at the eleventh hour, produce some sand or bushland *leelas*.

We walked in the pleasant grounds around the forest lodge. With a polaroid camera many color photographs of devotees, grouped around Swami, were taken — to become souvenirs of a journey when Eternity had put her indelible stamp on the fleeting hours. But that was the only miracle, for our next stop was "Brindavan," home.

Sitting in our apartment, we decided that an important lesson of the safari was: "From the Lord there will always be showers of blessings, but they will seldom, if ever, be those you expect." Yet it had been a wonderful trip, revealing many new aspects of the Avatar's caressing hand.

Narada, who moves always by and with the Lord, feels that God is beyond his understanding. Balarama, who incarnated as Lord Krishna's own brother, could not fathom His Personality. How then can you grasp my Mystery?

If you have faith, the Lord who is the core of your being will manifest Himself. He is within your grasp. Be aware of Him who is the eternal Witness: He sees and knows all.

SATYA SAI BABA

14
SHAKTI

Energy is Eternal Delight.

W. BLAKE

Soon after our return from the Nilgiris a party of Americans arrived at Whitefield. Among them were several old friends — Elsie Cowan, Camille Svensson and Robert Silver, an attorney from Ventura, California. We hoped that their arrival would bring some group interviews for Westerners, and that we would be included. And so it turned out.

Swami was fully aware, of course, that I still had a list of questions to ask him on the subject of the Spiritual Path, and at the interviews he sometimes began by saying, "Any questions?" — and looking straight at me.

One question I asked led indirectly to a short talk by Baba on the concept of *Shakti*. The word means energy or power. Brahman, the Absolute, is One and beyond all dualities, such as male and female. But, to begin Creation, Brahman, who has no beginning but is eternally *there*, limits an aspect of Its Infinite Self, and a dualistic polarity, a positive and negative, is formed. According to which philosophic treatment you are studying, this positive-negative polarity may be known as Purusha and Prakriti, spirit and matter, yin and yang (Chinese) or Shiva and Shakti. Sometimes they are called the Father and Mother of Creation. Why the power or energy aspect of creation should be personified as a female is not explained, but it is so, and always has been. At the top level, of the Supreme God-with Form, so to speak, the Shakti is called the World Mother, and down the scale through the lesser Gods it is always represented by a female figure.

Brahman, the Divine Ground of all existence, is said to have three basic aspects: *Sat-chit-ananda* (absolute Existence, absolute Consciousness and Divine Delight). The Delight aspect is manifested as Energy, the great

Shakti that creates the multiplicity of the cosmos. It is the Mother of all the energies that show themselves in a million ways throughout the universe. As the mystic, Blake, perceived, all the energies around us in nature, and within ourselves, are an expression of the Divine Ananda, the Eternal Delight. Man who could, and should, be a channel for the Divine Delight, the boundless Shakti, often blocks its free flow through his own ignorance.

"Where is your Shakti?" Swami suddenly asked Robert who was sitting close. I thought Robert might say: "My wife's back in Ventura," but instead he pointed to some part of his body. Swami asked others who indicated various parts of their bodies. But Baba laughed and shook his head. "Your Shakti is not just in one place, but everywhere. You are Atman, and Atman is identical with Brahman, but the energy-force that maintains your continually-changing body and mind is Shakti."

In his marvelous way of unifying diverse notions, Swami then went on to explain the Shakti figures in Hindu religion. The supreme, manifest, personal God, the Father of the Universe, is known as Ishwara or Mahesh. His three functions of creation, maintenance and destruction (continual destruction being essential for continual regeneration) are personified as the Gods: Brahma, Vishnu and Shiva (often called Rudra at this level, as the name Shiva is sometimes used for Ishwara.) Don't expect consistent Aristotelian logic in Indian metaphysics which has a higher paradoxical logic of its own.

Each one of this Trinity has his power aspect represented by a goddess form: Sarasvati, Lakshmi and Kali (also called Parvati). In mythology they are known as the consorts of the Gods and each goddess reigns over certain departments of life. But in their deeper significance they are symbols of the Divine Shakti. Generally, but not always, the prefix *Maha* (great), is used when this deepest meaning is intended. Thus Mahasarasvati is the Shakti of Brahma, Mahalakshmi the Shakti of Vishnu and Mahakali the Shakti of Rudra.

The three great Goddesses can take various forms. Mahalakshmi, for instance, has sometimes the form known as Durga, which is depicted in sculpture and iconography as a fierce Goddess with eight arms, each bearing a weapon, and riding on a lion. The lion which, in this case, symbolizes righteousness, is trampling a demon underfoot. Durga, the Mother Militant, is appropriately the great Shakti of Vishnu who in several Incarnations destroyed demonic power and re-established righteousness on earth.

Durga's main exploit in mythology was the slaying of the powerful, earth-destroying demon Mahisha. To commemorate this great event India's leading national festival is held. In Bengal it is known as Durga Puja, and in other parts of India as Dasara or Navaratra. For nine days at this festival Durga is honored by gorgeous pageantry and rituals that seem to touch something deep in the subconscious life of India.

The Goddesses, like the Gods, are usually depicted, not with eight, but with four arms. Sarasvati, for instance, who is associated with the color white, and is considered the Goddess of learning, speech and the arts, has four arms, with a book and a vina in two of them. But a rosary sometimes takes the place of the vina when the stress is on spiritual endeavor.

Swami paused in his talk and asked several people if they had seen Shakti. They all shook their heads. Whereupon he waved his hand, palm down, in the familiar but ever-thrilling manner. There was a metallic rattle as he closed his fist; then he held up in his fingers for all to see a gold circular pendant, with a figure embossed on front. Baba passed it around for our close inspection.

. The pendant was about one and one-half inches in diameter and had seven gold metal beads hanging from it on short chains. The embossed figure was sitting on a lotus. She had four arms but I could not determine what objects she was holding in her hands. Later we were told by an Indian that it was Lakshmi. If so, as well as being the Shakti of Vishnu, the Preserver of the Universe, she is the Goddess of Plenty, and three of the hard-to-distinguish objects in her hands would be: a sheaf of corn, a bowl of nectar and a lotus.

Baba had continued talking as the pendant went around, and as I stopped concentrating on it, I heard him say: "God is in all."

"And *you* are the all! Now don't answer back!" Elsie Cowan replied. The remark was made lovingly, as a mother might talk to a child. It could have been Yasoda admonishing the little boy Krishna, I thought.

Sutra Number 82 of the *Narada Bhakti Sutras* states: Devotion, or Divine Love, though in itself one, can manifest itself in these eleven different ways: Love of the Glory of God's Divine qualities; Love of His enchanting beauty; Love of worship; Love of His remembrance; Love of service; Love of Him as a friend; Love of Him as a child; Love of Him as the Beloved — as the wife or husband; Love of total surrender to Him; Love of total oneness with Him; and Love in the form of anguish at separation from Him.

One commentator writes: "It does not mean that there are only these eleven types; there are possibilities of as many types as there are human relationships . . . and different attitudes may be found in the same person at different times."

The commentary also says that the different types of Love by different people may be attributed to tastes, preferences and predilections due to the past *Samskaras* of the individuals, or perhaps to some inscrutable Divine purpose to be worked out only in particular ways. Thus, for instance, Narada and Vyasa are always found delighting themselves in singing the glories of the Lord.

One very important type of Love that has been left out of the list of eleven is, I believe, the Love of a child for its parent — either father or mother. This is a very well-known and wide-spread type of Love of God. It was, for instance, Sri Ramakrishna's kind of Love for the Divine Mother. And many Christian saints showed their Love of God as that of the child for the Father.

Most commentators mention the parents (Vasudeva and Devaki), and the foster-parents (Nanda and Yasoda) as supreme examples of people whose Love of God was in the form of parental love for the Divine Child Krishna. The Virgin Mary's Love towards Jesus, though she realized his Divinity, was also of the parental type.

But, though Divine Love runs through these different channels, as it were, and to some extent, is colored by the channel, it is in reality much broader and deeper than ordinary human loves of the same type. At its highest level it is, through the profound influence of the Object of the love, purged of all selfish considerations, and becomes pure Divine Love.

Among Sai Baba's devotees I have observed some of these different types of love for him — love as a friend, love of service, love of him as the Divine Parent, and love for him as the Divine Child. Several old ladies of India — particularly those who knew him as a very young man — exhibit this parental type of love for Swami, while at the same time being aware, at the back of their minds, that He is an Avatar.

Elsie Cowan's love for him seems to be of this type, at times anyway, as shown by her remark. Baba's response to it was a half-smile, showing that he understood the feeling behind it.

This maxim of Bhakti yoga — that man's love for God often bears strong overtones of different types of earthly love — is actually a reflection of Divine Love, and the more we can bring the Reality into the reflection the better. Thomas a Kempis writes: "Neither is that love true and pure which is not knit in Me (God)."

We should, therefore, practice the wonderful, transforming art of seeing God in the friend, the wife, the husband, the child, the parent, and all objects of our earthly love. If we can do this, for instance, with the marriage partner, the perennial problems of personality conflicts in the marriage situation would be solved. That is, ultimately, their only solution.

Baba looked around the group to see what had become of the Shakti pendant. It had travelled full circle, and was resting on Elsie's knee close to him. He picked it up. "Has everyone seen it," he asked, looking around. Yes, all had seen it. And all were waiting to see what he would do with it. Some of the ladies, no doubt, hoping that it would come to them.

One person sitting in the back row of ladies, neither hoping nor expecting (she told me later) was Iris. Swami suddenly tossed it over the heads of the group to her. The shock of surprise was so great that she almost failed to catch it. But then her expression changed to joy, and she bowed low to Baba in deep gratitude.

Later she said to me: "I think Swami gave the Shakti pendant to me because, in the first place, you asked him the question that led to his talk on Shakti."

Maybe. But I think there were other and deeper reasons why she received this gift and grace. Actually only Swami knows why he does things. Sometimes, long afterwards, we may discover his reasons.

God dwells in you as Joy. That is why you seek Joy always in every object around you. To become as full of Joy as Radha or Ramakrishna or Vivekananda, you have to sacrifice your ego, and saturate yourself with the Lord, with the consciousness that the Lord is your being.

So long as you have a trace of ego in you, you cannot see the Lord clearly. Egoism will be destroyed if you constantly tell yourself: "It is He, not I. He is the force, I am but the instrument." Keep His name always on the tongue; contemplate His glory whenever you see or hear anything beautiful or grand; see in everyone the Lord, Himself, moving in that form. Do not talk evil of others, see only the good in them. Welcome every chance to help others, to console them, to encourage them along the spiritual path. Be humble; do not become proud of your wealth or status or authority or learning or class. Dedicate all your physical possessions and mental skills and intellectual attainments to the service of the Lord. Then your ego will be wiped out.

SATYA SAI BABA

15
KARMA YOGA

The world is imprisoned in its own activity except
when actions are performed as worship of God.
                    BHAGAVAD GITA

I was sitting with several Indians in an inner room of Baba's house at "Brindavan" when the tall, ochre-robed figure of Swami Karunyananda came in. He had close-cropped hair and the grave face of a medieval monk. I thought he must be about fifty years of age, but was told later that he was, in fact, over eighty.

I had already learned something of his background. He was one of the earliest disciples of the well-known Swami Sivananda of Rishikesh. After his time with the Master, he had spent many years in the high Himalayas, carrying out the austerities considered necessary for his spiritual advancement, and had then established an ashram at Rajahmundry on the eastern side of Andhra Pradesh State. As might be guessed from the fact that his ashram included an orphanage, his activities were concerned with practical welfare work among the people of his area. He was, in fact, like his great-hearted Master, a karma yogi, a man of compassionate, dedicated action.

I had seen men of the ochre robe around Baba before, and knew that some of the great swamis of India came at times to him. Now was my chance to talk with one of them, to find out perhaps, his thoughts and feelings about Sai Baba, and what the relationship was.

Swami Karunyananda spoke little English, his native language, like Baba's, being Telegu. But in the room with us was the honest-hearted, down-to-earth Dr. S. Bhagavantam, Baba's own chief Telegu-English interpreter.

The nuclear physicist was willing to oblige; was, in fact, quite keen to do so, and this I attributed to his admiration for the karma yogi who had played a big part in a Sai Baba operation that Dr. Bhagavantam intended to tell me about later.

In answer to my questions, Swami Karunyananda said that the first time he had actually seen Baba and received his darshan was in 1957. In the beginning he had thought that Baba's miracles were from some yogic power that was less than Divine. Nevertheless, powerful feelings had drawn him closer and closer to Baba. Then, after more experience of the miracles, experience of Baba's presence, and much meditation on the subject, he came to the conclusion, that the Sai Power was a Divine Power, and that, indeed, here was an Avatar.

With the development of this understanding and concept, he found himself dedicating his work to this incarnation of God. Furthermore, he soon realized that Sai Baba was working through him as a channel, and, in addition, sometimes playing a more direct role in Karunyananda's welfare activities among the people. He then related several dramatic examples of this wonderful relationship, two of which I give here.

A widow not far from Swami Karunyananda's ashram had a son, a promising young engineer, who was the only support for her younger children and herself. Then one day unexpectedly the son died of a heart attack. The shock struck the widow dumb.

Six months later, when the swami first heard about her tragedy, he called to see her. She still could not utter a word. He was at this time making a practice of always carrying some of Sai Baba's vibhuti in his pocket for use in emergencies. He believed in its power, and experience had several times justified his belief. Now he took out a packet of the vibhuti and applied it to the forehead, throat and tongue of the poor dumb widow. Her younger children and several members of her family were at the widow's home, and Swami Karunyananda stayed on, talking to them, trying to raise their spirits and hopes.

It must have been about half-an-hour, the swami thought, after the application of Baba's vibhuti, that the widow, who had been sitting listening to the conversation, began to speak, herself. At first her words came with difficulty, but very soon with normal ease and fluency.

Those in the room became so overjoyed and excited that some of them rushed from the house to tell their friends in the village. The news spread like a fire in dry grass, and soon a crowd had gathered to witness the results of the miracle. Some asked the swami for vibhuti to cure them of their own ailments. He had only one packet left in his pocket, and gave it where he felt the need was greatest.

A penniless laborer living in the forest near Rajahmundry died, leaving a pregnant wife and two little daughters. They were utterly destitute, so Swami Karunyananda brought them to live at his ashram. The two little girls were taken care of at the orphanage, and he made sure the widow, who was getting near her time, received all the medicines and tonics she needed.

When the birth seemed imminent, he had her put in the small hospital at his ashram. There were other patients present but no serious cases, so only one nurse was on night duty.

On the first evening the nurse felt sure, since there were no signs of labor pains, that the baby would not be arriving that night, so she thought it would be safe to take a couple of hours off. She made her patients comfortable, and at 10:30 p.m., when they all seemed to be sleeping soundly, she went to a late cinema show. A little after midnight the nurse returned, looked into the hospital ward where all was still quiet, then lay down in her adjacent bedroom and went to sleep.

It was just breaking day when she awoke with a start to hear the sound of a baby crying from the ward. She jumped up and ran through the door, almost colliding with a cleaning woman who had just come on duty. Together the nurse and cleaner hurried to the bedside of the expectant mother; the bed had been screened off.

The mother was no longer expectant; the baby had arrived and was lying beside her, still protesting loudly. Anxiously the nurse examined the mother and child; everything was in perfect order, just as if a very efficient midwife had been on the job. No mess, no placenta, and the baby had obviously been bathed. The crying stopped, and the mother smiled happily at the nurse, who was still speechless with amazement, and a degree of guilt.

"But who delivered the baby?" she asked, at last.

"Oh, when my pains got very bad, a kind lady came. She soothed me — made it all very easy — got hot water — washed the baby — did everything. A wonderful lady!"

"Lady? What lady was it?"

"I don't know her name but her picture is on the wall over there." She pointed to a large color photograph of Sai Baba which Swami Karunyananda had hung on a wall of the ward.

"That's no lady," the nurse replied. "You must be mistaken."

"No, I'm not, nurse. I could not mistake the hair and red robe and kind, beautiful face. . . It was that same lady!"

"Well, how long ago was the baby born?"

"Oh, not long. The lady was still here holding the baby a moment ago. She went away just before you came in."

The puzzled cleaner left to see if there was a strange woman in a red robe anywhere in the ashram. Most of the patients in the ward had been sleeping soundly until the baby started to cry loudly. No one had seen what went on behind the screen, no one had seen a strange lady leave the ward. After a while the cleaner came back to report that there were no signs of the mysterious red-robed midwife anywhere about the premises and no word of one having been seen.

The nurse looked at the photo of Baba. With that mop of frizzy hair, he might easily be mistaken for a woman – but how could such a thing as this take place?!

Nobody at the ashram could think of any explanation of the strange events in the hospital, except the incredible one that Baba had indeed come, and acted as a midwife. Swami Karunyananda, himself, could not wholly accept the miracle at first. He had heard stories of Baba appearing at places when his body was somewhere else far away. He knew of the yogic power of travelling in the subtle body, and materializing that body to appear and act just like an ordinary physical body. The great Yogis, the great Adepts, had this power. Sai Baba, who was an Avatar, would certainly have it in the highest degree. And one could not know where Baba's great compassion would show itself, but why should his own ashram and humble little hospital be so honored? It seemed incredible, and yet what other explanation?

Not very long afterwards Swami Karunyananda was in Sai Baba's presence and able to speak privately with him. Baba confirmed the visit to the little hospital for the birth of the child, and gave details that he could not have otherwise known. Then the swami's belief was complete and his cup of bliss overflowing.

After Swami Karunyananda had related these incidents, he was called in to see Baba. Then Dr. Bhagavantam told me the story of an event at Rajahmundry that seemed to have left an indelible impression on his mind. Colonel Jogarao was present, and helped to fill in some of the details. Here is the substance of their story.

Once a year Sai Baba holds a conference of the leaders of the groups within his India-wide organization. Several thousand delegates attend. By 1973 five such All India Conferences had already been held, and the sixth one was due to take place during January, 1974. At the time of the Birthday Celebrations in November 1973, some discussions were held at Prasanti Nilayam concerning the locale and the administration of the forthcoming sixth conference. At one of these discussions Baba announced to his group of workers and technical experts that he had decided to hold the conference at Rajahmundry.

The announcement was greeted with the silence of consternation. The previous five conferences had been held in cities where adequate facilities and amenities for the big crowd of delegates and visitors were available. Rajahmundry was just a country town. It was noted for its long bridge, stretching one and three-quarter miles over the Godavari river, but for little else.

The first to find their tongues were Bhagavantam and Jogarao. They advised Baba against the selection. His answer was that Rajahmundry would prove an excellent area, where spiritual teachings would take effective root.

"But, Swami, the facilities are totally inadequate . . . ."

"Don't worry. All will be well. I know because I've seen it."

They were not sure what he meant by that, but they could see he was quite firm about the choice of Rajahmundry. What could they do? Despite their misgivings about the place, they could only accept Baba's decison and try to make the best of it. Both of them offered to go to Rajahmundry immediately and try to organize the construction of facilities for the accommodation and feeding of the thousands of visitors who would be flocking there early in January.

But Baba said, no, there was no need for that.

It was about the end of November when Baba called two men of Rajahmundry, and put all preparations for the conference in their hands. One was Swami Karunyananda and the other Sri D. Ramarao, District President of the Sai organizations for East Godavari, in which district Rajahmundry lies. Though there was only a little over a month before the All-India Conference, they felt no apprehension. Baba had honored them with the task; Baba would guide them. Work was worship, as he often said, and the results lay entirely in his hands.

They knew well Baba's rule that there must be no soliciting of money from the public, and that delegates and visitors must not be charged entry fees for anything and must be given the traditional hospitality of free board and lodging. So they called a meeting of ten Sai devotees — men of substantial means who also seemed to be very sincere bhaktas of the Lord.

At the meeting the Ten agreed to contribute 5000 rupees each for a working capital. Would it be enough? Experts in areas where such conferences had been held before said: "No, definitely not! It will take more like 200,000 rupees to prepare things and administer the conference properly."

But suddenly amazing things began to happen. A timber merchant, who was not even a Sai devotee, offered timber free of charge for the necessary temporary buildings. Free voluntary labor came along to erect the buildings. Commercial companies offered warehouses and other space for the accommodation of visitors. As the date for the conference drew near, food supplies began to roll in by wagon-loads. Town and country, rich people and poor people, all were making spontaneous contributions. Fifteen cooks, for instance, appeared at the right time, as if from nowhere, and offered their services.

The first meal served at the conference was for 10,000 people. "And," Colonel Jogarao interjected, "They were all seated at tables, not on the floor as is the custom in India when there are crowds."

"After the meal," Dr. Bhagavantam went on, "Baba asked me, with a twinkle in his eyes, what I thought of the food served by this little town with its 'inadequate facilities.' My answer was: 'It's incredible, Swami. Not for twenty years have I had such a rich, sumptuous meal — and then only in the homes of the very wealthy, at marriage functions.'

"But just as amazing was the fact that the high standard of catering was maintained right throughout the days of the conference."

Added Jogarao: "All arrangements were perfect. It could not have been done better by a big organization of experienced executives and caterers — in fact, not as well. The conference was a huge success."

"Did the 50,000 rupees prove to be enough?"

They both laughed. "There were 20,000 left over!"

"So the Ten got some of their money back?"

"They refused to take it; the money was used to buy a unit in one of the new blocks at Prasanti Nilayam for use by visitors from Rajahmundry.

"So," concluded Bhagavantam, "We were shown again in this event how wrong it is to ever question Baba's judgment. We look only at the surface. He sees the depths."

"And the future," added the Colonel. "So He's always right."

Yes, I thought, the story shows us how Baba sees into the hearts of people and into the heart of a town. It also reminds us of what he so often says: that love of God must express itself in work for humanity. He has set up the machinery for such work, and He teaches us in what spirit it must be performed.

Briefly, the machinery consists of: at the top, a Central Trust, with a Council of Management to take care of the financial and policy matters concerning the Sai social, welfare, and educational activities. At state levels there are State Trusts and Councils of Management, linked to the

Central body. Below, and under the guidance of these, are various groups with different names and functions.

Some groups concern themselves with developing more spiritual and devotional activities, holding regular meetings and retreat camps for bhajans, meditation, study, lectures and discussions. Others put the emphasis on practical welfare and educational works. These activities include: organizing medical camps for the poor, working in hospitals, conducting free libraries, bringing spiritual instruction to the village schools, establishing technical institutes where free training is given in crafts and trades, such as carpentry, plumbing, tailoring, turning and fitting.

Sai Baba's followers are expected to use their own initiative to find out where welfare work is most needed in their communities. By keeping in constant touch with his workers Baba strives to keep alive the true karma yogic motivation for the humanitarian work done in his name. This is, of course, the most difficult thing of all. Charitable efforts are growing in the world, and that is certainly a good thing. But how much of it is done with the pure motive of love for humanity, which is equivalent to love of God?

Any taint of self-seeking in the motive, any desire for renown, fame, honors from the actions, detract from their good effects on those who perform them; instead of helping to free the performers from bondage, the secret selfishness, the hypocrisy in the "charitable actions" serves to bind them closer to the world of suffering and death.

But right motivation in our acts of charity and social welfare work should, says karma yoga, be broadened to include all our actions in the world. All of them should be dedicated to God or to the good of mankind. This may seem a very difficult thing, and, of course, it is . . . but not an impossible thing. It may be attained by degrees.

The vast majority of people must live, not in caves and hermitages, but in the work-a-day world. They must thus aim at the acquiring of goods for the sustenance and welfare of their families and selves. So it is obvious that in the modern world one of the proper motivations must be to make money.

Indeed, the *Sanathana Dharma*, the eternal verities of Hinduism, states that the duty of a householder during certain years of his life is to acquire wealth, and if his karma permits, he may become very wealthy. There is nothing ungodly in this. But in the storing up of earthly treasures there are two provisos he must keep in mind. One is that he must always remember that his worldly possessions are not really his, but are held in trust from God. His wealth must be used rightly, and part of it returned to

God in the form of help to his fellow men. Like King Janaka of Arya-vartha, and Job of the Old Testament, he should be mentally and emotionally unattached to the possessions and the position God has given him in this world — while, at the same time, using them with wisdom and humility.

The second proviso is that, as he approaches old age, the householder should detach himself still further from his treasures on earth and turn his mind wholly to acquiring those spiritual treasures that he *can* take with him through the transition called death. His life must become more and more oriented away from the material towards the spiritual. How foolish it is for a man to spend his last years greedily acquiring worldly wealth, merely to be left behind the moment Death makes the inevitable call!

"Free yourself from attachment to the results of work; make all your actions holy by fixing your heart on the Highest," says God in the *Gita*. Sai Baba is ringing again this ancient bell of wisdom. Its note should, and shall, be heard around the world.

As many as can take this seemingly difficult step, can re-orient their values, can dedicate all their actions and possessions to the Divine, will rise beyond the endless see-saw of life's fleeting joys and pains, of miseries and precarious sensuous pleasures, and find peace and happiness at last.

Karma is like the trail of dust behind the moving carriage. When the carriage stops, the dust will settle on it. But the carriage cannot forever continue fast along the road in order to escape the dust. The best course is to get on the paved highway, away from the dust-track. That is to say, man must acquire the Grace of God and move along the path smoothened by it.

SATYA SAI BABA

16
TWIN FRUIT
OF SURRENDER

Let only that little be left of my will whereby I
may feel thee on every side, and come to thee in every-
thing, and offer to thee my love every moment.
                    RABINDRANATH TAGORE

Swami, was again leaving for Prasanti Nilayam, where problems in his
building construction program were demanding his attention. Iris and I
had only five more weeks left in India and wanted to spend every minute
of the time near him. On the other hand, we needed a few days in Bangalore for some urgent dentistry, and for the complicated business of leaving
India — income tax clearance, innoculations, transference of money from
Australia to pay our passages, and so on.

As always, Swami understood the situation without painful explanations. He said: "You stay here and attend to your business in Bangalore. I
expect to be back in about a week."

As he passed through the ante-room, he smiled lovingly at all the sad
faces he had to leave behind; then with Dr. Keki Mistry, and a few other
lucky ones, he drove off through the painted gate, and along the curved
avenue of people, gathered for a farewell darshan.

I walked back through the emptiness of the garden, passed Sai Gita,
shedding her elephantine tears again, and across the bare ground where the
big pandal had stood. Now from the windows of our sitting-room we had
an uninterrupted view of the elephant under the tree where she spent the
hours of daylight, swinging her trunk and munching her great pile of
foliage. This was good because she could be our sign; while she was still
there, Swami obviously intended to come back, we thought. But if she
vanished, it meant problems at Prasanti Nilayam had multiplied, and he
had decided to stay there indefinitely. We hastened to get our affairs in

order to be ready to move, without delay, if the elephant disappeared on its northern migration.

Our dentist in Bangalore was Dr. R. S. Padmanabhan, a great friend and a great Sai devotee. We were anxious to spend time with him, not only because of his wizardry as a dentist, but also because he had known Baba since the year 1945 and was on occasions honored by the Lord coming to his home to dine. He had promised to tell us a few of his rich Sai experiences.

One thing that had intrigued me was that this close devotee of long-standing, when he and his family came to "Brindavan" for darshan, always sat in the outer courts with the big crowd. Only on rare occasions did he come into the private garden and house. Once I saw him in the ante-room, but his purpose was to present to Swami a large box of contact lenses sent by Dr. K. C. Pani, of Washington, U.S.A., for the Sai welfare work. Another time Padmanabhan brought members of his family in for Swami's blessings on the marriage of his son.

Yet, though he was content to wait humbly outside the private domain, he never wore the martyred look, the sad discontent, seen on the faces of some old disciples (even though their discipleship was shorter than Padmanabhan's). On the contrary, the dentist's was a smiling face, as if lighted by some secret joy – born, no doubt, of his Sai experiences.

Dr. Padmanabhan was only twenty-three and just launching out on his professional career in Bangalore, when he first met the nineteen-year-old Satya Sai Baba. It is obvious that from the start he treated the young Swami with the respect and reverence normally accorded to age and wisdom.

He said: "At the first meeting Swami penetrated my heart, and lifted my spirit, with Divine Love. Also, without my asking for it, he predicted some important events in my future. For instance, he said that I would be married in two months. Well, at that time I had no such plan."

The dentist went on to say that he did, in fact, get married in two months, the bride being a young lady he had met at a Sai Baba gathering. Both she and her father were followers of Sai Baba, and had long been devotees of Lord Krishna; they had developed the practice of reading a passage from the *Bhagavad Gita* every day, and Padmanabhan began to do the same thing.

In the years following their marriage the couple had many uplifting personal contacts with Baba, both at his ashram and at their home which he often visited. The young Baba took a fatherly interest in their temporal, as well as their spiritual, welfare. In 1949 he told Padmanabhan that he should open a second dental surgery, which should be in the suburb of Malleswaram.

"But, Swami," he protested, "I would not be able to get premises in that area."

"Try," Baba answered, pointedly.

Surprisingly, Padmanabhan found a suitable place quickly, but he felt sure the rent would be much too high — certainly about 200 rupees a month! To his astonishment, however, he found that it was only twenty-five rupees monthly. He reported progress to Swami, but added: "The difficulty is dental equipment for a new surgery. It's been almost impossible to obtain since the war."

"Don't worry, a friend is going to help you," Baba told him.

Padmanabhan did not ask who or how. Even then he knew that Swami expects you to find out and do something for yourself. So he thought a good deal about the lead Baba had given. Then he remembered that a dentist friend of his had recently stopped practicing in his own home and taken over an excellent practice in another area. Perhaps his original equipment was still in his home; perhaps he would consider selling it.

Yes, the friend would sell it, and Padmanabhan could pay on easy installments as his new practice grew. Swami, whose invisible engineering was behind it all, the dentist felt, came to bless the new surgery on its opening day. During the ceremony he materialized a little silver figure of Krishna — a replica of a large Krishna in a famous temple.

Another four years passed, during which Padmanabhan's dental practice flourished, his family life proceeded harmoniously, and he felt that he was, by Swami's grace, making some progress along the spiritual path.

Then in 1953 Swami made another unexpected suggestion. Padmanabhan should, he said, go overseas for professional experience. Such an idea had never entered the dentist's head, but now, knowing that his Guru's advice had always been right, he began to think about ways and means. If he kept alert, the opportunity would present itself no doubt, for Baba was ever the power behind the scenes of circumstance.

Some little time later an All India Dental Conference was held at Bangalore. Eminent men from overseas were attending — among them a Professor of Dentistry of Vienna University. Padmanabhan wondered if he should approach the professor about going to Vienna for further studies. Being a humble, reserved man, he hesitated, so a friend made the approach. The professor proved quite willing to endeavor to arrange a seat for Dr. Padmanabhan at Vienna University.

"Get everything ready to move as soon as the confirmation comes,"

Swami advised him. "You will be away for a year!"

Then the right man turned up at the right time to carry on Dr. Padmanabhan's Bangalore practice while he was absent.

During the year he spent abroad, he gained experience in Munich and London, as well as doing his advanced studies and practice in Vienna. And, as Swami had obviously intended, his skill and reputation were greatly enhanced, so that he quickly became a leading dentist of great renown, not only in Bangalore but far beyond.

Busy and prosperous though he was, he always found time to make regular visits to Puttaparti, taking his wife, son and daughter, to offer respect and devotion to the One who was their guide and mentor in all things. On occasions, also, Baba still came to family gatherings at Padmanabhan's home, or at the home of his cousin Sunderamma, daughter of the Seshgiri Rao who had played an important part in the rituals at Puttaparti during the early days.

The years passed by. Happy years of fulfillment for a householder who kept one foot firmly in the spiritual dimension. When real problems arose, Padmanabhan took them to the Lord not only in prayer but in person. For instance, in 1963 some trouble developed in the dentist's back. His doctor diagnosed tuberculosis of the spine and others confirmed this alarming verdict. They all told him he would lose one of his legs within a year. Feeling very depressed, he went to ask the Swami's help.

"It's not TB," Swami assured him. "The trouble in your spine is from too much standing at the dentist's chair. But there's no need to stop your work. I'll take care of you."

The occupational disorder, though at times painful, has, Padmanabhan said, never cost him a day away from his practice. And, eleven years later, he still has his two sound legs.

In that same year, 1963, when the doctors warned him he would lose a leg from T.B., Baba told him: "It's time you went abroad again."

"But, Swami, it's very difficult now – very hard to get the necessary foreign exchange for living and studying abroad."

"Don't worry. You'll be invited; and while there you will be *paid*. No need for any foreign exchange!"

Now, with full faith in Baba's predictions, the doctor awaited the invitation. It came soon afterwards through a member of the British Council in Bangalore for whom he was doing some dental work. Soon all arrangements were made for him to work and study in London and Edinburgh for three months. While abroad all his expenses would be paid, he was informed, and he would also receive a salary. In fact, the only expense he had to meet out of pocket was the cost of his return air fare. That was not difficult to arrange.

So another valuable refresher course came his way through, he felt sure, Baba's mysterious manipulation of circumstances — or what the young Americans call "fiddling in the *akasha*."

Another problem that the dentist took to Baba was in connection with his son who wanted also to be a dentist. Unfortunately, the boy was doing rather poorly at college. Padmanabhan had the idea of sending him away from home to a college on the west coast. But of course Swami must be consulted on that.

Baba agreed to the proposed change, and asked for the son to be brought to him. At this interview he waved his hand and materialized a fountain-pen. Giving this to the youth, Swami told him to study hard, and always use this particular pen in examinations; it would remind him that Swami was there with him, supporting him, and he would do well.

Whatever the reason, the pen seemed to be the right inspiration. From that time on, the young man attained first-class results in all examinations, and in his final year came out at the top of the whole university.

In 1973, ten years after his last journey abroad, initiated by Swami, Dr. Padmanabhan himself, made the approach about travel this time. He asked Baba if he could go to England to arrange for his son to continue dental studies there.

"Yes, with my blessings," Baba said. "But go also to America. It is *there* that his future studies lie, you will find."

Padmanabhan travelled to both England and America, and finally was able to enter his son's name for advanced studies at the University of Pennsylvania, U.S.A. He was very happy when he went to report progress to Baba.

"But he must get married before he goes," said Swami, who knew the snares that await handsome young Indians in the jungles of the west. As always the dentist devotee accepted his Lord's ruling. Where would a suitable bride be found? Well, he could safely leave that matter to Baba's human engineering.

It was just after Iris and I returned to India in 1974, that an old friend of Padmanabhan, an Indian holding a high official position in America, came on a visit to Bangalore. With him he brought his wife and his beautiful daughter. After seeing the daughter, Baba said to Padmanabhan: "That is the wife for your son, if parents agree — and the young people are happy with the arrangement." The young couple, in fact, seemed quite thrilled with the idea, and naturally both sets of parents, all devotees, were delighted with Swami's suggestion. The wedding took place while my wife and I were at "Brindavan" and we had the pleasure of attending it — a double pleasure because we drove there with our old friend Raja Reddy and his wife, whom we met then for the first time.

Relatives of Dr. Padmanabhan and his wife, who form a family circle in Bangalore, are all staunch devotees of Sai Baba. Once we had the rare joy of hearing a group of the ladies talking about their divine experiences during their years around Baba — some of them had met him even earlier than Dr. Padmanabhan had. I had a cassette recorder switched on at the time to record their stories for use in this book. But their voices were so charged with emotion and so often drowned out in bhakti tears that, when later in Australia, I played back the cassette, we could not understand any of it. It sounded as if we were all having a good cry together.

Still, the experience itself was an unforgettable *satsang*. As with Dr. Padmanabhan, himself, all projections of ego seemed to have been washed away by the pure bhakti stream. The love of the Lord flowing through them lifted our hearts high above the mundane world.

All I recall from the talk is that amazing experiences came to the family, particularly in the early days, before 1958, when Baba's *mahima* or miracle-working aspect was the dominant feature of his life and work. (Now it is the *upadesha* or teaching aspect.) Sri N. Kasturi relates, for instance, in his *Life of Bhagavan Sri Satya Sai Baba*, that in a room behind the old Mandir at Puttaparti Baba used to perform surgical operations, and that one of them was on Dr. Padmanabhan's brother for hernia.

Once when Padmanabhan was driving us through Bangalore, talking about the Lord's *leelas*, as he dodged the careening taxis and bouncing auto-rickshaws, Mrs. Padmanabhan was sitting in the back seat, telling Iris about her own wonderful experiences. One of these, which has to do with Baba's out-of-the-body travel, I will relate in another chapter.

Throughout his story, told without any display of ego, I gained the impression that Padmanabhan had found Sai Baba in his heart, and did not need the physical Form as most of us do. But if so, why did he go to see Baba at all!

He said: "Swami is like a father who loves to see his children. If I don't go for some time, he mentions it. So I go regularly to his darshans. Surely, that is the least I can do to show my gratitude for all he has done for me!"

"And mostly you sit outside, why?"

"Swami is extremely busy, and those who love him should try to help, rather than hinder him by taking up his valuable time. I go for an interview if I have a pressing personal or family problem, otherwise I just show my face in the line; sometimes he looks at me and smiles; sometimes he doesn't. But I know that he sees me, and knows I'm there. That's all that matters."

This was a very good lesson, indeed, to us who had a little earlier been feeling hurt because Swami sometimes ignored us. It spurred us on to try to take the important step forward, where we would think more of giving to the Lord, than always wanting to receive. What can we give him anyway — presents of flowers or fruits or gadgets? He often says that he does not want such things. He wants only ourselves — in complete surrender.

We have long known this in theory, and have tried hard in practice. But this devotee of nearly thirty years standing was a living example. In his life we could see the twin fruits of surrender. The outer fruit: divine guidance for worldly prosperity was, of course, the most obvious one. But the other, the spiritual twin, with its inner peace and joy, its understanding of life's meaning and purpose, was certainly the most valuable fruit. One fruit belonged to time; the other to eternity.

On the subject of surrender to the divine, Ramana Maharshi of Arunachala once said: "Complete surrender is impossible at the beginning. Partial surrender is certainly possible for all. In course of time that will lead to complete surrender."

These words help us to appreciate that there are stages along the road to surrender, that we must not despair at our own slow progress, but be content to take a step at a time. But some people may ask: "Why should I surrender myself at all? Why should I become spineless, with no will of my own?"

Such a question shows a complete misunderstanding of the situation. When we surrender to God (either to the Formless Divinity or to any form we choose), we are really surrendering to our own higher selves. We are, in fact, exchanging something shoddy and valueless, our little, manufactured desire-wills, for something great — the wise divine will within ourselves.

Small wonder that those who have surrendered their personal, egocentric wills acquire and demonstrate the strongest of wills; this is seen in the lives of the great saints and masters. Those who have given their lives to the divine gain a new life on a higher, happier level.

People who cling to their little egos, as if that is their only precious identity, people who feel loath to surrender to the divine in a Jesus, a Sai Baba, a spiritual guru in any form, should remember that they are not really surrendering to another person, but only to an outer symbol of their own inner divinity, their true selves.

Looked at in another way, the personal outer God or guru is a catalyst to promote the alchemical process of transmuting the lead of the lower self into the gold of the higher divine self. Baba knows and states that this transmutation is a slow and painful process, but that the crossing out of the false 'I' is the true cross of salvation.

Pondering these aspects of bhakti and divine wisdom, we awaited anxiously the return of Baba to "Brindavan." The end of the week came with no signs of his reappearance. Then Sai Gita vanished from under her tree, and we knew that Swami would not be returning that summer.

What you need to cross the sea of life is the bark of bhakti, of assurance of Grace, of surrender to His will. Throw off all burdens, become light, and you can trip across with one step on one crest and another on the next. God will take you through . . . . .

I ask only that you turn to me when your mind drags you into grief or pride or envy. Bring me the depths of your mind, no matter how grotesque, how cruelly ravaged by doubts or disappointments. I know how to treat them. I will not reject you. I am your mother . . . . .

SATYA SAI BABA

17
THE
VIBHUTI BABY

*Even a mind that knows the path can be dragged
from the path; the senses are so unruly.*

BHAGAVAD GITA

Soon after the disappearance of Sai Gita, we had a telegram from
Prasanti Nilayam, saying that Swami wanted us to come there immediately. We arrived the same afternoon.

At the first interview he told us that his building program was keeping him in Prasanti Nilayam, and taking much of his time; nevertheless he
would see us as much as possible now, during our last weeks in India.

When one is around Swami one sees so much of vibhuti production,
that soon it appears quite natural. He takes it from the air, wherever he
may be standing, as easily as, in his last incarnation, he used to take it
from the fire in his mosque dwelling at Shirdi.

But there is another aspect. Baba does not have to be physically present for vibhuti to appear, or for it to work its wonders. In many parts of
India and in far-off places, like New York, Los Angeles and London, vibhuti materializes on Baba's photos, and for that matter on other holy pictures, at the shrine of some Sai devotees.

The fabulous stories about such phenomena would fill a book, but I
leave them alone in general, because Swami, himself, is reluctant to discuss
them, and seems to want to play such experiences down. The reason for
this, I think, is that very few people are able to remain humble and reti-
cent in the face of such favors from the Unseen. Talking about them, writing about them, only adds fuel to the fires of their self-importance. Some
people, I understand, have so far fallen from grace that they have charged
a fee for the public to go in and see the vibhuti show.

So Baba plays it cool, implying that such events are private — only for the few who will gain in faith and strive to live purer lives through exposure to this symbol of Divine Power. Nevertheless, there are recipients who seem to want as many as possible to share in the joy of their wonderful experience in all humility. One morning in a coffee bar, in the bazaar outside the wall, I met a young Indian who offered to take me to a house where vibhuti was appearing in large quantities.

It proved to be a humble dwelling behind some shops. When we arrived, the only people present were the owner of the house — a modest, shy woman — her brother who was there on a short vacation, and an Indian lady doctor. I learned that all three were Sai devotees, and I was told later that the owner is a devoutly religious woman who has reached a high degree of self-surrender to the Lord Sai Baba. She spoke no English, so her brother and the lady doctor related the facts to me.

A few days earlier vibhuti had begun forming copiously on Baba's photos and other sacred pictures in the room where we were now sitting. From some of the pictures came also a colorless liquid which they called "honey." The quantities of both substances were so great that they fell off the pictures into containers placed underneath. As I watched, the pictures were still exuding both vibhuti and "honey."

I was given samples of each. The so-called "honey" was thinner and less sweet than ordinary honey. It had the consistency, but not quite the heavenly flavor, of the *amrita* that Swami sometimes produces in containers from the sands.

Word of the phenomenon had spread rapidly in the village, and crowds gathered — up to three hundred at a time, the brother told me. They packed the yard, verandah and small rooms to suffocation point. Many were given holy ash and "honey" to take away.

But on the evening following the first day of crowds, Swami appeared to the saintly house-owner in a vision, and told her he did not want her bothered by all these people; she must deny them entrance to the house and grounds. This she did. I, myself, was graciously permitted to come in to view the phenomenon because they knew my name as the author of *Sai Baba, Man of Miracles*. So I was made an exception, but no other visitors were present.

Then, soon after our arrival at Prasanti Nilayam the "vibhuti baby" made its appearance at the ashram — a phenomenon quite unique in my experience. Immediately I heard of its arrival, I hastened to investigate. A small crowd of people standing outside a building revealed the baby's location. I joined the crowd, but was told that no one was permitted inside.

Fortunately, Dr. S. Bhagavantam was staying in the house nearby.

He had met the young parents of the baby and seemed to have gained their confidence. They spoke his language, Telegu, so he kindly took me into their apartment and acted as my interpreter.

The baby, a boy, was only a few months old. From the time of his birth, the parents said, he had been exuding vibhuti from his head, face and other parts of his body. It appeared on his skin, quickly covering him from head to toe. When they wiped it off, more came immediately. They knew, as all Indians know, that some holy men smear their bodies all over with ash, but they had never heard of it appearing on the skin by its own power. As the weeks went by and the flow of ash continued unabated, they became more and more worried. How could their child possibly live a normal life this way!

It was not many miles from their village to Puttaparti, and some of their neighbors suggested that they bring the baby to Sai Baba. Perhaps he could stop the flow of troublesome ash.

So they came by bus to the ashram. On Swami's orders they were given this apartment very near to the Mandir, and supplied with meals by several ladies who often cooked dishes for Swami, himself.

When I entered the room, the little boy was asleep. Grey vibhuti covered his scalp in a thick layer under the sparse black hair; patches of it were forming on his face and hands as I stood watching him. After a few minutes he awoke and looked at me from the gleaming depths of eyes that were bright with intelligence. He was a very attractive baby, and some mysterious secret seemed to shine behind his dark eyes.

The parents were shy village folk; I could see that being in the limelight of public attention was painful to them. All they wanted, I sensed, was a quick miracle to end the vibhuti miracle, so that they could return to the quiet life of their village. But who on earth was this little boy that the sacred symbol of Siva should be sprouting spontaneously from his skin?

The crowd watched eagerly that evening as, after darshan, Swami walked over in the direction of the "vibhuti baby." But he went into Dr. Bhagavantam's house nearby. We waited and watched, thinking that he might visit the baby after leaving Bhagavantam's place. About twenty minutes later he emerged and walked straight back to the Mandir, without a look in the direction of the vibhuti mystery.

A few days later the young couple and the "vibhuti baby" vanished from the house in the ashram. If Swami had visited them, it must have been at night when no one was about — at least, I found nobody who had seen him go to the house. Nevertheless, I heard later, the flow of ash from the child's skin had stopped. Obviously, he who can initiate a flow of vibhuti at will, would have no difficulty whatever in stemming one — whether he was physically present or not.

But what could the strange phenomenon mean? A week or so later, during an interview with Baba, I had the temerity to ask him about it. There was nobody else present except my wife and Dr. Gokak, so I thought the time might be auspicious.

"The baby," said Swami in a gentle, thoughtful manner, "was a yoga brashta."

The word and Swami's explanation, are part of the concept of reincarnation, which is a tenet of the Hindu and Buddhist religions. The Christian churches accepted the concept for the first five centuries of their existence. Then, at the Council of Constantinople, in A.D. 534, the doctrine was voted out of the church creeds by a small majority. Since then the Christian churches — with a few exceptions — have been silent on the subject. Even so, many church leaders, including some popes, and some ministers of non-conformist denominations, have declared their belief in the rebirth of the soul. Moreover, several Western philosophers have accepted it, and some great poets and writers, such as Masefield and Kipling, have shown in their works their belief in this doctrine. Furthermore, it is basic to the writings of many mystics, including some of the Muslim faith.

Liberation from the enslaving desires of the flesh, and the reactions of the mortal mind, is the aim and purpose of human life, according to the Hindu spiritual philosophy and Sai Baba's daily teachings. Such liberation is part of an evolutionary process and takes many lives on earth to achieve.

Sometimes during some lifetime, an individual will become consciously aware of his true life goal, and make conscious efforts to achieve it — thus aiding the upward thrust of the evolutionary force. His efforts will embrace the arduous spiritual self-disciplines which the Indians call yoga. If the yoga is of the bhakti and karma varieties, practiced by the Christians (though many do not even know the names), the disciplines will still be arduous, as the lives of Christian saints have fully testified.

But supposing an individual has made good progress along the yoga path, and has almost reached the goal of *moksha* or liberation, when some latent desire or pride turns him from the path and he dies, a fallen yogi. Are all his efforts lost? Does he have to start again at the foot of yoga's steep, stairway when he is reborn into another life on earth?

Five thousand years ago on the battlefield of Kurukshetra, the warrior Arjuna asked this question of his friend and charioteer, Krishna Avatara. The Avatar's reply was that no achievements on the spiritual path are ever wasted, no forward progress is ever lost. In his subsequent life, the one who has fallen away from yoga will be born into circumstance favorable to the continuance of his yogic endeavors, starting from the high point he had previously reached.

"He comes to be united with the knowledge acquired in his former body and strives more than ever for perfection."

A brashta yogi is one who has fallen from his high estate, and will be given by Fate, or the Lords of Karma, another good chance to get back on the yoga stairs, to continue his upward climb from the step off which he had previously tumbled.

The "vibhuti baby" was, Swami said, such a brashta yogi, reborn. He must, I thought, have once been a very holy man indeed, high up on the yoga stairs, to return to this world exuding from his skin the sacred symbol of Lord Siva, the God of the yogis. His auspicious rebirth had taken place only a few miles from Prasanti Nilayam, and he had been brought into the orbit of Sai Baba Avatara during the first few months of his life!

Sadhana (spiritual or yogic exercise) will disclose to you your true identity as one with God. But be careful; sadhana can foster pride and envy as a by-product of progress. You calculate how long you have done sadhana, and you are tempted to look down on another whose record is less. You are proud that you have written the name of God ten million times, perhaps; you talk about it, whenever you get the chance, so that others may admire your faith and fortitude. But it is not the millions that count; it is the purity of mind that results from genuine concentration on the Name. You must make sure that your sadhana does not become like drawing water from a well with a cane basket. You will get no water this way no matter how many times you pull the basket up. Your vices are the holes in the basket. Keep the heart pure, keep it whole.

All religions exhort man to cleanse the heart of malice, greed, hate and anger. All religions hold out the gift of Grace as the prize for success in this cleansing process. Ideas of superiority and inferiority arise only in a heart corrupted by egoism. If someone argues that he is higher, or that his religion is holier, it is proof that he has missed the very core of his faith. Sadhana will reveal the unity in the fundamental teachings of all religions.

SATYA SAI BABA

18
THE HOUND
OF HEAVEN

I fled Him down the labyrinthine ways of my own mind.
FRANCIS THOMPSON

Sai Baba has said that we come to him only when he calls us, and it is reasonable to assume that he calls only those who are ready. Yet sometimes it appears that they, themselves, do not know they are ready. And when the earthly ego hears the call, it is inclined to flee, for this is a warning of its own impending annihilation. The situation may be understood as the flight of the self from the voice of the Overself, allegorized by Francis Thompson in his poem, "The Hound of Heaven."

Mr. Vemu Mukunda was a brilliant student of modern science at Indian universities. Then he went on to do post graduate research in nuclear physics and engineering at Strathclyde University, Glasgow, Scotland, following which he worked in atomic energy establishments in England. Thus he became a son of the west, a limb cut off from the tree of his own native spiritual culture.

Yet he was not happy in this empty western life-style where progress of technology was the god, and the social round of cocktail parties the ritual. Its soul-killing inadequacy struck him like a Titan blow when his brother and sister both died back in India. Questions about the true meaning of life and death hammered at the door of his mind. But where were the answers? For the nuclear mind they could not be found in temple or church.

He became more and more disillusioned with his profession as a nuclear engineer; it had, no doubt, a practical value to mankind as an energy provider, but its dark side could lead to world destruction. Periods of suicidal depression hung over Vemu like a black cloud. The only thing that saved him was regular escape into the sweet music of his veena, an instrument he had played since he was a boy. Now it became his solace in a dark, loveless world.

Then the first of a series of strange events took place. He was living in London and one day the manager of the Royal Shakespeare Company there invited Vemu to come to his home and have a look at his wife's veena which needed some attention. He agreed and was taken there by car, along with a few friends. The veena, he found was in very bad shape, with a twisted bridge, uneven frets and other damage. He could not get one clear note from it. But he felt he would like to repair the instrument, and offered to take it home for that purpose.

On the way home his friends wanted to call at a Sai Baba bhajan session, taking place at the house of a Dr. Dakshinamurti. Vemu had no interest in Sai Baba, though his parents had for long been devotees of Sai Baba of Shirdi, but he could hardly refuse to go with friends in whose car he was travelling. He thought, however, that the bhajans were in honor of Shirdi Sai.

When he walked into the room and saw the photo of Satya Sai Baba, his mental reaction was: "Oh, no, not him!" Though his feelings towards Shirdi Sai were neutral, he felt a kind of hostility towards Satya Sai Baba, because his parents would not accept the latter as a reincarnation of the former. They considered Satya Sai an imposter. They belonged to that group of Shirdi devotees who, Swami says, are too attached to the old form; they worship the outer appearance without understanding that the same spirit can return in an entirely different body, and show different personality traits. The same Divine Spirit has been made manifest in all Avatars, yet the outward appearance of each has always been unique.

Vemu sat down behind the singers, taking no part in the bhajans. Presently the hostess put a veena in his hands, and asked him to play something. The singing had stopped, and he began absently to strum the beloved instrument. A tune came into his mind and he played it. On request for an encore, he again launched spontaneously into the first composition that came to mind. At the end he realized that the two pieces were old classical numbers by two saint-musicians of different parts of India. The title of each, in the languages of the composers, was "No one is equal to you."

Looking down at the veena he had been using, he observed, for the first time, that it was the badly-damaged one he was taking home for repair. One of his friends must have brought it in from the car, and the hostess, not noticing that it was damaged, had handed it to him to play. But how strange! Not a note had been wrong in his performance! A feeling of awe swept through Vemu, and his hair seemed to stand on end. He tried the veena again, but now could not produce a true note on it.

"Sai Baba!" he thought. "What power! Is he a black magician?"

Soon after that incident he began to get invitations to play, professionally. He accepted as often as possible, and, oddly, wherever he went he met someone who talked about Sai Baba. And at home in London, friends kept pressing him to attend Sai bhajan meetings at the different Sai Centers. He began to get the feeling that Sai Baba was at his heels, pursuing him.

Part of him wanted to surrender, but another part resisted. What was the world of the Spirit but a foolish dream, he asked himself — an escape from the harsh realities of life? Yet the world of the harsh realities held no enticements for him. He was in a dark night of limbo, desperately unhappy, sleeping badly, eating little, losing weight, torn between thoughts of suicide and the hope that some power would come to his aid.

Eventually, he sat down and wrote an airmail letter to Sai Baba, addressing it to the ashram at Prasanti Nilayam: "I feel you are chasing me, Sai Baba. Would you please give me an answer to an important question about my future: should I continue as a nuclear engineer, should I become a full-time professional musician, or should I give up both and become a *sannyasi*?"

Baba, he had been told, did not write answers to letters, but gave replies in other ways — if you could read the signs. Now that he had paused in his flight, and spoken over his shoulder to the Hound of Heaven, would he get some sign, Vemu wondered, as he caught a plane to Paris for the week-end. He was giving a public veena performance there.

A few days after his return to London, he felt an inexplicable urge to go out to Pinner, on the outskirts of London, and pay a visit to Mr. and Mrs. S. Sitaram. He had been taken there once to a bhajan session, against his inclinations, so why did he now feel a strong desire to go there? He resisted for a time and then, late one afternoon, submitted to the persistent urge, and caught a train to Pinner.

He took a taxi from the Pinner railway station to Cuckoo Hill Road, and had no difficulty in finding the Sitaram house, with "Om Sai" written clearly on the front. Mrs. Sitaram answered his knock.

"Oh, I'm so glad you've come," she greeted him; "I have something for you."

She led him into the shrine-room, where Sai gatherings were always held, and handed him a photograph.

She said: "A visitor who came to our last meeting — I don't remember his name — left this. He asked me to give it to you as soon as possible — so I've been hoping you would come."

The photograph showed Satya Sai Baba playing a veena.

"At that moment," Vemu told me, "I surrendered. I prostrated before the life-sized photo of Baba standing in the room, and wept."

Vemu Mukunda understood this to be Baba's answer. He gave up his engineering job and became a full-time professional musician. In the ensuing months many engagements came his way, taking him to all the main cities of western Europe. Soon his reputation was such that he was also giving performances in Russia, and other countries of eastern Europe.

Now his life seemed to gain meaning. Not only was he happy in his profession, but he felt that the "One to whom no one is equal" was watching over him. From that inner Sai Source, he said, came the idea to start research into the effects of sound on the human mind. This he did and found great satisfaction in the work.

Inexplicable events, faith-fostering events, emerged from the new dimension that had opened through — he believed — his inner contact with Sai Baba, and he felt a strong urge to go and see this Man of Power in the flesh. Another reason for going to India was that his parents, who lived in Bangalore, were begging him to come home and see them. But underneath his desire was a fear that Baba might not see him if he went. What a frightful disappointment it would be if Baba ignored him — if, after all, his new-found faith was built on nothing but his own imagination!

Finally, he wrote to a friend in India who was a Satya Sai devotee, and begged him to ask Baba, at the first opportunity: "Should Vemu Mukunda come here to see you, Swami?" Soon afterwards, while in Geneva on tour, Vemu had a vivid dream in which Baba rubbed vibhuti on his left shoulder beneath his shirt and said: "Come to India." The dream seemed very real, but — he told himself in the days that followed — it might have been merely a psychological, wish-fulfillment dream.

These experiences are hard to interpret with any certainty. Are they manufactured by the dream-consciousness, or are they true visions created by Sai Baba? If the latter, do they have a literal or an allegorical meaning? Those are the questions.

One of my own early dreams of Swami was certainly allegorical or symbolic. In it I was standing before Baba and we were exchanging bodies. One moment I would be in his body and he in mine. Then we would return to our own bodies. This went on several times. It was an unforgettable experience. I thought about it a good deal afterwards, and felt it held several lessons. For instance, although I knew and understood, philosophically, the great truth that the body is only a vestment, and that our real selves are immortal, being one with God, no doubt, I was in practice identifying too much with the body.

Swami's dramatic illustration in the dream was, I think, to help me really experience the truth I knew. It brought to mind the words of Christ: "I am in the Father and you in me and I in you," expressing the same truth.

A dream of the literal type was told us by Mrs. Padmanabhan of Bangalore. She and her dentist husband had for years made a point of always attending the great Dasara Festival at Prasanti Nilayam, and though the crowds were constantly enormous, Swami had always given them a room to themselves.

But in 1973 their son and daughter, and several lady friends asked to go along with them. This might, she thought, create an accommodation problem for Swami, yet it would not be kind to go without them. Normally she used to go before the festival, and her busy husband would come a few days later. This year she decided, with her husband's agreement, to solve her dilemma by not going to Dasara at all. Then Swami came to her in a dream and said: "Come, I will give you a flat."

She was greatly elated, yet, though a devotee for twenty-eight years, she could not feel quite sure that the dream was real. It might be a creation of her own desire-mind. "Trust the dream!" her husband told her; so after much thought she decided on a compromise. She would go for the night, taking two of the ladies with her. If the dream was true, the others could come later; if not, the three of them could crowd for the one night into a corner of her cousin's undoubtedly overcrowded permanent quarters at Prasanti Nilayam.

The festival had already begun when they arrived.

"We don't expect anything, but is there something?" she asked the official in charge of accommodation, diffidently.

He shook his head. "How many of you?"

"Three now. Seven more would be coming later."

"Oh, that's quite hopeless."

She took her friends to her cousin's room, from which they could watch the morning's festival events. With these Swami, himself, was fully occupied. After lunch the accommodation official reappeared at their door.

"Come!" he beckoned Mrs. Padmanabhan and her friends. "Swami told me there is a flat he has been keeping for you. I have just been able to see him a minute ago."

When devotees of long experience, like Mrs. Padmanabhan, find it hard to be sure when a dream of Sai Baba is actually a message from Baba, who can blame Vemu Mukunda for his wavering doubts? But after some days of hesitation, he made up his mind, cancelled all engagements for the next few weeks and took a plane to India.

A large crowd was sitting along the tree-lined drive at "Brindavan" when Vemu arrived there. He sat on the sandy earth at the end of the row of men. His neighbor informed him that he was very lucky as Swami had not yet given his morning darshan, and was expected at any moment.

Time passed, punctuated by the caw of crows and the rumble of trucks and buses outside the wall. But around Vemu was peace and a happy feeling of expectancy. Then came a stir at the far end of the lines, and he caught a flash of flame-colored robe. His heart beat with excitement as Baba walked slowly down the avenue, stopping here and there to talk to people, to bless some object held up to him, to materialize vibhuti.

When the figure drew close, Vemu's heart was leaping into his throat; he could no longer bear to look towards the face, the halo of hair, the light movements of the delicate feet. Instead he looked down at the yellow earth. But now the naked feet were standing right in front of him, pointing towards him from the rim of the shining robe. Still he continued to sit there, like one struck dumb and rigid.

Gripped in Vemu's hand was a letter he had earlier written to Baba. He felt the letter taken from him. He felt Baba raising him up. He heard a gentle voice say, "Go inside and wait."

When at last they were alone together in the interview room, Baba produced vibhuti from the air and rubbed it on Vemu's left shoulder under his shirt — just as in the dream, thus confirming the truth of the dream. Then he listened in awe as Baba talked and showed full knowledge of the young man's struggles, problems and his great depression until Baba directed him into the career of musician.

At the end of the talk, Baba circled his hand in the air again. Out of it this time came a five-faced rudraksha in a gold setting, hanging on a gold chain. He gave it to the young musician to wear constantly, saying that great success would attend his career and his spiritual progress. Finally, he invited Vemu to give a veena concert in the Satya Sai College at "Brindavan."

On the day of the concert Vemu's eighty-year old father came with him to "Brindavan." He would just sit in the outer grounds, he told his son, and wait.

But when Swami learned the old man was there, he called him inside and, in Vemu's words: "For a whole hour Swami talked to my father like a loving mother to her child. After that my father was a changed man."

Vemu Mukunda concluded his story, a happy smile flashing through his black, pointed beard: "Not only my father, but my mother, my brother, who is a doctor in Bangalore, and, in fact, all members of my family are now followers of Satya Sai Baba."

Mr. C. Mahadevan of Colombo, Sri Lanka, was another who tried at first to ignore the signs of the pursuing feet. The first sign was when his young son of twelve tried to interest Mahadevan in a photo of Sai Baba. His response was utter indifference, and an attempt to quash the boy's enthusiastic interest.

Then a little later while Mahadevan was walking along a railway platform, a magazine fell off a bookstand right at his feet. Picking it up, he saw that in falling it had opened at a large color photograph of Sai Baba.

Such events struck him as odd, and he began to feel an urge to go to India and see Sai Baba. Thinking this very foolish, he tried to ignore it, but the urge eventually became so strong that, in the next vacation from his work with the public service, he yielded. With him on the trip to India he took his son, who was absolutely delighted at the prospect of seeing Baba, and also his wife who was suffering considerable pain in her back from spinal trouble.

During an interview, Swami materialized a locket for the wife. Overcome with joy and gratitude, she forgot her spinal malady and fell at Baba's feet. He raised her up, and at the same time, Mahadevan said, cured her back. Anyway, from that moment on it never gave her the slightest pain.

This miraculous event and the Love and Grace radiating from Baba, changed Mahadevan's outlook. Back in Colombo he felt an inner compulsion to begin holding bhajan sessions in his own home. He wanted to share his new faith with his friends. But there was to be a tremendous test of his faith within a short time.

He contracted cancer of the right jaw. Several specialists confirmed that the growth was malignant. Perhaps an operation would help, they said, but they could not be sure. He decided to try it.

He spent twenty-eight days in hospital with this operation, and then a few months after he was discharged, the growth began to spread again. In a second operation surgeons removed part of the lower left mandible, and put him on nasal feeding. This time he spent thirty-two terrible days in hospital, during which he lost fifty-six pounds in weight.

Soon after leaving hospital the second time, he began to suffer an acute pain in the side of his head, and a discharge of pus oozed continually from the area of the operation. Radium treatment was tried without effect; then came a third operation for corrective surgery. But this brought no relief; the pain and discharge continued.

The third operation had taken place in February, 1974, and another attempt at corrective surgery was scheduled for the following April. But Mahadevan was beginning to lose faith in the surgeons. The continual shocks to his system, the worries, the great loss of time that had cost him promotion and a salary increment, all combined to bring on diabetes.

He doubted if a fourth operation would be any more successful than the others. How long must all this go on? How long could he survive if they could not prevent the spread of the malignancy? The surgeons had said, at the outset, that they could not guarantee the success. Obviously the knife had failed, and his life seemed as good as finished.

His only hope now lay in the compassion and mercy of Sai Baba. He cancelled the fourth operation, and flew to India, alone.

Swami was at "Brindavan" when Mahadevan arrived, and took his place in the line for darshan; and — he prayed — a touch from the Healing Hand. When Baba paused in front of him for a moment, Mahadevan summoned up the courage to say: "Swamiji, the doctors want to do a fourth operation for my cancer."

"Poor fellow!" Baba replied, and walked on.

As the feet moved away from him Mahadevan felt as if the end of his life had come. But suddenly Baba stopped, turned, and shot back towards him like an arrow. With a look of power and tremendous determination on his face, Swami twirled his hand and materialized a large quantity of vibhuti.

"Eat this!" he commanded, pouring the vibhuti into Mahadevan's palm. Then he stood watching as the man from Sri Lanka ate.

"The vibhuti tasted like a mixture of ghee and honey," Mahadevan told us later. "After I had eaten it, Swami walked away, and the pain in my head left with him. Also, from that day, there was no more discharge. I knew I was cured!"

Even so, he found it hard to leave. He followed Swami to Prasanti Nilayam and was still there when we talked with him several weeks later. Almost every day we saw Mahadevan, and every day he seemed to grow in strength and in devotion to Sai Baba.

Such Divine convalescence after cure is, I believe, a most important thing. The healing of the body is wonderful, but only a temporary relief unless the person's thinking and way of life change too — as Jesus often made clear to those he cured. Unless the soul itself turns towards the healing light, the demons of disease will creep back to the impure places that invite them.

At the end of Mahadevan's stay at Prasanti Nilayam, Swami said to him: "I fought for your life three times, and, finally, cured you at Whitefield. I know you have lost promotion and salary increments, but don't worry: Swami will help you in all ways."

Giving him some packets of vibhuti to take home, Baba continued: "Keep up your good work with the bhajans. I am always there with you."

So the gentle-mannered Mahadevan returned to his home in Colombo. Some months later we received a letter from him, telling us about the great joy of his family and friends, and of the sensation caused among his office colleagues by his miracle-cure. Also he wrote: "Baba not only cured my cancer, but did away with my diabetes, too. After my return from Him, it was found that my blood sugar had dropped to normal."

His son, he writes, was delighted that his own early efforts had borne such wonderful fruits — "bringing us into the Sai Family so that my life was saved by Baba."

His wife, a Methodist by upbringing, was now leading the singing at their regular home bhajans, where more and more people were gathering for the Sai meetings.

"We had a grand bhajan on Baba's birthday, November 23, and fed the poor with lunch packets put together by the Sai devotees . . .

"Baba appears to me often in dreams, especially in the early morning hours . . . Now I don't worry about anything. I leave everything in His hands . . . "

Yearn, yearn hard for success in achieving the real purpose of life, and success will be yours. Remember you are all certain to win; that is why you have been called, and you have responded to the call, to come to me.

The Lord is the Sun and when His Rays fall upon your heart, unimpeded by the clouds of egoism, the lotus bud of the heart blooms and the petals unfold. Remember, only the buds that are ready will bloom; the rest have to wait patiently.

SATYA SAI BABA

THE HOUND OF HEAVEN   139

19

A SCHOOL
FOR IMMORTALITY

*When one sees Eternity in things that pass away
and Infinity in finite things, then one has pure knowledge.*

BHAGAVAD GITA

"How can I reach Sai Baba? It may be a very long time before I can
go to India: is there anything I can do to reach him before that?"

Camille Svensson asked this question in 1971, just after I had given a
talk on Baba at the East-West Center in Los Angeles. We had heard the
question before, but not often. Such an idea is usually born only in minds
that have made some progress in the spiritual search. Camille, herself, had
been a Theosophist for many years, and, particularly, a keen student of
Madame Blavatsky's life and works. From the eager shine in her corn-
flower blue eyes during my talk, I felt that Baba had struck a responsive
chord in her heart.

"Yes," my wife and I assured her. "You can reach him through
meditation. For many this has proved a quicker and surer road than the
journey to India. Through it you can set up what one might call the 'hot
line' to Baba. There are, however, some external aids to the meditation
route. You can, for example, sing bhajans and join in discussions with one
of the groups here in Los Angeles, and read about Baba's life, and study
his own written words . . . "

Unlike some who listen to this answer with mental reservations, and
go their way, Camille tried the prescribed formula wholeheartedly. Soon,
she told us in letters, she began to feel, without any doubt, the out-
stretching power of Sai Baba. It helped her in personal problems and
inspired her in lectures on Theosophical themes, which she often gave.
Then the great two-way traffic of love began to flow – the love *from* and

to the Guru that eventually becomes the law of life.

When, in 1974, we met Camille in India, it was her second visit to Sai Baba. Much had happened. An ardent student of Theosophy, which is in essence a combination of Raja and Jnana Yoga, Camille had been transformed into a devotee of Sai Baba. This Path requires much more of Bhakti than of any other type of yoga. It works primarily on the heart center.

Now many of her lectures, to Theosophical and other audiences, were about Baba. She had already come to regard him as an Avatar, and, to the disapproval of one or two conservative Theosophists, expressed this idea in lectures. It is a subtle, elusive concept that some will accept, swiftly or slowly, and others reject out of hand.

During an interview that Baba gave to Westerners, including ourselves, at "Brindavan," Camille sat near the back of the group, making notes — as she usually does. At the end she knelt at His feet. Swami helped her up, saying, "Good woman," as if he was voicing a thought to himself. Then he moved towards the door.

Camille picked up a packet of vibhuti lying on the floor and found that it had "Sai Ram" printed on it. Thinking that Baba had dropped it, she hastened after him.

"Is this yours, Swami?" she asked, with reverence and concern in her voice.

Swami smiled. "You keep it," he said, and went on to explain the import of the printed mantra on it. Then he circled his hand three times before her, closed it, opened it again, and there on his palm was a shining ring, with the same mantra, "Sai Ram," engraved on it. He slipped the ring on her finger, smiled at her again, and walked away.

Camille could not stop looking at the ring, which fitted her finger as if made to measure. She had read a great deal about materializations, precipitations and other wondrous phenomena in the Theosophical literature. But this spontaneous miracle, so timely and specially for her, held the numinous of Divine Love in the voice and eyes of the Avatar. Her own blue eyes were moist, and her face shone with even more than its usual radiance.

During the days we spent together later at Prasanti Nilayam, our friend, Camille, told us of many wonderful things that had happened to her since her feet had found the Sai Path. She also told us about a remarkable man who had appeared in the Theosophical and Sai Baba circles of California.

This was Dr. Benito F. Reyes, a superlative lecturer, and an educator of brilliant academic background, holding doctorates in philosophy, literature and several other areas of learning. But what interested her, and us, was that, combined with his distinguished academic achievements, was a deep-probing interest in the spiritual verities. At this time he was President of the Institute of Avasthology* which he and his wife, Dr. Dominga Reyes, had established in Ojai, California.

Following a visit to Sai Baba, Dr. Reyes had been asked, without warning, to give a lecture on his experiences in India to a group in California. He spoke spontaneously, without written notes, so that there was no record of his lecture, except the copious notes that Camille had taken at the time. These she graciously gave me, and from them I have written about Dr. Reyes's Indian adventure — as much as possible in his own words and those of his wife. After writing the first draft, I was fortunate enough to visit America, meet Dr. Reyes, and have the account checked and agreed to by the learned gentleman, himself.

But before reproducing the story of his first visit to Sai Baba, I should give a few points about his background, relevant to the birth of what he has called a "School for Immortality." In his early career at the University of the Philippines Dr. Reyes lectured on Botany, Clinical Psychology and Philosophy, including Asian Philosophy and Comparative Religion. Eventually, he held the position of president of that university. Also, during his academic career in the Philippines, he founded, and was president of, the University of the City of Manila.

When the government of the Philippines came under a dictator, Dr. Reyes left the islands of his home. He went to California. There, having been a Theosophist for some forty years, he was asked to take charge of "The School of the Wisdom" at Krotona, Ojai. After some time in this work, he founded his Institute of Avasthology.

Though Dr. Reyes had heard of Sai Baba while still in the Philippines, and, as he said, "got the strong feeling that he was an Avatar," it was two people of California that brought him into closer contact. One of these was Robert Silver, an attorney in Ventura; the other was Indra Devi, to whose house, just over the Mexican border in Tecate, the Reyes couple were taken.

"There I saw the vibhuti," he said. "Something began stirring in my heart. Then we had bhajans in the Baba Room! After we went home to Ojai, I would dream of Baba the whole night. Having been a teacher of psychology, I would interpret these dreams as some kind of wish-fulfillment. I did not understand what it was to dream of Baba until much later."

About his work and ideals Reyes said: "I have been an educator for the last thirty years, but in our modern system there is a kind of moral bankruptcy. I was anxious to bring about some sort of transformation towards a more spiritual education. But, of course, I knew that first the transformation must come within me, myself."

He wanted to develop his institute into a spiritual university, something on the lines of the colleges Sai Baba was starting in India. But there were many difficulties. One was the need for funds. The Reyes couple had been able to bring nothing with them from the Philippines, except, as he put it, "an ideal and a longing. I had only fifteen dollars in my pocket. Can you start a university on fifteen dollars?!"

Their dream, he said, "was to educate people not only for these three-score-and-ten years of earthly life, but in terms of man's eternal *dharma*; to educate people not for a profession, or a vocation, not even for culture — but for immortality."

Some people told him he was crazy.

"I am the product of universities. I studied a lot of algebra, for instance, but in all my life I never used algebra. There is not a school that teaches man how to die correctly — not even that! They teach us how to survive on this planet, but not how to face eternity. They teach us how to find a place in our locality, but not to find a place in the universe. So many millions wasted on education that does not prepare us for eternal life."

Dr. Reyes felt that his preparation for the work ahead required an early visit to Sai Baba. "It was high time that I saw this great being and asked for his blessings on the work."

But there were problems here, too. Primarily there was the question of money for the trip. When the Lord calls, however, he opens the way — and then often throws up a road block along the route to make the approach difficult. This happened to myself and to a number of other people I know. For Dr. and Mrs. Reyes the way was opened when Sai devotees presented them with two return air tickets to Bangalore, India, and invited them to go with a group from California.

As the Californian party would be setting off soon for Sai Baba country, the Reyes decided to make the first leg of the Indian journey, that is, as far as New York, immediately. Their daughter, Anita, lived in that city and was about to have a baby. She wanted her mother to be with her for the birth. So it was a good opportunity to grant that wish.

Explaining their state of mind, Dr. Reyes said: "We had lost our country and our home — so many things — through that drastic change of government in the Philippines. All we had left to us was our own family. It seemed of the greatest importance to our daughter that her mother should be with her at the time of the baby's delivery."

But the baby was in no hurry to oblige. Robert Silver phoned daily from Ojai, urging them to be quite ready, with their injections and all other requirements completed, to depart with the Californian party in a few days. On the day before they were due to leave for India there was still no baby. "My wife felt she must stay, and I did not want to be apart from her on our first visit to Baba. So, when Robert phoned that day, I told him I had decided not to go without my wife, and now she could not go as the baby had not arrived."

That night the Reyes couple went to bed feeling very sad; the door that had opened invitingly for India and Baba was now certainly closed. Next morning Mrs. Reyes woke up with the red swollen eyes of trachoma. She said to her daughter, "I cannot stay here with this contagious disease, Anita. I would infect the children, even the one about to come."

Anita replied sadly, "No Mom. I think you had better not stay any longer."

About two o'clock that afternoon Dr. and Mrs. Reyes met the Californian party at the airport and left New York for India. En route they would have a stop-over in Zurich, Switzerland.

Dr. Reyes's talk continues: Let me tell you a strange thing, when my wife opened her eyes next morning in Zurich, they were perfectly well. We thought of Baba and laughed. It seemed to us the condition had just been sent to persuade our daughter that it was better we should go.

We arrived in Bangalore, a beautiful, beautiful city. The city of Baba, I called it. In the afternoon we went out to "Brindavan," in Whitefield. Baba had left an hour before our arrival. Dejected, we sat there on the earth. "You could have waited just one hour, Baba," we said.

Next day we went to Puttaparti. When I first saw this elusive Man walking, I saw beauty in motion. I cannot describe how this One moves — this motion of Beauty and Spirit. He was not walking; He was gliding, floating. There is something airy, other-worldly about the way He walks. I thought, then, He is not of the earth, but has come to the earth to bless it.

My heart was floating out to Him, but I was a stranger and did not know how to behave. I decided it was best to do just what the group did. If they prostrated I would prostrate. If they took the dust from His feet into their mouths, I would do the same.

That night the temperature was about a hundred-and-twenty. I saw the others setting out their mosquito nets, and looked around for an extra net, but there was not a single one. I looked at my wife; she was sleeping. I thought, this wife of mine did not even take care to find out if I was all right.

The heat was like an oven in the little cubicle where I had to sleep. I knew that, as everyone else was under a net, I would be the sole target for the squadrons of mosquitos that night. I took a handkerchief, wet it, put it on my forehead and asked Baba to take care of me. Using my little rosary, I began saying, "Sai Baba, Sai Baba, Sai Baba." Repeating it, I went to sleep about nine o'clock. Several times during the night I became more or less conscious and felt a strange layer of cold around my body; it seemed to cover me from head to toe. I did not get a single mosquito bite.

By five in the morning it was already hot. I went to the bathroom and then straight into meditation. There came a call that Baba would see us immediately. My heart began to beat fast. How does one meet an Avatar? Should I talk? If so, what should I say?

The American group gathered in the interview room. Baba looked at us and began giving us vibhuti from his hand, saying "Eat it – eat it." So I ate it. Then He said: "You have not had breakfast. You must be hungry." He waved his hand and gave to everyone some kind of substance that had the consistency of peanut butter. I took a big lump as I *was* hungry. It did not taste like peanut butter; it was very delicious, like some kind of sweet with powdered nuts.

Everyone in the group seemed intent on sponsoring me and my idea for a university. One began by saying, "Dr. Reyes is an educator, Swami."

Several times Baba asked, "What is education?" but every time I attempted to answer, He would say, "No, no, no!"

I mentioned that meditation was taught at our institute.

"What is meditation?" He asked. Again, immediately I tried to answer, He said, "No, no, no!" All the time, whenever I began a sentence, He would stop me. At last I got the message and remained silent.

Then for three hours He talked to us. No doubt people outside were thinking: what a blessedness! But I was thinking of the frustration of not getting across to Him what I had come to say. When Baba prepared to go, He said, "I will meet you this afternoon privately." My heart revived.

Afternoon – three o'clock – four o'clock; still no sign. But at last He called us – my wife and me. "What do you want?" He asked me. "Please, a university for . . . " "Approved, approved, approved! But what do you want for yourself?" "Nothing, Baba – just to kiss your hand." I did not have the strength to tell him I wanted to kiss His Feet. I have never kissed anyone's feet.

"Approved, approved," he said.

I took his hand and kissed it. It had the smell of jasmine. Then I did ask for several things in connection with the university and He kept saying, "Approved, approved." My heart was singing with joy. Before leaving, Baba said, "Tomorrow we go to Anantapur. You come. You can talk with Dr. Gokak and Dr. Bhagavantam."

It was a beautiful morning when we drove to Anantapur. Baba's car was out in front; we were in the second car. I was thinking that He had not given me anything to show to my friends back in California — so what was the evidence? I could not show them "Approved, approved!"

I focussed his face in my mind and said, mentally, "Baba, please give me a ring, even just a little one. I ask you this way, but I will never ask you with my lips."

And so we arrived at Anantapur. We sat in a room with hundreds of others, waiting for Baba to come in. When He came, He called my wife and me to sit near Him. Then He looked at me and asked, "Do you like Krishna?" "Yes, Swami, I have read the *Bhagavad Gita* and *Mahabharata* — I like Krishna very much."

He took my hand, materialized a ring, and put it on my finger. It had a picture of Krishna on it. I was overcome, but I said, "It is *your* picture I want, Baba!"

"Krishna, Baba, there is no difference. You were asking for a ring in the car; I have given you one. Whenever you want anything, always ask me with your mind, like that." Something in me exploded. I sat there almost fainting.

Then He looked at my wife and materialized for her a beautiful medallion with his picture on it. She was crying. "You have a pure heart," He said. "That is why you always cry. Go on, cry; you are happy! This is for you, too." Something was coming out of His hand — whitish, opalescent. When it fell on the floor, I saw it was an ear-ring. Then I watched Him release the other one from the side of His hand. The ear-rings bore the lingam, the symbol of Siva and creativity in the world. Tenderly He put them on my wife's ears. Baba does not only give; He gives with his heart.

Then he began lecturing on creativity, sex, vegetarianism . . . We eat, He told us, not only with our mouths, but with our eyes, nose, touch, hearing. We become what we eat, so all must be purified. When the senses and the mind are pure, the great energy of the universe descends.

He paused after the lecture, then spying a little brass container in the hands of a woman, he pointed, saying, "Hah!, that is my creation." "It's broken, Baba," she said sadly. "I've done something wrong, haven't I?"

Baba had given her, some time earlier, the little container filled with vibhuti, and promosed it would always be full, but it had stopped producing vibhuti. "Small, anger, small ego." He took the container from her and inverted it, bouncing it upside down on the table. It was empty, all right. He put the lid securely back on the container then holding it covered in his two hands, said, "This is my creation."

After waiting a few moments he took the lid off the container again. The ashes came spurting out, jumping onto the table. My wife took her handkerchief and began wiping up the spilled ashes. "Very precious," Swami remarked. "Wipe!"

Later the woman shared with us Baba's comments and instructions to her. "Anger, from body weakness," he said, and instructed her regarding diet. "I am helping," he promised. Ego – "you tried to test Swami. You gave little packages of vibhuti to empty the container and see if it would fill again. You forgot this was my creation. I told you, for healing – but not for everyone. You must listen!"

Baba replaced the lid – then began rubbing the container with his bare hands. Discoloring spots, there a moment ago, disappeared – the surface was a burnished gleam again. "I am to have it again, Swami?", the woman beamed, her face aglow. "Take, – and remember – to listen!" Tears of joy filled her eyes.

Later he showed us the beautiful buildings of his Anantapur College; then he said, "Your university will come. My strength is behind you."

In the past the way had not been easy, and Baba knew there had often been fear in my heart. Now He said, "No more fear; just do your work. When you need anything for the university – even funds – write to me. Now what else do you want?" "Nothing, Baba," we both cried, "Only to kiss your Feet!"

He held back the edge of his robe. "Approved, approved."

We prostrated and kissed His Feet. I had been curious about something as his Feet were always naked and walking on the ground. But they were so clean, and the smell was of vibhuti and jasmine. When we stood up, He said, "Now, you can go."

But being with Baba, one never wants to go far away. So we did not leave the place immediately.

Well, that is my experience, Dr. Reyes concluded. My interpretation could be wrong, but there is something in which I am not wrong: in my heart there is joy; in my mind there is peace; and there is a new energy surging through me to share with all people.

Following her husband's lecture. Dr. Dominga Reyes gave a short talk. Here are some of its highlights, showing aspects of their great experience from her point of view.

At Indra Devi's place in Mexico, while watching the film on Sai Baba, I saw his figure suddenly change, taking on a beard and a different face. When he turned, showing his profile, I saw that it was my own Master – the Master Jesus. At the same time I heard a voice say: "Can't you recognize me in *any* Form?" Tears filled my eyes and the vision ended. From then on I had the yearning to go to Baba.

When we were at Puttaparti and able to talk to Him, I said that I had been trying to meditate for forty-four years. He replied: "But your meditation is incomplete. You must just keep quiet." (This calls to mind how Shirdi Baba often used to say – pointing out the Sai Path to God – "Just keep quiet, and I will do the rest.")

I told Baba about how at our institute we are trying to get the students to realize the unity of life, the grandeur of man, the divine origin of man, that man is not just a rational animal, but a Divine Being. Then I said. "Baba, please purify me for that work."

He replied, tenderly, "Whatever you ask of me I shall grant."

In the car going to Anantapur I wrote about seven poems to Him. When He took them in His hand, He said, "Much beauty! Send some more." So I have written twenty-four poems, and will be sending them soon.

I have told my children – my son who is a doctor of medicine, and my daughter, Anita – that if God walks on Earth, He is Baba. To realize that you have to see Baba, kiss His feet, look into His eyes, see His walk. Then you will know that you have seen God.

When Jesus walked on earth, not only was He not recognized, but they killed Him.

We are very fortunate; we have seen Baba's face.

The lotus on the lake is far, far away from the sun; but distance is no bar for the dawn of love; the lotus blooms as soon as the sun peeps over the horizon.

SATYA SAI BABA

20
THROUGH AND BEYOND THE DOCTORS

The countless Gods are only my million faces.
BHAGAVAD GITA

Back in 1970, just before we left India the first time, I met the late Mr. P. C. Kamani, head of one of the leading industrial families of India. When I first saw him, I was walking, with several other people, behind Swami towards the darshan line at "Brindavan." Tall, distinguished-looking, elegantly dressed, Mr. Kamani pressed forward among the crowd that was standing just outside the first gate. Evidently Baba already knew the industrialist, who came up eagerly and bowed low as Swami spoke to him and invited him to go inside.

It was in the long room later, while Mr. Kamani was waiting for his interview, that I had a chance for a brief conversation with him. He began to tell me enthusiastically about some marvellous experience to do with healing that he, and members of his family, had had with Baba a few weeks earlier. But before I could gather the salient points of the story, Swami called him in for the interview. I left India soon afterwards, and never saw him again, nor heard the details of the story from his lips. While in Australia, I was told that Mr. Kamani had died.

In 1974 I met two of Mr. P. C. Kamani's brothers, his eldest son, Ashish, and his widow. It was easy to see that the whole family were now ardent Sai devotees, and were spending as much time as possible away from their comfortable Bombay homes in the austerities of ashram life at Prasanti Nilayam.

Even when the Kamani men returned to the city to keep the wheels of their industry turning, the widow remained behind for long periods, basking in the ambience of Baba's presence; she was one of the small group of quiet, gentle women who wait and watch for an opportunity to serve

Baba. The women who long ago moved around Jesus the Christ, anxious to serve Him, must surely have been something like these, I used to think.

Ashish, pale of skin and delicate of features, like his father, agreed graciously to tell me the story that had been interrupted four years earlier. He prefaced his account by saying that the Kamani family were nominally Jains by religion.

There is a quality of gentleness about the Jains — even nominal ones. I think it probably comes from the *ahimsa*, or principle of non-violence, that is perhaps the main tenet of the religion. I have seen strict Jains wearing cloth-mesh masks over their noses and mouths, to prevent the killing of the minute life in the atmosphere as they breathe.

Another aspect of their religion is that they do not believe in a personal or creator God. The universe has existed eternally in some form, they say. It did not need a Creator. But they do believe in perfected men — the enlightened ones. The aim of life is to reach the level of these men. Such an achievement requires many lives on earth, many reincarnations, says Jainism, which is an offshoot of Hinduism. Among India's 500 million souls there are about a quarter of a million Jains.

It was appropriate that I should, finally, hear the story from Ashish as it was his wife, Nilima, who had played the main role in it. The drama began in 1969, soon after the young couple were married, when Nilima began to feel great pain in the area of her kidneys.

As the pain persisted, she was taken to the family doctor in Bombay. The diagnosis startled them; serious congenital kidney disease as a result of which her kidneys were enlarged to seven-and-a-half times normal size. What could be done? They sought the opinion of a panel of leading specialists of Bombay. (Ashish gave me the names of the five doctors on the panel.) All confirmed the original diagnosis, and stated that the only possible cure was a delicate operation on both kidneys, but this required highly sophisticated equipment not available in India. The operation could, however, be performed either in England or America.

There was risk, of course, in such an operation, but Nilima was suffering a great deal of pain and the condition might worsen. Furthermore, unless she was cured, she could not have children, and the young couple were very anxious to have a family. It was finally decided that she should go to England for the operation.

A leading specialist in London was contacted, and arrangements made for Nilima to enter St. Paul's Hospital, London, for the operation. But several weeks were lost in the tangle of official red-tape required to obtain government permission for the journey — with the foreign exchange of money involved. There had also to be another medical check-up, and recommendations for the operation to be done in England, certified by government doctors.

Before all the arrangements had been completed, there was another event which, at the time, the family thought of little importance. It was during the month of May, 1969, and Satya Sai Baba was on a visit to Bombay. A friend invited Ashish and Nilima to his house to meet Baba, but, being completely absorbed in their personal problem, they did not feel inclined to go. They had heard of Baba's miracles, of course, but had no belief in them, nor were they interested in spiritual matters.

Finally, however, their friend persuaded them to visit his house on the morning Swami was expected there. In a large room there were a lot of people sitting on the carpet waiting for Baba to arrive. Ashish and Nilima joined them. Eventually Swami appeared in the room and, after walking around the group greeting people, sat down in front of Nilima. He began telling her about her chronic health problem. This astounded her because her illness had been kept secret, discussed only within the family circle. Yet Baba seemed to know all about it.

Before leaving the house, he materialized a rudraksha for Nilima, and instructed her to dip it in water and drink the water. If she did this once a day for ten days, he said, she would obtain great benefit. Neither Nilima nor members of her family, or her husband's family, believed in the power of any such ritual, but something deep inside the young woman made her carry out Baba's instructions.

Ashish, Nilima and her parents left for London at about the time the ten-day rudraksha ritual came to an end. Their Harley Street specialist, Dr. Ferguson, had already examined the X-rays and reports of the Bombay doctors, but, like all specialists, he wanted to make his own tests before doing the operation. So he spent four days doing more X-rays and other tests while Nilima lay in hospital, waiting to be told the date of her operation. One night she had a dream in which Sai Baba came to her and said: "Don't worry, I am with you." This somehow made her feel less anxious — more at peace with the situation.

It was early on her fifth day in hospital that Dr. Ferguson brought the incredible news to her. Instead of naming the day for the operation as expected, he said that her kidneys were now quite normal and that there was no need whatever for an operation. He confessed that he could not understand what had happened. The congenital disease certainly had been there, as all the data from Bombay had clearly shown. There was no possibility of any error in that diagnosis. But now — inexplicably — the disease had vanished.

Nilima was filled with happy relief and gratitude but the others could not really believe their ears. Could this great London specialist be making a mistake? They had come a long way, and wanted to be quite sure before returning to Bombay. An Indian doctor friend of theirs was practicing his profession in London; they begged him to discuss the case with the Harley Street specialist. This he did, and was able to assure the family that everything was really all right, as the specialist had told them.

Ashish immediately got on the phone to his father in Bombay to tell him the great news. But Mr. P. C. Kamani would not believe the miracle, either. It required a telephone conversation with Dr. Ferguson and also with the Indian doctor friend in London to convince him.

Still bewildered, but with a new joy surging in him, Mr. Kamani told his wife. They remembered the rudraksha ritual in which they had certainly not believed. Sai Baba had helped them in spite of their unbelief. They felt very humble as they set off immediately for Bangalore to offer Baba their thanks.

Soon they were waiting with the crowd in the outer grounds at "Brindavan." Their hearts filled with gratitude, they were content to wait for as many hours as necessary. But soon in the distance by the gate a bright red dot appeared and a hush went through the crowd; Baba was walking between the curved lines of people. When he neared the place where they stood, he came straight towards them, and said, smiling, "Well, your daughter-in-law is all right now. Are you satisfied?" Before either could find words to express their feelings, Swami went on to describe in detail the recent events in London. He knew it all.

Too overcome with emotion to speak, Mr. and Mrs. Kamani went down on their knees at his feet.

When Ashish told me the story, five years after the events, there had been no recurrence of Nilima's kidney disease, and, he said, happily, "With Swami's blessings, we now have two fine children, Chetna and Harsh."

On the surface this would seem to be a case where Swami cured someone who had no faith. But faith lies deep, beyond the grasp of the conscious mind. Nilima's actions in carefully carrying out Baba's instructions for ten days suggest that a subconscious, underlying faith was there, deep in her heart.

Furthermore, Baba knew the spiritual potential of a family that seemed, outwardly quite lacking in religious interests. Though it was the miracle of Nilima's cure that brought them to him, it is something else that keeps them there as his devoted followers — something that provides understanding, joy and peace.

For Nilima, Baba worked ahead of the eminent doctors; their part was to specify the existence and nature of the disease, and to prove beyond doubt the reality of the cure. In the next case the Divine Power works *through* the doctors, and yet also goes beyond the understanding of medical science. The work of the Divine Hand is always unique and mysterious.

In America, near the end of 1970, we met the brilliant Indian biophysicist, Professor Y. T. Thathachari, and his charming wife, Madhuri. At that time he was a senior member of the research faculty of Stanford University, California. He had previously held similar positions at the Massachusetts Institute of Technology, Cambridge, and at the University of California. "I have been seeking," he wrote, "to understand life processes, in health and disease, in terms of the spatial structure of the molecules of life. I have also been interested in the problem of the structure, manifestation and goal of knowledge. There is a need to re-examine this ancient problem in the context of the new, spectacular advances in the life sciences."

The professor and his wife were devotees of Sai Baba, and this was the link that took us to their home near San Francisco, and led to further meetings later in different parts of the world. At "Brindavan," in 1974, I asked Professor Thathachari to write me an account of how he came to Sai Baba. He is the type of reserved scientist who shuns publicity, but at the same time he is a man of compassion, with a deep respect for truth. Finally, he did as I asked, stating: "I have written about the true story of my blessing, with the faith that it may kindle a ray of hope in those in trouble and despair, and save them even as I have been saved."

Here is the story. Soon after going to America from India, early in the year 1960, Thathachari began to get severe pains in his hips and knees. The doctors suspected rheumatoid arthritis and treated him with saturation doses of aspirin. But the symptoms continued.

By mid-1961 his doctors were prescribing drugs like butazolidin. A few months later several bumps appeared on his scalp and he was having frightening attacks of double vision. So he was put through a series of tests in an attempt to discover the real basis of his illness. The tests included dozens of X-rays, a brain scan with radioactive mercury, a surgical excision and biopsy of the scalp lesions.

In October, 1962, the medical team involved in the tests announced its terrible verdict. Thathachari had tumors in the skull, neck, ribs and hips. The tumors were aggressively malignant and had metastasized. The cancers had the features of both Ewings and Reticulum Cell Sarcoma.

"Even if the disease had been discovered in its initial stages," wrote Thathachari, "nothing could have been done. When the first cell turned malignant, the die was cast." So, now, there was no possibility of cure through medical science. But, oddly, after two years of being haunted by a fear of the worst, now that the worst was known to exist, "the trepidations vanished. Madhuri and I knew for certain that only God's Grace could save me. We sought that Grace intensely." The doctors, telling him that the very best he could hope for was about two more years of life, advised him to return to the bosom of his family in India, and spend the time left to him there. He was about thirty years old.

Thathachari took the doctors' advice and the couple returned to India. In a Madras nursing home the Indian doctors gave palliative treatment to the professor — intravenous injections of nitrogen mustard. Any relief, they warned, would be only temporary, and later flare-ups would become resistent to the drug. Also, there could be very severe side-effects.

But, fortunately, the only side-effect experienced by Thathachari was a feeling of nausea for a few hours after each injection. And his body responded tremendously to a treatment that was not expected to cure, but merely alleviate his suffering. In two or three weeks there were no bumps left on his scalp, no more attacks of double vision, and no pain!

The professor gained weight quickly, and began to feel so healthy that in the latter part of 1963 (about a year after the first discovery of the cancers), he joined the Madras University faculty to continue his research work.

But the next year brought two major relapses. In the first of these an X-ray examination of his hips revealed large destruction of the pelvic bone. Cobalt irradiation was used on him for six weeks; again there were none of the expected side-effects and his response was immediate. All pain vanished. The second, and worst, relapse began with symptoms of jaundice. It took the doctors three weeks to discover that Thathachari's liver had become affected by the cancer. "Surgical intervention was not feasible, and the involvement of the liver is considered terminal in many cases of cancer."

So his hopes of a complete cure, that had been riding high six months earlier, were now dashed to the ground. Even so, it must have been

Divine intervention that had helped him before, and this could surely come again. The professor and his wife prayed for help with renewed fervor and faith.

The doctors decided to try the oral administration of endoxan (cyclophosphamide). Immediately the jaundice began to subside. No bad side-effects appeared, as had been feared, and within three weeks the professor had thrown off all symptoms of the cancer and was regaining his lost weight.

"I feel," he wrote, "that my recovery at all stages was due to God's Grace, since the treatments could well have evoked no response, or triggered serious side-effects." The doctors thought that he should continue with the endoxan for a time. They monitored his blood count frequently, and whenever that dropped very low, the drug intake was interrupted.

The professor's former colleagues and the medical specialists at Stanford wrote to express their great happiness at his amazing recovery. Some called it miraculous; others used the phrase "spontaneous remission," which means the same thing but sounds more "scientific." Thathachari and his wife know that it was nothing short of Divine Power, working through and beyond the medical men.

"But," the professor wrote, "though I felt in perfect health there was a constant, gnawing fear that the 'remission,' as they called it, might not last. I seemed to be living on borrowed time. I longed for an assurance that I was fully cured, and that there would be no more relapses. Such an assurance I knew could not come from medical science.

"During the year 1965 a friend made a chance reference to Sri Satya Sai Baba. Madhuri and I suddenly realized that we had heard about him before, and now we felt an urge to seek his blessings. For several months we made frantic, but unsuccessful efforts to meet him."

A letter to Sri N. Kasturi, saying that Thathachari needed Baba's assurance about the cure of disease that seemed to be arrested, brought vibhuti and blessings from Baba. But the professor felt the need of a personal contact with the great Man of Power in whom his hopes for an assurance now lay.

"By January 1966 we had decided that we must go to Prasanti Nilayam, to sleep under trees, if necessary, until Baba talked to us. Just as we were about to set off, I received a letter from Stanford University suggesting that I return there to work. I replied that I was leaving Madras for a while, but would consider the suggestion and give an answer after my return.

"On arrival at Prasanti Nilayam we had darshan from Baba, and were given accommodation on his instructions. Early next morning we sat with a crowd of some four hundred people, waiting for Baba to appear. I was praying that he would select me for an interview. My prayer was answered.

"Madhuri and I moved joyfully into the interview-room with about fifteen other people who had been selected. First Baba materialized vibhuti and gave some to everyone in the room. Then he took Madhuri and me to an alcove behind a curtain. There he talked about our many attempts to see him, and said the doctors had frightened me.

"Then he mentioned a recent unhappy event about which we had spoken to no one at all. This jolted me. When we came from behind the curtain, I knelt at Baba's feet. Madhuri saw him wave his hand above my head, in a gesture of blessing, and, at the same time, produce a photograph of himself, containing his name and address. This he gave me. Then he referred to the recent invitation to return to Stanford, and advised me to accept it.

"But the most important thing was, he assured me that I would have no more health problems. 'God's Grace will be with you always,' he said. 'Your work will be very successful too, and remember — work is worship.' We asked him if I should continue with the medicine. He replied 'Yes, there will be no side-effects.' "

Before they left for Stanford, the couple visited Baba twice more. On one occasion he spoke to them in Telegu. The professor, who did not know the language, looked confused, but Baba turned to Madhuri: "You were born in Proddatur; why do you not understand Telegu?" he asked. The fact that Madhuri was born in the Telegu-speaking village of Proddatur was known to few except the immediate family. Yet Baba knew it. "Incidents like this, trivial as they may seem, helped greatly to strengthen our faith in Baba."

The couple returned to Stanford. A physician there who had treated Professor Thathachari during his terrible illness, wanted to put him under a Stanford specialist in cancer chemo-therapy for "management." Obviously the physician did not trust the "remission." But Baba's assurance had brought complete trust to the professor's mind. He would continue, he told the physician, with the endoxan (Baba had agreed to this) and have check-ups to monitor his blood count once a month, but nothing else.

The physician thought this a strange response, but he finally agreed, saying, "After all you have solved your problem in your own characteristic Indian way, and I will let you continue in the path that has done you so much good."

During the next three years the professor continued with the treatment agreed by Baba. Only rarely did his blood count call for a temporary suspension of the drug. Then, in 1970, he returned to India for a brief visit, and Baba told him to stop using the endoxan as it was no longer necessary.

The physician in California was dubious about this, thinking that Thathachari was taking a grave risk, but reluctantly agreed to stop the drug treatment. Regular check-ups showed that Thathachari's blood picture was quite healthy, so eventually even the blood checks were reduced to one about every twelve months.

The professor concludes: "A few months after we first met Baba, I suddenly realized that I had not been bothered by fears of a recurrence for some time. Whatever my conscious worries might be, deep within me there has been, and is, the confidence that Baba is protecting us and guiding us as he promised.

"I have been enjoying excellent health during the ten years since my recovery, in 1964. I often work for some fifteen hours a day; I can walk briskly for several miles, and I have no need for any kind of pain-killers. When I recall that, during the years 1960-62, just to get in and out of a car was an agonizing experience, and that even strong drugs, like codeine, could not fully relieve the pain, I realize how kind God has been; for only Divine Grace could have brought about such a complete cure of an 'incurable' disease."

When Professor Thathachari agreed to tell me his story, in 1974, he was again working in India, but seeking Baba's guidance on the question of whether or not he should return to America once more. He does not like to make important decisions, where imponderable factors are concerned, without first consulting Baba to obtain his advice and blessings. This indicates the degree of his surrender to the wisdom of the Divine Mind.

My reason for asking the professor for his story in the first place was because during an earlier meeting Madhuri had said to my wife: "Swami cured Thathachari of cancer." So, obviously, though they had not actually met Sai Baba in the flesh at the time of the cure, Madhuri identified Him with the Divine Power that worked the great miracle.

Professor Thathachari has not, himself, stated to me that he makes this connection, but his attitude to Baba suggests that he does. Moreover, it has been my experience that all intelligent, spiritually-perceptive Indians accept the Vedantic concept that there is but One God who is basically formless, but who can take on any form whenever He chooses. Whatever the form taken, it is the one Supreme God.

I am the servant of every one. You can call me any Name, I will respond, for all Names are mine. Or, rather, I have no particular Name at all . . . . .

One man's mind prefers Krishna; another's mind likes Siva; another prefers the Formless Allah. I never call on people to worship me, giving up the Forms they already revere. I have come to establish Dharma, and so, I do not demand or require your homage. Give it to your Lord or Guru, whoever He is. I am the Witness, come to set right the vision.

SATYA SAI BABA

21
TWO WESTERN
RESEARCHERS

*The touch of Earth is always reinvigorating to the
sons of Earth, even when they seek a supraphysical
Knowledge.*

SRI AUROBINDO

At Prasanti Nilayam I heard that two research scientists had been
there a few months earlier, investigating the Sai Baba phenomena, and I
talked to Mr. S. D. Khera who was their interpreter during the interviews.
This old devotee of the Lord told me about some miracles that took place
before the eyes of the two western researchers, and I was anxious to find
out what their reactions had been. From a card one had left behind I
found that their names were Karlis Osis, Ph.D., Director of Research for
the "American Society for Psychical Research Inc.," and Erlendur Haraldsson, Ph.D., Research Associate of the same Society. Through correspondence I obtained the kind permission of both these gentlemen to use the
reports of their investigations.

Their unhesitating cooperation may have been partly due to the fact
that they had both read my earlier book, *Sai Baba, Man of Miracles.* In his
letter to me Dr. E. Haraldsson wrote: "We found your book very helpful,
and we interviewed a number of persons you mention there. We were glad
to find your reporting careful and accurate." His letter came from the University of Iceland where he had been appointed Associate Professor of Psychology. He also wrote: "Your book is being translated into Icelandic and
will be published here. I suggested this to a publisher after my first trip to
Puttaparti in late 1973."

Dr. K. Osis said in a letter: "Your book, in which you portrayed
Baba and his phenomena so well, was indeed a great experience for me. Of
course a research man, as I am, would not simply take a writer's state-

ments for granted. I interviewed some of the people whose stories you told, and found their testimonies consistent with what you wrote. That certainly spurred me on to a serious research effort."

I was very happy to have these comments from two trained, experienced research men, and I give them here in the hope that such a recommendation will stimulate confidence and narrow the credibility gap my readers might feel regarding a subject so far outside everyday experience.

Dr. Haraldsson sent me a copy of the "Preliminary Report" prepared to be presented at the Parapsychological Association's Convention. Here are some extracts from it.

> In a series of interviews we had opportunities to talk with and observe Satya Sai Baba. He speaks English but prefers to use an interpreter. He tends to belittle the significance of his alleged psychic phenomena, calls them "small items," and repeatedly stresses the importance of religious and moral issues.
>
> During the seven interviews we had with Sai Baba, he spontaneously displayed to us, generously, a number of his alleged materialization-phenomena.
>
> Babá's interview room is bare with concrete walls and floor, without any decorations. The only furniture is one armchair.

Dr. Haraldsson goes on to state that the number of people at the interviews varied from nine to just the three of them — presumably meaning the two scientists and Mr. Khera as interpreter. They all, he said, sat on the floor — this would include Baba who usually sits there with the people he talks to.

One of the four "materializations," fully described, concerns a rudraksha, the berry — considered sacred — of a certain tree, used for making rosaries. Dr. Haraldsson writes: "Before this, however, Baba presented both of us with some vibhuti (holy ash, probably comparable to 'bread and wine' in Christianity). This he gave after a typical wave of his right hand in small circular movements that lasted two or three seconds. Then, after a short discussion, he presented Karlis Osis with a large golden ring, again after waving his hand in a typical manner.

"While we were debating with Baba the value of science and controlled experimentation, he turned our discussion onto his favorite topic — the spiritual life, which, in his view, should grow together with daily life, like a double rudraksha.

"We did not understand this term, nor could the interpreter explain it properly. Baba seemed to make several efforts to give us a clear understanding, then, with some sign of impatience, he closed his fist and waved his hand. He then opened his palm and showed us a double rudraksha, which we are told, is a rare specimen in nature, like a twin orange or twin apple.

"We observed Baba closely all the time while we sat on the floor. Two or three minutes later, still holding the rudraksha in his hand, he turned to me and said he wanted to give me a present. Then he closed his fist still holding the rudraksha, made a quick short circular movement with his hand and opened it towards me. In his palm we saw again a double rudraksha, but now with a golden ornamented shield on each side. The shields were about an inch in diameter, and were held together by golden chains. On the top was a golden cross, with a ruby-like stone fixed in it. Behind the cross was a hole, so that this altogether beautiful ornament could be carried on a chain.

"Sai Baba wears a one-piece gownlike dress with sleeves that reach his wrists. We observed his hands very closely and could not see him take anything from his sleeves, or reach towards his bushy hair, clothes, or to any other hiding place." [I have myself often seen him pull his sleeves up to the elbow when producing something in front of a sceptic. His sleeves are loose fitting and do not have cuffs.]

"On one occasion we had an opportunity to examine two old robes Baba had worn. He reportedly always wears robes of the same sort, and when they start to wear out, he gives them to someone. The two we examined contained no pockets of any kind.

"We became acquainted with a former Professor of Chemistry in Bangalore, Dr. D. K. Banerji, and learned that one day Baba had visited him and his wife unexpectedly. He had 'produced' some things for them, as he does almost wherever he goes. As he retired for the night in their house, he asked Mrs. Banerji to wash his clothes, so that he could use them again the following morning. This she did, and during the washing, Baba's robe was examined carefully by Mrs. and Doctor Banerji and also by a friend who was there, Dr. P. K. Bhattacharya (doctorate in chemistry from Illinois, U. S. A., and at that time Director of the Chemistry Department of the All India Institute of Science, a leading research institute of India). These three persons found that Baba's robe contained no pockets whatever. They reported this incident to us during two interviews we had with them."

[While staying with Baba in the Horsley Hills, my wife once ironed one of Swami's silk robes for him. We observed at that time that there were no pockets, attachments or anything at all in which objects could possibly be held.]

Another of Dr. Haraldsson's descriptions deals with the disappearance of a stone from the ring Swami had given Dr. K. Osis earlier.

"This ring had a large stone with a colored picture of Satya Sai Baba on it. It was held firmly in the ring as if it and the ring were one solid article.

"During an interview when we were trying to persuade Baba to participate in some controlled experiments, he said to K. Osis: 'Look at your ring.' The stone had disappeared from it. We searched for the stone on the floor, but no trace of it could be found. The frame and the notches that had held the stone on the ring were quite unharmed.

"For the stone to fall out of its frame, it would have been necessary that at least one of the notches be bent, and probably the frame as well. Otherwise, the stone would have to be broken so that it could fall out in pieces.

"As Baba made us aware of the stone's absence, we were sitting on the floor, about a yard or two away from him. We had not shaken hands as we entered, and he had not touched us. I had noticed the stone in the ring as K. Osis rested his hands on his thighs earlier in the interview. Two other persons in the room — Mr. D. Sabnani of Hong Kong and Mrs. L. Hirdaramani of Ceylon — whom we had met for the first time at this interview — certified that they had observed the ring, with the stone in it, on the left hand of K. Osis during the interview.

"When the stone could not be found anywhere, Baba remarked, somewhat teasingly, 'This is my experiment.'

"At our next interview, two days later, Baba asked Osis if he wanted the stone back. The latter admitted that he did. At Baba's request, K. Osis handed him the stoneless ring. Holding it in his hand, Baba asked: 'Do you want the same or a different stone?'

" 'The same,' Osis replied. Baba closed his hand around the ring, brought it to within about six inches of his mouth, blew lightly on it, stretched his hand towards us, and opened it. We recognized the stone as like the one that had previously been in the ring. The ring, itself, however, appeared slightly different.

"We observed Baba's hand carefully from the time he closed it till he opened it again. We failed to notice anything that might indicate fraud. The six other persons at the interview reported the same to us afterwards."

An interesting phenomenon observed by the two researchers was Baba's production of a long necklace for a Los Angeles lady. This followed immediately after he had produced a gold ring for her husband. Another person present at the interview had this to say about the experience of the Los Angeles couple, a Mr. and Mrs. Krystal: "Baba turned towards the couple and asked them if that day was not the thirty-third anniversary of their wedding. They were stunned; it took a few seconds for them to say, 'Yes.' He created a ring with his portrait embossed on it, and placing it on the trembling palm of the wife, he asked her to put it on her husband's finger. Then he waved his hand again, and a necklace with a golden lotus flower strung in the center, carrying a portrait of Baba, came sliding out of his palm. He instructed the husband to put it around the neck of his wife. Baba then pronounced his blessings in Vedic Sanskrit, and patted the backs of both when they knelt at his feet."

Dr. Haraldsson's "Report" on this says: "At close range we observed that Baba had to loosen the grip of his fist so that he could hold the large bulky necklace in his small hand. The necklace was about a yard long, and contained a variety of different stones, interspersed with small golden pieces. Attached to it was a picture of Baba, surrounded by a golden, rose-like frame, about two inches in diameter."

Describing another careful observation of the supraphysical, Dr. Haraldsson writes: "We sat crosslegged on the ground in a long line of people as Sai Baba walked by. He stopped in front of a friend of Dr. D. K. Banerji. This person was sitting second on the left of Karlis Osis and third to myself. Baba waved his hand. As we were sitting on the ground and he was standing, his right hand was slightly above the level of our eyes. His palm was open and turned downwards and his fingers were stretched out as he waved his hand in a few quick small circles. While he did this, we observed, a grey substance appeared close to his palm. Baba grasped it with a quick downward movement of his hand.

"Karlis Osis, who was sitting closer than myself, observed that this grey material appeared first as granular lumps that then turned into the fine-grained, almost dusty, substance called vibhuti. Baba then presented the vibhuti to Dr. Banerji's friend."

[Princess Nanda of Kutch told us that once when she was sitting before Swami, below the level of his waving creative hand, she had a glimpse of what went on beneath it. First, she said, a small, luminous cloud appeared close to his palm. This quickly condensed into a solid glittering object, over which his hand closed. When he opened his hand, the object was seen to be a gold ring.*]

The two researchers estimated, from their observations and extensive interviewing, that Baba's materializations number about twenty to thirty daily. And, from reports of devotees, this is known to have been going for nearly forty years. They remark, "One interesting phase of these phenomena is the appearance of greasy substances, like oils and greasy foods, that would be very hard to conceal in a thin silken dress." They state that, under the given conditions, they were "not able to detect fraud" in their close personal observations of some fourteen phenomena.

The "Report" concludes with the sentence: "Only further research, and co-operation by Sri Satya Sai Baba can give scientific answers to the very important questions raised by our observations, and the reports we have gathered from numerous first-hand witnesses."

In his "Report to the Convention of the Parapsychological Association" in 1975, Dr. Karlis Osis deals with his research into Out-of-the-Body Experiences, usually called OBE's in India. About Baba he says: "Sri Satya Sai Baba is a 49-year old religious leader who claims to be an avatar and is said to have six million followers. He seems to have been born with unusual gifts, and his powers were not acquired through training with a guru.

"Sai Baba ostensibly appeared to Mr. Ram Mohan Rao, the Director of a technical school in Manjeree, Kerala State, who then invited about twenty neighbors to a devotional meeting with him. We were able to interview eight witnesses who had been present, three of whom were children at the time. This incident occurred ten years ago, and memories of it have become rather inconsistent.

"However, on the main points there is reasonable agreement: a sadhu who looked like Sai Baba, whom they had seen only in pictures, was present in the school Director's house, sang some Sai Baba songs with them, produced holy ash in the way characteristic of Sai Baba, and remained there for an hour.

"A few months after this incident, a local investigator showed a picture of Sai Baba to a high-school girl who had been present and asked: 'Who is this man?' With no hesitancy she answered that she had seen him at the school Director's house. Two observers, who are now dead, are said to have doubted that the visitor was Sai Baba.

"In this case, the sadhu taught them Sai Baba songs, handled objects, and gave presents which the hosts still have. We were able to establish the fact that Sai Baba, at that time, was on the other side of the Indian peninsula at the Palace of Venkatagiri, where there are records registering his visit.

"The hallucination hypothesis would not appropriately explain this case because of the multiple observations of the stranger for more than an hour, and because the visitor moved physical objects and also left gifts."

In giving me permission to quote his research brief on this case, Dr. Osis wrote: "I only hope you realize that what I said in it was phrased for a skeptical audience, the culture gap being so great."

Dr. Erlandur Haraldsson's "Preliminary Report" had to be condensed somewhat for presentation to the convention, but, he wrote: "*The Journal of the American Society for Psychical Research** has accepted a paper by myself and Karlis Osis on Sai Baba's physical phenomena that we have observed. It is a longer version of the preliminary report I sent you originally."

Though both researchers kept their investigations as objective as humanly possible and presented their reports in the cool, detached language of psychic research, I gained the impression that both were touched by Baba's spiritual love and by the numinous quality of his presence that can never be measured and assessed by human yardsticks.

Dr. Haraldsson wrote: "I am glad to know that you started on a new book on Satya Sai Baba." He told me that he was taking his nineteen-year old son to India to see Baba, and asked if I would grant him the favor of being the first to hand to Baba a copy of the Icelandic edition of *Sai Baba, Man of Miracles*, which had just come out.

Dr. Karlis Osis wrote an article for the *Garland of the Golden Rose*, a book produced at Prasanti Nilayam at the time of Baba's fiftieth birthday. In it he reveals something of his feelings about Baba's greatness, and makes a plea for a thorough "scientific" investigation of the Sai phenomena which, he believes, would change the whole outlook of science and, consequently, the world.

He writes, *inter alia*: "I have been an active researcher for twenty-five years, have travelled widely, and nowhere have I found phenomena which point so clearly and forcibly to spiritual reality as do the daily miracles around Baba . . . .

"Suppose Baba would truly reveal his nature in the best laboratories in the world: what new, breath-taking insights would be gained, and what an impact would be made on the scientific world view — new facts forcing science to accept the spiritual reality . . . .

"Of course, in the scientific community, as in every establishment, there is inertia, conservatism and hostility to anything radically new. I, personally, am convinced that such thought habits will be overcome because Baba's powers are so strong that he could provide the definitive experimental facts which no one with integrity would be able to explain away. Good scientists have integrity, and science is built on it. They will try to tear apart anything as 'outrageous' as Baba's miracles. But if the facts prevail, in spite of the closest scrutiny, science will incorporate them in its modern world view . . . "

Is Dr. K. Osis right in thinking that "experimental laboratory proof" of the Sai supraphysical phenomena would force science to accept the existence of a spiritual reality?

I am determined to correct you only after informing you of my credentials. That is why I am now and then announcing my Nature by means of miracles, that is, acts which are beyond human capacity and human understanding. Not that I am anxious to show off my Powers. The object is to draw you closer to me, to cement your hearts to me.

SATYA SAI BABA

22
SAI SCIENCE
AND SPIRITUALITY

*He comes to the thought of those who know Him
beyond thought, not to those who imagine He can be
attained by thought: He is unknown to the learned and
known to the simple.*

"KENA UPANISHAD"

Scientific investigation is time absorbing. Our two psychic researchers were able to investigate only one case in which Swami was seen away
from his physical body. But dozens of such cases have been reported to
me, and that must be but a fraction of all those experienced by devotees.
Many may not be provable in the scientific sense, but they have been described by reliable eye-witnesses, and the number and variety of them
through the years is strong evidence that they are not all imagination.

A typical example that rings true, though it could never be *proved*, is
the story told us by Mrs. Padmanabhan, wife of our dentist friend in Bangalore. With Swami's permission, she went on a tour of Europe with the
Women's Rotary Club of which she was a member. Visiting Sweden, she
stayed a night in the house of another member who was away from home.
In the middle of the night she awoke stifled with heat, scarcely able to
breathe.

She realized that the central heating was turned far too high.
Weakly, she staggered to the heater in the room with the intention of turning it down. But the type of equipment was strange to her, and there
seemed to be many knobs. She was afraid to turn any of them lest she
cause an explosion. She tried to open the windows but these, too, were of
a strange design, and she could find no way of opening them.

Now she began to panic. She started towards the door, but, almost
unconscious with heat exhaustion, collapsed on the bed, and was unable to

move. She thought she was dying. With tears streaming down her cheeks, she began to pray, calling on Sai Baba, and repeating his name.

She heard, she thought, a footstep outside the door, then could see Baba standing just inside the door. There was a luminosity around him in the darkness, so that she could see his form quite clearly. He said: "Why fear when I am here! I am always with you." Then he vanished. The room quickly became cool and Mrs. Padmanabhan slept.

Back in India, some weeks later, Swami asked her: "How was the trip?"

"It was fine, Swami."

"What about Sweden?" He gave her a pointed look.

"Oh, I want to thank you for that, Swami . . ."

"I know, I know!" He laughed and changed the subject.

Then there is the late Mr. Walter Cowan of Tustin, California. Highly successful in his business ventures, Walter had become a millionaire, but was, at the same time, a keen searcher for spiritual Truth. When I first met him in India, he had practically retired from business, and was devoting his mental energies and powerful will to laying foundations for the life in realms where dollars are of no avail. He was then nearing eighty years of age, and a devotee of Satya Sai Baba.

Both Walter and his wife, Elsie, had sought the occult verities along various avenues and under other masters before coming to Baba. They had both learned to travel consciously out of their bodies, and bring back into waking consciousness memories of their OBE's. It was this that brought them to Baba.

Over dinner at their hotel in Bangalore they told us of their strange and wonderful first contact with him. One night, they said, they were both out of their bodies on some plane of the astral realm, and found themselves in a dangerous situation. In fact, they needed help very badly. They called on the name of the Indian teacher who was at that time their master. But he did not come. Yet, unexpectedly, they were helped out of their predicament by the timely arrival of one who bore no resemblance to their own master. They had, in fact, never seen this unusual being before.

Some weeks later they happened to see a photograph of Satya Sai Baba and immediately recognized their helper on the astral. They made enquires about his name and address, and, as soon as possible, went to India to meet him in the flesh.

But it was during their third or fourth visit to India and Baba that we came to know them well and hear about this first meeting with one whom they now regarded as an Avatar, and their spiritual guru. We, too, were staying in Bangalore at the time, and we used to travel with the Cowans each morning by taxi to Whitefield, where we usually spent the whole day, seeing as much of Swami as possible.

Once we were sitting in the long ante-room at "Brindavan," hoping that Swami would pause and have a few words with us as he passed by on his manifold activities, or better still, take us into an inner room for one of his beautiful talks, when time ceases to be. Sometimes it happened, sometimes it did not. No two days were ever the same.

Once when Baba was very busy, and seemed to have no time to spend with us, Walter said to me: "I often feel lonely for Swami here in India. I see more of him back in Tustin."

Knowing that Sai Baba had never been to America, I asked Walter to explain.

"Oh, almost every day he comes into the room where I am and talks to me. I see him sitting in a chair as plainly as if he were there in the physical body."

Elsie collaborated this, saying that she, herself, would "feel" the presence of Baba, and be able to communicate, but did not have the clairvoyant vision to see him — which she seemed to regret greatly.

On one of the Cowans' many visits to India, after Iris and I had left that country, Walter took seriously ill and shortly was pronounced clinically dead. Sai Baba brought him back to his physical body and life. Details of this "raising from the dead" have been given in a number of journals and books, including, *Sai Baba, the Holy Man and the Psychiatrist*, a fine book by the psychiatrist Samuel Sandweiss, M. D., so I will not state them again here.

Sometime after Walter's return to his home in Tustin, his private secretary, Sharon Purcell, wrote to us, saying that she considered the greatest miracle was the rejuvenation of Mr. Cowan's mind. His mind was, she declared, twenty years younger than before his "death and resurrection." Walter, himself, was delighted to find that he had left his severe diabetes and other ailments behind, and, through his experiences on the "other side," had lost all fear of death. Some eighteen months after his death experience in India, he died at home in America at the age of eighty-two.

Later, on a visit to India in 1974, I asked Baba if he would tell me his reason for bringing back to life, for a short period, this old devotee who was nearing the end of his life's span anyway. From his answer I gathered that the main reason was his compassion for Elsie Cowan whose great faith and love of the Lord bring to mind the sisters of Lazarus, whom Jesus raised from the dead.

"I wanted to save Mrs. Cowan the pain and bother of taking her husband back home, dead. It was better that he should die later in his own country," Swami said.

After nearly a century of collecting evidence on thousands of cases, the Society for Psychical Research, London, could not say that life-after-death, or other psychic phenomena, had been *scientifically* proved, or disproved. I was, myself, a member of that Society for some years, and talked to other members on these matters. I found that some of them believed, personally, in the post-mortem survival of the "soul"; others did not. Some believed in telepathy, clairvoyance, precognition and other extra-sensory perceptions. Others did not. Nothing had been definitely proved through the methodology of science.

Dr. J. B. Rhine tried to gain acceptable proof through the use of special cards and statistical analyses of results. He gathered a great mass of evidence to establish the existence of extra-sensory perception (ESP), including precognition. Some sections of the scientific world accept that these occult faculties of the human psyche have now been proved. Others say that true scientific proof has not yet been established.

Uri Geller's ostensible psychokinetic powers have been investigated *scientifically* by research workers at Stanford University. Some scientists say results prove the genuine quality of Geller's mysterious metal-bending powers of the mind. Others contend that the researchers must have been fooled in some way; such outrageous phenomena are too far outside the conceptual framework of scientific thought to be acceptable. So the scientific "proofs" have made little impact on scientific thought.

Then again, precognition, or prophecy, has been experienced by human beings for thousands of years. But the world of science does not accept it as a reality. It makes too many mistakes for the stomach of science. Astrologers, crystal-gazers, tea-cup readers, and the rest, are constantly making predictions, somewhere. Part often comes true; part does not. Who can read the future with one hundred per cent certainty? If all is pre-ordained, then such a thing would be a possibility. If only the main outlines are fixed, and the rest remains plastic and malleable, then even the greatest prophet could foretell only the main, the inevitable events with accuracy and certainty. Yet, even that would be evidence for extra-sensory power and knowledge.

But how is scientific proof established? History has shown that the unlikely event, the expulsion of the Asians from Uganda, in fact, took place. As told in an earlier chapter, Sai Baba predicted this four years before the event. Yet even though Dr. Patel, and others who were given the warning, regarded Baba as an Avatar, they did not have sufficient faith in his prophecy to act upon it. Scientific research would require that the prophecy had been put in writing by at least one of the recipients at the time it was received. Even then, what would it prove? Hundreds of true predictions have been collected by the psychic researchers through the years, but, whatever common sense might say, cautious, sceptical science says that they could all have been lucky guesses, coincidences.

Scientific requirements apart, man has always been fascinated by prophecy — those that have been fulfilled, and those that await possible fulfillment. I was privileged to hear of some interesting prophecies from Mr. S. D. Khera, a cultured gentleman, retired from the Indian Civil Service, and interpreter for the two psychic researchers from America.

Back in the year 1934, Khera, who was living in the north of India then, had a great Guru who prophesied that the next big event in the world's history would be the raining down of fire from the skies onto Europe and parts of Asia. There would be great destruction. When World War II came five years later, in 1939, with its massive bombings, Khera considered that the prophecy had been fulfilled.

Another prophecy given by his Guru was that the second great and terrible event of history would see the world become as hot as the sun for a period of 24 hours. No one would remain alive except the true, sincere devotees of God.

Khera asked how these would be saved, and how many would be left alive in the world. The answer was that their consciousness would be altered and they would be protected by Divine Power. About one-fifth of the world's population would be saved. The guru did not say when this cataclysmic event would take place. But Khera thinks it was a prevision of either a world-destroying atomic war or else a natural catastrophe.

There was a third prophecy — a personal one. Khera was told that later in his life, after his guru had passed away, he would meet an Avatar in the south of India. Some years ago he met Sai Baba and, he said, the prophecy was fulfilled. Furthermore, he added, at their first meeting, Baba told him about his deceased guru, and seemed to know all the important things that had passed between them. Baba did not, however, either confirm or deny the prophecy of the colossal world catastrophe.

It is of interest that, unlike some Christian prophecies of a similar nature, this Hindu prediction does not state that only members of a specified religious sect will be saved. Those protected by a miracle of Divine Power will be the "true, sincere devotees of God," whatever their religion.

Sai Baba must be well aware that the miracles he has been performing daily for the last four decades could not be *proved* to the satisfaction of the *scientific* world. In any case, like Jesus, he does not regard them as the most important feature of his work. They flow from his compassion, from his outpouring Divine Love. At his level of cosmic consciousness, he does not regard them as miracles, but as a part of his Divine Nature. He was born with such powers; they have been manifesting continually since his childhood. Anyone in the world may come and witness them, taste the joy of the Divine Love that flows to the recipient along with the material gift, and, if ready for it, experience the supreme miracle of the inner transformation that changes character, life-style and destiny.

Scientific acceptance must move along its slow, steady tortuous path. That is its nature. But in the meantime thousands, including many eminent scientists, know from personal experience that Sai Baba's miracles are genuine. Scientists, like Dr. S. Bhagavantam and Dr. D. K. Banerji, say the Sai phenomenon is something that goes beyond the present formulations of science, but that science must accept facts even though it cannot explain them. To the yogi the Sai miracles are not the *yogic siddhis* acquired in this life through yogic disciplines. Coming to earth with the Incarnation, like the powers of Krishna and Christ, employed only for compassionate and benevolent reasons, never diminishing in strength through years of use, the Sai Powers are one of the signs of Avatarhood.

To the philosopher and metaphysician divine miracles, if accepted, are a proof that the straitjacket of causality can be broken. Though the axiom of cause-and-effect holds true on normal levels of existence, at the level of the absolute it breaks down. There we find a primal cause that itself could have had no cause. The Absolute, Brahman, had no cause, no beginning. It always *was*. This is a concept beyond the rational capacity of the human mind. Yet, says the philosopher, though the divine miracle may appear random and causeless, it does in fact have a cause — the Divine Will.

To children, before the prison-house closes around them, miracles are as acceptable as fairy tales. To the adult devotee the *leelas* are breaches in the prison walls. With the divine traits that attend them, the Sai miracles open windows to other worlds, through which Light, Faith and Love can flow. They are something more tangible than words to tell of mysteries in heaven and earth beyond the dreams and understanding of our worldly philosophy.

In the numinous presence of Sai Baba, not fear of the unknown, but a rejoicing in the unfolding depths of life comes to the devotee with these new insights.

Welcome all faiths and religions as kith and kin; all faiths are but attempts to train men along the Path; all aspire to win the same illumination through the cleansing of the mind by means of good works. The seeds of all religions are in the Sanathana Dharma (Eternal Truths) of the Vedanta. That Dharma examines all possible approaches to the Divine, and arranges them in the order in which they can be utilized by the aspirant, according to his level of equipment and attainment.

The Vedic Dharma is the great grandfather, Buddhism is the son, Christianity is the grandson, and Islam is the great grandson. If there is any misunderstanding between them, it is but a family affair. The ancestral property, of which all are co-sharers, is the same.

SATYA SAI BABA

23
FAITH AND
LOVE IN ACTION

*In any way that men love me in that same way
they find my love: for many are the paths of men, but
they all in the end come to me.*

BHAGAVAD GITA

On the second Saturday of November, 1971, Mr. R. S. Khare of Dehra Dun, north India, tried to thread a needle to make a garland, but could not do so; his sight had faded. He rubbed his eyes in panic and tried again, but the hole in the needle was not visible.

What could it be? He was only in his forties, in the prime of life, with a good job as supervisor in the electricity division of the Public Works Department. He was the father of four children.

An eye specialist in Dehra Dun, after a thorough examination, pronounced the condition of his eyes as very serious indeed, and getting worse. Alarmed, he sought a second opinion at the Dehra Dun hospital. The specialist there told him he would be quite blind in a week. He was.

But hoping that this blindness could be cured, Mr. Khare went for treatment at the Sitapur hospital, near Lucknow, one of the most famous eye hospitals in India. Though not a wealthy man, he said, he was admitted to a private ward, and treated as a private patient by a great eye specialist, who had had considerable overseas experience.

After seventy-four days in hospital he was discharged. Modern medical science had done all it could for him; it had, in fact, restored enough of his vision for him to see a man at a distance of ten feet, but not to be able to identify the man. Khare hoped that with time his sight would improve.

But within ten days his condition relapsed to total blindness. He returned to Sitapur hospital, and for several days was put on the same treatment as before; this was the best known treatment for his condition, the eye specialist assured him. But as there were no positive results this time, and seemed absolutely no hope of any, he was discharged, still completely blind. That, as far as the specialists understood, was the condition he must accept for the rest of his life.

Mr. R. S. Khare had heard of Sai Baba before his blindness, and "regarded him as the greatest holy man of India." But he had never had personal experience of Baba's presence and powers. Shortly after he was finally condemned to permanent blindness, he was to learn that his daughter, Madhu, had been accepted for Baba's first Summer Course at Whitefield. In fact, she was the only student accepted from the State of Uttar Pradesh.

A few days after Madhu arrived on the campus at "Brindavan" for the course, in the month of May, 1972 Swami came up and talked to her while she sat having breakfast with the other students.

"You are worried about your father's blindness," he spoke with gentle compassion, "but don't worry; everything will be all right." Then he circled his hand, materialized vibhuti, and gave it to her.

"Post this to your father," he said.

It was the first time Madhu had witnessed Baba's powers. Thrilled, she packed the ash carefully and sent it to her father, with a letter, describing what Baba had said and done.

When R. S. Khare received the vibhuti and letter, he felt quite certain that this was his cure. Where material science had failed, Divine Science would succeed. He took a bath, asked for some of the vibhuti to be placed on a piece of paper and put in his hand. Then he held his head well back and poured vibhuti into each of his eyes.

Within an hour he began to see a little. This reinforced his faith; daily, thereafter, he poured a little more of the vibhuti into his eyes. At the end of seven days the supply of vibhuti was finished, *but so was his blindness – his vision was back to normal!*

Khare went again to the great eye specialist who had tried to cure him. The specialist examined his eyes in amazement. "This is indeed a miracle!" he said. The other doctors who knew the case agreed wholeheartedly.

Khare wrote to his daughter, saying he wanted to come to "Brindavan," as soon as Swami would permit, to offer his devotion and gratitude. On the day she received the letter Madhu asked Swami if her father could come to see him.

Swami smiled. "He has already made arrangements to come, and will leave before you could get a reply to him. Expect him in four days from now."

Khare arrived at "Brindavan" on the predicted day. He was eager to see Sai Baba without a moment's delay, but the guards at the inner gate did not know him. He had no letter, they said, no badge of office, nothing to recommend him; no, he could not go in. At that moment Baba himself appeared, and — without any need to ask Khare's name — took him inside. What passed in there is between Khare and his savior.

When, some two years later, I saw the tall, trim figure, with the clipped greying moustache, moving serenely among the people at Prasanti Nilayam, I would never have guessed that he had once been totally blind. Hearing scraps of his experience from those who knew him, I invited him to our rooms. Though a quiet, reserved man, he wanted the world to know of his healing miracle — for the greater glory of God.

His experience had brought complete surrender and devotion to the Divine Power and Love that Khare saw in Sai Baba. And from this flowed many other signs of grace. Vibhuti materialized on the sacred pictures in his prayer-room, and help came to his daily life at all times — help that he knew was from the Divine Hand.

A humble, happy man of simple faith, he seemed to me to have found the secret formula for meaningful living — surrender yourself to God, discern His Will, and accept it as right for you in all things.

In his vacations from the public service, Khare wants nothing more now than to come to Sai Baba's ashram, not to ask for interviews or any special favors, but just to see the beloved form and breathe the blissful atmosphere.

Members of all the great world religions may be seen in the crowd around Sai Baba. He never tries to convert any of them to another religion, but rather to convert each truly to his own religion — to deepen and spiritualize their understanding of it. At base, Baba says, there is only one religion, that is the religion of the heart, but men of different temperaments and development require different approaches to God, hence the different forms of the one religion.

In the seventh and eighth centuries A.D. the followers of the ancient Zoroastrian faith in Persia came under severe persecution from the Moslems. Many of them fled to India in the early part of the eighth century, and in her tolerant, great-hearted way India accepted them — as she had accepted early Christians and others before. The group from Persia became known as Parsees, and are so called today.

Colonel H. S. Olcott of the Theosophical Society, who studied and sought the core of truth in all religions, writes of the Parsees: "The key-note of the religion is purity; purity absolute in thought, word and deed. To worship the one Supreme Deity and to hate all bad, opposing influences, whether human or superhuman, are the fundamental articles of Parsee Creed. Prayer, obedience, industry, honesty, hospitality, alms-giving, chastity and the great virtue of truthfulness are enjoined, and envy, hatred, quarrelling, anger, revenge and polygamy are strictly forbidden. . ."

The Parsees are a small but influential group in India. By nature they are enterprising and astute in commerce — many acquiring considerable wealth. They are found in the professions, too; often at the top of the ladder. One of these is Dr. Keki M. Mistry, a leading orthodontist of Bombay.

I had first met Dr. Mistry at Sai Baba's World Conference in Bombay in 1968 — a tall figure, of dignified but humble mien, with the pale Parsee skin that twelve centuries of Indian suns have failed to darken. Then I met and talked briefly with him on several subsequent occasions.

On one of these, just after the Summer Course at "Brindavan" in 1974, I asked if he would tell me about how he first came to Baba. I had heard from others that it was an interesting story, with its full share of the strange and miraculous.

He was hesitant at first, but having obtained Swami's permission to do so he decided to speak out. His story had its beginning in 1964 when his sister was having difficulty with the birth of a child. A mutual friend, who was a follower of Sai Baba, asked Keki to give his sister a packet of vibhuti and a photo of Baba, as these would help her through the danger-ous delivery. "You give them to her, yourself," Keki said, gently, wanting to have nothing to do with such matters.

Several months later he developed a nasty, hacking cough. Ear, nose and throat specialists told him that there was a swelling, larger than a golf ball, in his nasopharynx. It was probably malignant, they said, and should be removed immediately.

This frightening diagnosis put Dr. Mistry in a dilemma. He was plan-ning to get married as soon as possible and wanted no set-backs in his pro-fession. The proposed operation would certainly be a set-back; he would lose his voice for a period, and, from what he had observed in others who had been through such an operation, the voiceless period could be as long as two years. Who would come to an orthodontist who could not speak? On the other hand, if the growth got worse, and was malignant, as the special-ists thought, delaying the operation until later might make it too late!

He talked to his fiance and her parents about his problem. The parents said he must have the operation as soon as possible; they were certainly against the marriage, and rightly so, he felt, until the situation was clarified. His fiance, herself, took the opposite view. She said: "Let us first get married, Keki, and then we'll face whatever comes, together."

He loved her for these words, but asked himself if such an action was really fair to her. His problem was not solved, he was still undecided and miserable, when someone gave him a copy of the book, *Sathyam, Sivam, Sundaram*, the Life of Sai Baba, written by N. Kasturi. Not feeling interested in the subject, he put it aside. After a few days, however, something made him take the book up and glance through it. He read a few lines, and gradually became so enthralled that he read on and on through the night.

When daylight came, a new yearning had been born in Keki — a yearning for spiritual guidance. Thereafter, he began to pray regularly, and found that his prayers were mainly in the name of the one he had previously brushed aside — Sai Baba. But for good measure he added prayers addressed to Zoroaster, and to Paramahansa Yogananda, the great yogi from whom his fiance had earlier gained spiritual nourishment.

Prayer, meditation, soul-searching led him to the conviction that his fiance was right; they should marry without delay and face the problem of his health and career together.

During their honeymoon at Bangalore, Dr. Mistry heard that Sai Baba was at Whitefield, a few miles away. He felt an urge to go there, but hesitated. He thought that his wife would not agree; she had received a modern, Western-type education and would probably be sceptical of the Sai Baba miracles. In the end they returned to Bombay before he had brought himself to broach the subject of a visit to Sai Baba.

But the happiness of marriage had not removed his health problem. His cough got worse, his voice became extremely hoarse, the pain increased. He saw his doctors again, and was strongly urged to have the operation immediately. But, still thinking of its ruinous effects on his dental practice, he kept putting off the evil day. Yet he knew this was foolish, the longer he left things the worse they would get, and the more dangerous to his life. Though aware of this, something inhibited action, and as the weeks passed, a cloud of gloom settled over him.

It was while he was in this depressed state, that he heard Sai Baba was in Bombay; a ray of light shot through the gloom. Now, he felt, he really must speak to his wife on the question of a visit. First he told her about his feeling while they were in Bangalore. She looked at him in thoughtful silence, and then said: "Keki, I had the same wish to go at that time, but did not like to mention it to *you*. How foolish of us!"

They both agreed that they must now try to see Baba without further delay. Mrs. Mistry told her parents of their intention, and was surprised to find that they, too, wanted to go to Baba.

So enquiries were set afoot. It was found that Baba was staying at the home of one of the government ministers. It would be a big house with a large garden, where the inevitable crowds could gather.

Perhaps there would be great difficulty in getting an interview there. But they must try.

Arriving at the house as early as possible in the morning, the four of them joined the large crowd already in front, and stood waiting for a sight of the great man. The day began to grow oppressively hot; midday came; the older couple became very tired and went home. Soon the crowd began to thin out with the cruel heat, but Keki and his wife decided to stay on. They would wait till two o'clock, but if Baba had not appeared by then, they would go. The sun beat down on them as the minutes dragged by; they stared hopefully through the shimmering heat at the balcony above, praying that he would appear soon.

"Fifteen minutes to two," Keki croaked, glancing at his watch. He looked around at the devoted few who were still standing there patiently. Then he looked up at the balcony again. His heart leapt; there was the little red-robed figure, his face shining like a lamp under the dome of black hair. Baba's eyes moved lovingly over the people, and his hands made gestures of blessings. This was the darshan for which the people there had waited in such discomfort through the long hours.

Baba's large, luminous eyes came to rest on Keki, and his hand made a beckoning gesture. Keki dashed forward eagerly, but was soon stopped by a policeman on guard near the door. The policeman had not seen Baba's gesture on the balcony above, and he would not accept Keki's word for it. Called by Baba, and yet unable to reach him, Keki felt desperate.

When he was about to give up, Baba appeared at the front door, downstairs. This time he called loudly to Keki, telling him to come and bring his wife, too; the policeman, hearing, let them through. They stood before Baba on the front verandah in silence, while he looked at them, and *through* them, it seemed. Keki knew not why, but tears began streaming down his face, while the world around faded, time stopped, and Eternity took over.

Then Baba smiled, and said the unexpected: "Your mother is not well." The remark was directed to Dr. Mistry.

Keki agreed: "She has asthma, Baba; she's had it for many years."

"I know. Bring her here tomorrow at nine in the morning."

Then Baba went inside. Nothing that one could name had happened, yet it seemed to Keki that the world had changed.

Dr. Mistry arrived with his mother and wife in good time the next morning. Shown into a large room, they found, to their dismay, that about two hundred people were already waiting there. After a few minutes Baba came in and started distributing vibhuti to everyone. He came last of all to Keki's mother. Then he beckoned to Keki, who was among the men, and took both mother and son into a private room.

Swami looked at them invitingly, waiting for them to speak. After a few moments the mother said: "Please, Baba, tell me — does my son have cancer?"

"This boy!" Swami almost thundered the words, power and love ringing in his voice; "He's *my* son. How could I let *him* have cancer!"

Then, giving Keki a large supply of vibhuti, he told him to take some in water three times a day.

"Now, any other questions?" he asked, as if the problem of Keki's growth had been completely settled.

"My wife is not well," Dr. Mistry said.

"I know. She is pregnant. Call her in."

When she came in Swami told her that her health would be all right now. She must not worry. "On August the 22nd you will have a son who will live a long life."

After only three days of taking the vibhuti, Keki felt much better, and decided to leave off all medical treatment, to rely wholly and completely on the power of Divine healing. Soon the pain had gone and his voice was clear. Also, his wife kept in good health for the remainder of her pregnancy, and on August 22nd gave birth to a son.

Six months went by; then one morning Keki coughed and spat blood. His temple of faith shook; the old doubts streamed back into his mortal mind. Unable to fight them off, he returned to his ENT specialist.

After an examination, the specialist demurred: "I must make a thorough examination under anaesthetics before I can be sure of the present condition." Arrangements were made, and Dr. Mistry was given the thorough examination without delay. Afterwards the doctor came and sat by him to give the verdict.

"Well," he said, "I don't understand it. Something strange has happened. The growth that was in your nasopharynx has vanished completely. There is nothing the matter now."

One of Narada's Sutras states that a means of promoting devotion and love towards God is the hearing and narrating of the glories of God, even while attending to the affairs of ordinary life. Dr. Mistry's story, told to Iris and me, began at his surgery, continued while he drove us through the crazy traffic of Bombay, and was completed as we sat in his car outside our hotel. Iris sat on the rear seat making notes, while I plied Keki with questions.

When the account was finished, the car seemed to be full of Divine Love, uniting us all as One, and we felt profoundly the Truth of the Narada Bhakti Sutra. We understood too, the thought expressed by St. John when he said: "We love each other because He first loved us."

When man taps the energy of the Divine in Himself, he can easily master Nature, which is only the vesture of the Divine.

Through Truth you can experience Love; through Love you can visualize Truth. Love God and you see God in every creature.

SATYA SAI BABA

24

TO PART IS
TO BE TOGETHER

*Lo, I am with you always, even unto the end of
the world.*

MATT. 28:20

One morning, towards the end of our time at Prasanti Nilayam we
were called to a group interview. About a dozen people gathered in the
room, the ladies mainly westerners, the men — except myself — all Indian.
Swami sat down on the floor and invited us to join him there.

I contrived, as I usually do, to sit next to him. This is not now, as it
was in my early, skeptical days, to watch closely for any sleight-of-hand,
but simply for the pleasure of being as near to him as possible. The other
men sat in line to my left, while the ladies crowded in front of us, with
their eyes fastened on Swami's face.

As usual the room was bare of furniture, except for an armchair,
standing in a corner. Swami began by inviting questions on spiritual subjects. Someone asked about "love," and he explained that real love is
innate in everyone; it arises from the Divine Center in every person. You
can think of it as being like a cloth with its threads going out to wife,
husband, children, parents. If the threads are centralized through the Love
of God, they will spread out to reach, not only members of your own
family but also members of the whole human family and, indeed, to all
life.

I noticed that the eyes of many of the ladies were moist, maybe
from the timbre of tenderness in Swami's voice. Then he stopped talking
about love, and suddenly turning to me, said: "Give me that ring."

He referred to the ring he had materialized for me years before, at
my first interview with him at Prasanti Nilayam, a beautiful ring of panchaloha — the sacred five-metal alloy — with Shirdi Sai embossed in gold

on it. I had worn it constantly through the years.

As I pulled it off my finger, he remarked: "It's too tight now." Then, holding it up to look at the circle that had bent with time and use, he smiled, and commented: "More like a chapatti."

Everyone laughed but me. I was becoming afraid that he might take the ring from me.

"But I like it, Swami."

"You need a new one," he said emphatically. Then holding it in his closed hand, a few inches from his mouth, he blew on it once.

The eyes of the ladies popped as he opened his hand and a new, broad, shining ring lay there. Now, instead of Shirdi Sai in gold, it bore a large colored picture of Satya Sai on a sky-blue background. It was certainly a gorgeous, impressive ring. But I mourned the one that had vanished somewhere into thin air.

"It's of different metal," I complained, as I put it on my finger.

"No, the same – panchaloha," he said.

When we went outside, the conspicuous ring on my finger was quickly spotted by friends, and the story of its origin went crackling around the ashram like fire through dry grass.

Back in our rooms I sat thinking about the phenomenon; the old ring had been a symbol of something. When I had received it, I realized that Swami knew of my love for the old Shirdi form, born in my heart before I had even heard of Satya Sai. On that same far-off, memorable day Swami had struck the dry rock that I used to call my heart, and something that felt like a warm fluid gushed forth to flood my being. Hitherto, my search for spiritual truth had been an intellectual affair. But on that day Swami had opened my heart, changing my life. The ring had been a reminder and symbol of that wonderful occasion.

But perhaps I had grown too attached to the material sign. Perhaps I was now beginning on a new phase. All I was sure of was that Swami knew more of my inner life than I did, myself. I began to like this large, attractive picture of Baba, adorning my hand.

The next day he called us to another group interview. Some of the same people, and some new ones, were there on the floor around him. He began by talking about the eternal, spiritual religion of the heart that knows no barriers of creed, caste or color. Someone asked about the meaning of the symbol of the cross. Swami had his own unique interpretation. The upright post of the cross stands for the 'I,' the personal ego, he said; the cross-beam represents the crossing out of the ego. This crucifixion of the ego brings suffering until the true Self, the Divine Spirit within, rises from the tomb of the old self. The aim of all religions is to crucify man's false ego. Only when this happens, and the inner God reigns in the heart, can there be true brotherhood and peace.

I had often listened to his figurative explanations of the great Truths, but one can't be reminded of them too often, especially while basking in the sunshine of his presence. Only by experiencing the enigma of Baba can we begin to know him, and only to the extent that we know him, do we know our own deep, inner Selves.

After a while he stopped talking, looked lovingly around the group, waved his hand in the well known circular gesture, and produced a large handful of sweets. As usual the product was warm, as if brought straight from his akashic oven, and as usual there was ample for everyone.

Then he looked at me, in my usual place by his side and said: "That ring doesn't fit you well; it's too big."

It was, in fact, a little loose on the third finger where I was wearing it.

"It fits the middle finger well, though, Swami," I answered quickly, slipping it onto that finger to demonstrate.

"No — that's not the correct finger! Give it to me." I handed it to him, hoping that he would merely shrink it — as he has been known to do. I had already become rather fond of this big, bright ring.

"Would you like gold or silver?" he asked.

"I want your picture, Swamiji."

"Yes — but gold or silver?"

"Gold."

The sea of eyes in front were fastened on him eagerly as he went through the same ritual of holding the ring in his lightly closed hand and blowing into the hand. There were not more than three seconds from the time he closed his hand till he opened it again, but the change was fantastic. In place of the bulky ring, now lying in his palm was a gold ring, modest in size, but shining with the nine sacred stones of India, encircling an oval colored picture of Swami. The sacred stones are named by Indian jewellers as, emerald, diamond, pearl, white sapphire, ruby, coral, cat's-eye, blue sapphire and gomedak. The picture of Baba was smaller this time, and the stones were small, but the ring had an exquisite, glistening, delicate beauty.

When he saw that it fitted my finger neatly, Swami seemed satisfied. The group had enjoyed the excitement of watching his creative hand ringing the changes on the rings, and the ashram later enjoyed the serialized story of the miracle play. I, myself, hoped that Swami would let me keep this last beautiful production.

Our time was getting short and Baba was, in his infinite grace, favoring us with many interviews. At one of them in the last days, with only Iris, Dr. Gokak and myself present, I asked him the meaning of the perfumed leaves that I had found in my bed. Why had he chosen to send leaves, and not something else, to greet, cheer and bless us some months earlier, in Madras?

Leaves, he explained, have many important spiritual associations. They were used by the ancient rishis in their forest hermitages, and they played a part in some great sacred events of scriptural times. The lives of an individual, Swami went on, are as numerous as the leaves of a tree. Leaves that are plucked, or have fallen, represent the lives that have been lived already. The last incarnations, as a man reaches his journey's end, should be perfumed with holiness, as symbolized by the perfume on the leaves.

In more detail and more precisely, Baba related the leaf phenomenon of Madras to our own lives, but that is too personal to write about.

There were events in the past that made me think Baba attached some other occult significance to leaves. I had thought, in my early Sai days, that the devotees put garlands of fresh mango leaves above Swami's doorways to celebrate his return home. But when we were living for a few weeks at "Brindavan" in 1968, and Swami himself was at Prasanti Nilayam, I observed that the caretaker, Sri Rambrahma, hung garlands of fresh mango leaves over the outside doorways each morning. Asked why, he said that Swami had instructed him to do so, regularly without fail.

The last days of our sojourn in the world of Sai Power and Love were drawing to a close. Some of the new friends we had made at the ashram had already left, but some were still there, gathering daily in the semi-circle before the Mandir. Coralie Leyland still limped here and there, happily. Asked about her health, she would raise the bad arm above her head to show that it was improving. She was delighted because she had been promised a job in India, supervising in a cheese factory in Bangalore. This would enable her to see Baba often.

Jon Gilbert, a young New Yorker, still sat in the darshan line resignedly. Jon had incurable Hodgkin's disease (a progressive malignant condition of the reticulo-endothelial cells). As a last hope for a miracle-cure, he had come to Baba. When I first met him, Jon had already been some months at the ashram, sitting daily, usually in the front line of men, making sure of Swami's darshan, and hoping for an interview.

But there had been no interview. Swami would look into his eyes, sometimes smile, sometimes speak a few loving words; occasionally produce some vibhuti for him to eat.

Talking to the pale young man whenever opportunity offered, I found that — at the mental level — he had no faith or belief in a miracle-cure. He had resigned himself to death. I tried hard to make him appreciate that nothing was impossible to God, that the higher law of Divine Spirit had on many occasions refuted the material laws and facts of medical science. He *could* be cured, I assured him, but he had to play his part by opening himself with love and faith to the flow of Divine Grace. But my words seemed of no avail. His intellect found reasons to question, to doubt.

"But it has been well worth coming here," he said. "Back in New York I used to resent terribly the idea of dying so young. But here, something has happened. I have no fear or anger about dying now. I've accepted it."

Dr. K. C. Pani of Washington, D. C., who was at the ashram, also talked to Jon Gilbert and finally gave him a medical examination. The doctor, deciding that Swami, for reasons of his own, was evidently not going to cure Jon Gilbert, went to him and said: "Swami, I have examined Jon Gilbert and give him only another ten days to live. I would like to have him admitted into hospital in Bangalore, if you agree."

In his own inscrutable way Baba agreed to this move. Howard Levin decided to go with Jon in the taxi, and stay in Bangalore as long as necessary to give the dying man any help he could. Dr. Pani went with them, too — on the way back to America.

The sun was shining with mocking brightness on the morning we went sadly to our last interview. Several others, who were leaving the ashram, were present. Soon, after some general talk, Swami took each person in turn into a private enclosure, screened by curtains. The others left behind in the room can hear only a muffled murmur from behind the curtains. What takes place there is personal, between Baba and the devotees concerned. They come out with eyes shining or wet or both, and with a bloom of joy on their faces. But their experience there will not be put into words; indeed, it cannot be.

Of our own behind-the-curtain experience I can only speak in general terms, leaving out the personal aspects and the indescribable overtones. We were, of course, no longer surprised to see farewell gifts sliding into Baba's hands, coming from somewhere outside this three-dimensional world of the five senses, proving the limitations of those senses, and the mortal mind behind them. But we were ineffably happy in the flow of

Love that came with the gifts.

One gift was a circular container, seven cm. in diameter by three cm. high. Iris saw it coming into the world – half of it first, and then the whole of it, just as one might see a package coming in through a letter slot in a door. I, myself, did not see it until it was wholly there in Swami's small hand. Then he removed the lid, and we were enveloped by a heavenly fragrance from the light-grey, fluffy vibhuti that filled and overflowed the container. He gave us instructions about how to use the vibhuti, daily, in the future.

Our hearts were warmed by his loving concern for our welfare. He gave us directions on our work in the world, our lives, and our spiritual exercises. Such directions are always individual, applying only to the persons concerned.

His general spiritual teachings are expounded in his talks to groups and crowds. These apply to all. But for each individual there is an *upadesh*, a spiritual guidance, that fits the disciple's particular stage of development, temperament and background. Every individual has his special spiritual work and sadhana to follow. To speak or write of such *upadesh* might mislead others for whom it is not suitable.

"Remember, wherever you are I am always with you," he assured us. He has often used these words before, to us and to others, and by now we know that they are not just words of consolation to relieve the sorrow of parting. They state a reality.

"You are always in our hearts, Swami," I agreed.

"Not only in your hearts but in every cell, right through you – above, before, behind and all around you." He spoke with tender but powerful assurance.

I have thought a great deal about this great Truth that Sai Baba enunciates, as other Avatars have done before him. It does not, of course, mean that he is *always* with all of us in a subtle body, in the way, for instance, that he showed himself to Walter Cowan in Orange County and to others in other places.

The Form may be there at times, but when he says, "I am with you always" he refers to the formless, all-pervading Spirit, which is the ultimate state of Divinity. When Jesus was taking His Form away from the sight of his disciples, He told them He would send the Holy Spirit, the formless God, to be with them till the end of time. Baba expresses the same Truth, for He, himself, is that formless divine Spirit much more than he is the little red-robed figure that moves about the grounds of Prasanti Nilayam and "Brindavan."

So, being one with the Divine Consciousness, he is always with us, and can tune his own individual consciousness into our daily thinking whenever he wishes, just as we select a particular radio station by pressing a switch. What causes him to tune-in to a devotee or group of devotees at a particular time?

"Wherever and whenever you think of me, I shall be with you," he has often said; and "Whenever you call to me, I shall respond." Every devotee has a direct, "hot line" to the Avatar, and can call whenever he wishes. The answer, the Divine help comes — sometimes even before the devotee has called.

Our hearts warmed by his blessings, we left the interview room, but for me it was not quite the end. Swami said we should not leave until afternoon, and I was able to go up to his bedroom, and spend about half-an-hour with him after lunch. As it was a rule that ladies did not visit this room, Iris was not able to go. Only a retired judge and I were there, sitting on floor mats in front of Swami.

Baba, himself, was sitting on a couch, identical to the two in the rooms we were just vacating. He was going through a pile of correspondence, and reports on his college students. The judge had some personal and family questions to ask, and Baba's replies brought tears of joy to the old man's eyes. I, myself, had no more personal questions to ask, and was completely happy just to sit there at the Lord's feet, while eternity shone sweetly through the thin fabric of time.

The room was bare, except for the couch. "Where do you sleep, Swami?" I asked.

"Sleep? This is my bed," he smiled, patting the couch. Though not as narrow and hard as the suspended plank he used to sleep on when in the Shirdi body, it was austere enough, I thought. But Swami has never shown interest in luxurious comfort, though devotees have tried to provide it for him. I remember, for instance, the comfortable, air-conditioned room that Mr. V. Hanumantha Rao had constructed for Swami in his new Madras home. One day after lunch there, Baba invited me up to the special room for a siesta with him. While Raja Reddy, one or two others, and I lay down to sleep on soft mats on the floor, Swami sat on his bed. I did not see him lie down, and when I awoke from my siesta, he had gone. I do not think he slept at all.

Once, on a hot night in Hyderabad, Swami had his bed taken onto the flat roof of the house where we were all staying. The devotees slept there too, around Swami. In the middle of the night a few drops of rain awoke my wife and sent her downstairs to find a waterproof cover. When she passed by Swami's bed, she saw that he was sitting up in a cross-legged position on the bed. He did not speak, and she thought he might be in some kind of Samadhi. But next morning he asked her if she had been unable to sleep, showing that he had seen her movements.

"Sleep never overpowers an Incarnation of God," writes Swami Ramakrishnananda, disciple of Sri Ramakrishna. "He sleeps only when He wills." And any sleep He might have is not the same as ours. "He has mastery over his mind when He is dreaming, and He has mastery over his consciousness in deep sleep."

I have, personally, never found anyone who has ever seen Baba asleep.

At last Swami stood up and said it was the right time for us to leave. I kissed his hand. We both touched his feet, the Hindu gesture of reverence and devotion. He patted us lovingly, and we stumbled down the winding stairs to the waiting car – in which the judge was also travelling to White-field.

As we left the ashram and threaded through the hills of polished stone, the outside world seemed no more than the fabric of a dream. And, indeed, what else is it but a mayavic dream compared with the divine eternal world that casts its aura over Prasanti Nilayam!

One day in Bangalore, before taking plane to Australia, we called to see some American friends at a hotel run by a Sai devotee. Many western-ers, on their pilgrimage to Whitefield and Prasanti Nilayam, stay there. We were surprised to find Jon Gilbert among them.

Sitting together out in the garden, Jon told us that he could not bear being in the hospital, and after a few days, he had come to stay at the hotel. He made it clear to Howard Levin that he preferred to be alone, so Howard had left, and Dr. Pani had returned to America. Jon evidently had no plans for the future, whatever small future there was left to him. He was simply living each day, as it came, and found the hotel a more pleasant place than the hospital for this purpose.

Handing him our Australian address, I said: "When the Divine Power heals you, write to me, Jon. You'll be top of the miracle list for the year."

He smiled wanly. "*If* I'm cured, I will certainly write and tell you all about it." I could see that he did not expect to be putting pen to paper.

No letter ever came, and no one we knew in Australia, or California, seemed to have any information about Jon. We often thought of him and wondered, but as the months passed in silence, we assumed that he had died there in Bangalore as decreed by the facts of physiology and the material laws of nature.

Man is the Divine poured into the human mould, just as everything else, alive or inert, is; but it is the privilege of man, alone, to be able to become aware of this precious truth. This is the message of the Upanishads to man. The same message is echoed by the scriptures, and the declarations of countless saints.

SATYA SAI BABA

25
SIGNS
IN AMERICA

Throughout all generations both before and after the Christian era, The Christ, as the spiritual idea — the reflection of God — has come with some measure of power and grace to all prepared to receive Christ, Truth.
MARY BAKER EDDY

During the year after we left India my wife and I were able to make a trip to America. From Los Angeles, California, an old friend drove us up the coast road to the sunny valley of Ojai. This place has some interesting spiritual associations. According to Mary Lutyens' book* J. Krishnamurti went through a severe psycho-physiological process towards Enlightenment or Self-realization under a pepper tree at Pine Cottage, Pine Lane, while he and his brother were living in this lovely valley.

His brother Nitya wrote, soon after they first went there: "Our valley lies happily, unknown and forgotten, for a road wanders in but knows no way out. The American Indians called this valley the Ojai, or the nest, and for centuries they must have sought it as a refuge."

Krishnamurti, himself, once wrote, after heavy rain, "the green of England is nothing compared with this . . . this is a truly wonderful country."

Dr. Annie Besant was caught in the spell of the valley's beauty and peace, and bought acres there for a trust called The Happy Valley Foundation. This was to be for work connected with Krishnamurti's mission, including the establishment of a school, known as The Happy Valley School. At Ojai, today, there is also a theosophical colony, called Krotona.

In a cottage standing in a garden we met Dr. Benito Reyes. We sat in his lounge, facing a large portrait of Satya Sai Baba and learned some interesting things. The first was that his dream had come true — his Institute of

Avasthology had become The World University in Ojai, of which he was President. He was also Chairman of the World Congress of University Presidents being held in Boston a few days later. He was presenting a paper on his ideas for spiritual education to that meeting, and afterwards going on to India to see Sai Baba again.

After approving my account of his lecture and experiences with Baba (as given in Chapter 19), he related a recent miraculous story which he said I could use. I give it here.

One day the doctor and his wife went out in a car with two friends, leaving no one at home at their cottage. When all returned in the evening, unlocked the front door and entered, they found the whole house filled with what looked like grey smoke. They ran into all the rooms, searching urgently for the source of the fire. None could be found. But now the "smoke" was settling, making a thin film on floor and furniture. In the bathroom, where the grey deposit had covered the bath and tiles, Dr. Reyes ran his finger over the surface, gathering some of the deposit. He smelled it; he put some on the tip of his tongue. In smell and taste and appearance, it was Baba's vibhuti! The others also tested it in the same way, and came to the same conclusion.

Dr. and Mrs. Reyes were very thrilled. In fact, they felt quite awed and overcome with the stupendous phenomenon. But why had Baba filled their house with a cloud of vibhuti? The doctor searched his mind for a reason. Then he remembered two things. First, some days earlier a little vibhuti had appeared on one of his pictures of Baba. He had been delighted and grateful, but had said, mentally, "Please give me a whole lot of vibhuti, Swami, so that I can share it with my students and friends." Second, in India on their first visit Swami had said to him: "Whatever you ask me with your mind, I will grant."

I thought, myself, that, as well as the wonder of it all, there was a touch of typical Sai humor in startling the good doctor with a house full of vibhuti in answer to his mental prayer for more.

Dr. Reyes suggested we confirm this story with the two people who had taken him out in their car, and returned to the house to see the cloud of ash with the taste and smell of Baba's vibhuti. They were, he said, Douglas and Marybeth Mahr. She was an astrological writer and lecturer at the World University in Ojai and he a business man and publisher, giving much financial support to the university.

A day or two later we dined with Mr. and Mrs. Mahr in Encino, California, and thus found two new, delightful Sai friends. They confirmed in all details the doctor's vibhuti story; then, at our request, told us about how they, themselves, had come to Sai Baba, and what it had meant to them. Like all Sai stories, it was unique.

Back in 1973 the couple had reached a crisis and a turning-point in their lives. Doug was in the real estate business and things had not been going well. In fact, though he lived in an expensive house in the hills above Los Angeles, and drove the latest model Cadillac, as he put it, "I was down to my last nickel and tremendously in debt to the tune of some $20,000. Our house was in foreclosure; we were very depressed."

As the scriptures say, "Man's extremity is God's opportunity." At this time Marybeth began looking for a new spiritual teacher and having "visions" about one. Her former teacher — an Archbishop of the Catholic Church — had passed away. Her spiritual hunt took them to Krotona where they heard a lecture by Dr. Reyes. Marybeth immediately recognized him as her next teacher.

Now the couple began going up to stay in Ojai every weekend and in conversations Dr. Reyes mentioned his dream of establishing a college for teaching the deeper spiritual truths. Both the Mahrs were thrilled with the idea.

Soon afterwards the Reyes couple made their historic first trip to see Baba. When they returned, they were, Marybeth said, "both radiating like suns." They had wonderful stories to tell — tales of a man with powers and love like Christ.

"We felt very close to Dr. and Mrs. Reyes." Doug explained, "so we believed their fantastic stories. We went to the Sai Baba Center in Hollywood and saw a film on Baba, then we read your book and other books. We started to meditate on Baba, to sing bhajans, to study his teachings. We longed to go see him, but we had no money — only big debts!"

After getting in touch with Baba on the inner plane through meditation and yearning for him, Doug formed a new philosophy towards money, status, and life-style. "I began thinking along the lines of doing something good for humanity instead of myself. I changed my attitudes and method of work; instead of selling properties, I began to represent investors. The most important thing was: I decided on a program of giving away time and money to worthy causes — like this project for a spiritual college dedicated to the uplifting of humanity to a more loving state of consciousness."

After he had made this great decision, the money began to roll in, and Doug was able to pay off his debts as well as helping, financially, the birth of the new university in Ojai. As finances improved, the trip to India to see Sai Baba began to look like a possibility. "One day," Doug said, "a business phone call brought us in a couple of extra thousand dollars, and we decided to go to India. We were lucky; Indra Devi was taking a party of about a dozen people over to see Baba, and we joined the group."

Neither of them had been in the East before and their exposure to India was a great cultural shock, — its material poverty and spiritual wealth bringing them, Doug said, an experience of "the agony and the ecstasy."

Marybeth described her first sight of Baba as a shock, too. She had seen photos and films of him, but these did not do him justice. "He was so beautiful, so delicate; he seemed to float. I thought 'I will be able to judge his spiritual stature by looking in his eyes.'

"He floated towards me and stood there, looking into my eyes. Then I knew that he knew everything about me, and there was nothing I could do about it. But I didn't mind; he was so full of love."

They experienced and witnessed miraculous events, and heard of many others. But I will tell here only one such experience that each had.

"In our first interview," Marybeth said, "I saw Swami produce vibhuti and start to distribute it to all in the group. I had been thinking that all I wanted was spiritual advancement, but I held my hand out like all the others. Swami touched me on the forehead, and passed me by, not giving me any vibhuti. Then, back in his seat, he looked at me and said: 'Oh, would you like some vibhuti too?'

"When I said, 'Yes, please,' he came and put his hand down towards my outstretched palm. Then I saw the vibhuti coming out of his finger-tips in little soft puffs, and falling into my hand. I just sat and stared at it. Swami said: 'Eat, eat!'

"Later in the interview, during his spiritual talk, someone asked Baba a question, to which he replied, 'We create our own world, ourselves. The real world is within us; that is the spiritual, Divine World. Nothing else really exists.'

"I had heard this teaching before, in other or similar words, and accepted it philosophically. But now it was not as if I understood it with my mind, but actually experienced it within myself. I realized it, for a moment, in a way deeper than mental understanding. Then I really knew the Truth of it.

"Also, while with Baba, I understood the deep truth of what Dr. Gokak once said: 'In Swami you recognize your real Self. Then come the tears of self-recognition — tears of joy and gladness that you have found your long-lost Self."

Doug said: "I had always felt that there must be more in life than making a million bucks, that you can't take with you, anyway. Surely the accumulation of power, status, prestige, fortunes and other worldly items isn't the answer. One has to develop one's inner spirituality.

"When I met Baba, I knew that he was the key to the right way of life. I had been worried about the Indian scene — the terrible poverty compared with our own land of plenty. I wanted to do something to help, but it was such a huge problem! Basically the trouble was man's ignorance, greed, refusal to share with his brothers. So the foundation for a world change was a deep spiritual understanding in man — in enough people. This was what Swami was trying to bring about — the new world order he had come to establish. It was the only worthwhile work. How could I best help him?

"I was thinking along these lines during a group interview. While enjoying the ecstasy of Baba's presence, I was remembering the agony of the world. Swami was talking earnestly to some other people at the time. Suddenly he stopped talking, turned towards me and said: 'This will help you carry out the work you're thinking about.' He waved his down-turned hand in a few circles and materialized a small copper disk. Handing this to me, he said: 'Put it in your wallet and carry it with you always. It will provide you with all the money you need if you use it for humanitarian purposes.'

"All at once, my heart, my soul, my body were filled with Baba's pure selfless love. I heaved a huge sigh and verbalized a faint, inadequate, 'Thank you.' It is in these moments that we realize the magnificence of Baba — his totally unselfish love for all of us. At that moment I was sitting before God incarnate — and I realized it for an instant. What an incredible thing it was.

"When we returned to America, I found that my partner had negotiated some big deals, and the money started pouring in — like Baba's unending stream of vibhuti. It was his gift, his blessings, anyhow, and I gave as much as possible back to his work — towards the establishment of the spiritual college at Ojai, for instance."

Money, in this modern age, is an instrument of power. I think it was Sri Aurobindo who said that it had been in the wrong hands so far, but now it must be put into the right hands, so that the Kingdom of God may be established on earth. It seemed to me that Doug Mahr was one of the channels Baba was using to bring some of the money into the right hands for the spread of spiritual understanding, and the expansion of consciousness.*

California, we found, was still performing well as the potential cradle of the new race of higher consciousness — as the prophecies of some great occultists have foretold. Though Baba has not been to America, yet, he sent Dr. V. Gokak as his envoy at the end of 1974. On our visit to California in 1973, we found that the Satya Sai Centers had grown in number, in size and activities since we left in late 1971.

In Honolulu we had a warm welcome from architect Steve Au and his wife, Irene. They had both lived for months at "Brindavan," where Steve did some work for Baba on the design of the permanent building for the Sai College at Whitefield. He had also constructed the friendly interior decor of the apartment where we lived, with its window opening on Baba's Summer Course for Indian culture and spirituality.

The Sai Family in Hawaii had grown, too, since our last visit four years earlier, and now spread over several islands. It was in this luminous land of the gods that we heard another remarkable story.

Back in India in the late 'sixties we had known John Worldie, a lovable character known generally as Big John. There were tales among his young American contemporaries about the wild life he had lived before he came to Baba and saw the Light. When we first met Big John he was already a devoted disciple whose only desire seemed to be to carry out the Lord's Will. He was also a keen amateur photographer producing work of professional standard. He left India before our own departure in 1970.

One sunny morning in Honolulu Big John came to see us at Steve's house, carrying a large rolled photographic print. But he would not unroll it until he told his story. It seems that during a recent year he had returned to India for the great Mahasivarathri Festival. He was, as usual, armed with a high-grade camera and intent on getting some good portraits of Baba. This is how he tells the story.

"On the morning of the festival at Prasanti Nilayam, I was following Swami around trying to take a picture. He was moving about here and there in the crowd, very busy. Every time I held the camera in front of him, he put up his hand in the 'Stop' gesture, and said: 'Not *now*, not *now*!' Anyway, I kept trying.

"In the afternoon the crowd was thicker so, to watch Baba's movements better, I sat up on the platform of that open rotunda — you know, where he produces the lingam. What's the name of it?"

"Shanti Vedika."

"Yes, right. Well, it was hot and I was feeling drowsy; but I woke up with a start when I saw Swami coming from the direction of the Mandir. There were several men with him and they came my way. When he was a few yards off, Swami stopped, faced me, and called, 'Now!' — like an order it was.

"I scrambled to my feet, to a squatting position, and took a picture of him. As I clicked, I felt a tremendous power, like a strong current, coming from Baba, and I fell over backwards onto the floor of the Shanti Vedika. For a moment I seemed to go unconscious, but I had the sense to hold the camera up high in my hand as I fell, and no damage was done.

"My unconsciousness must have only lasted a second because the people around, who had seen me fall, were still laughing when I got up. Swami had left, and I left, too. Later when I developed the film and made a color print, back in America, do you know what I found? Well, I'll show you the picture."

He unrolled the print which was about twenty by fifteen inches in size. It was a good head-and-shoulders portrait of Baba, with a half-smile on his lips and a look of power in his eyes. Starting about the middle of his left eyebrow was a thin, curved blue line leading to the space between his eyes. And there, in outline but quite clear, was the third eye — the eye of Siva.

Sai Baba — considered an incarnation of Shiva-Shakti — had on the day of Siva's great festival, revealed his third eye through the lens of Big John's camera. I could see that John was still awed by the phenomenon, and I, myself, felt the same way.

"The blue line is not a fault on the film," John told us. "You can see nothing there on the film. But it came out on the three prints I made. It's sort of like a pointer to the third eye. I'm not going to make any more prints of this portrait. It's too special. But this one is for you."

Iris and I were more than thrilled. We are still wondering what we did to deserve such an honor from Big John, the disciple about whom there is a mellowness and a mystery that seem to belong to some far-off background — perhaps to a former life that only Sai Baba knows about.

The rare photograph of Swami, showing his third eye, hangs on the wall of my study as I write these lines.

It is good to be born in a church, but it is not good to die in it. Grow and rescue yourselves from the limits and regulations, the doctrines, that fence in your freedom of thought, the ceremonials and rites that restrict and direct. Reach the point where churches do not matter, where all roads end, from where all roads run.

Pardon the other man's faults but deal harshly with your own.

SATYA SAI BABA

26
THE GOAL
AND THE WAY

*For even the immortals when they put on mortal-
ity are but a little part of themselves, a spark in the
immensity of their own fiery being.*

A. E.

"What is Sai Baba trying to do?" a New York publisher asked me,
expecting, I felt, a quick, brief answer.

A brief answer is difficult, but, if I can mentally stand back and take
a look at the situation – at Baba and the world as I see it today – perhaps
I can offer a few thoughts about Baba's mission to our troubled times.

Before I met him I had heard the Perennial Philosophy brilliantly
expounded by great spiritual teachers at many ashrams throughout India.
Inspiring words they were, opening windows on new worlds. But words
though they weave a web of noble theory and thought, always leave one
searching for more.

When I encountered Baba, I found that he not only taught the same
eternal verities, in his own unique way, but through his life and actions,
demonstrated the truth of the teachings. The truth became a reality
beyond words.

I am not referring only to the miracles, though these, themselves,
disclose the reality of the Indian spiritual philosophy. Sai Baba had been
born with the powers he reveals. The philosophy teaches that when a
human being reaches his true goal and becomes identified with the Godhead, he need be reborn no more. Yet sometimes from the Godhead comes
One to live a life on earth to help man extricate himself from a dangerous
situation into which his ignorance and lower nature have led him. The
incarnation is voluntary, the only motive being Divine Love for mankind.
And in the life of the great Volunteer those powers over nature that are

normal to him, but miraculous to us, will be constantly apparent.

"The miracle has the characteristic of conveying to us something about God: it is a form of His self-disclosure," writes philosopher Ninian Smart. Was I then, I asked myself, in the presence of a Divine One, an Avatar?

Part of the same philosophy, however, is that certain disciplines, austerities and mantric practices can develop supernormal powers in an individual who is still at the level of selfish human desires. The powers will, in such cases, almost certainly be used for selfish, or even criminal, aims, and what is termed "black magic" ensues.

But such powers are always limited, and after a period of misuse they usually weaken and vanish. I have talked with people who have been witnessing Baba's powers since his youth, and now, after half a century his dominion over nature shows no signs of vanishing. His powers are as copious and constant as ever.

Apart from this, it did not take me long to discern that the supernormal powers were never used for selfish reasons. Always there was Love shining through the miracle – the Love that wants to bring joy, build faith, foster understanding of the great truths, and bring more and more people into the fold of Divine Life.

From early morning until late at night, every moment of Sai Baba's day gleams with an altruistic love of man. He is always offering joy, happiness, understanding, contentment – to an individual, to a small group or to a crowd. If not occupied with these activities, he is supervising the construction of accommodations for his devotees, or working on the educational organization through which he plans to spiritualize the new generations in special colleges throughout India – and now taking root abroad. His dedication and colossal energy are themselves superhuman.

What is Sai Baba trying to do? Spending time with him, one realizes that all his efforts are aimed towards one goal: to raise human consciousness to a new level, lifting mankind above the mire of ignorant selfishness, setting up a vision and understanding that will revolutionize the human life-style.

What is his main message and method in striving towards this stupendous aim? Well, each one of us is searching for an identity. We may find it, temporarily, as a musician, a business man, a writer, a famous actress, a good mother, or in many other ways. But whatever the identity, the self-image, we are never completely satisfied with it – at least not for long.

The reason for human dissatisfaction about the worldly self-image is that we have not found our true identity. All we have found is a pleasing part to play in the cosmic drama we call life. The drama is a transient, passing show and the part we play in it even more transient.

Baba's main message is to remind us again and again, in all manner of ways, that our real identity is the Atman, which, in plain English, means the immortal Spirit. We are part and parcel of God, images of God, sons of God — as eternal as God, Himself. The temporary projection of ourselves into the world of matter, our bodies and minds, we have mistaken for our real Selves. Most of us live through our lives quite unaware of our true identity.

The sleeping dream is a useful analogy to life. In the dream, itself, everything seems quite real, and we are utterly identified with the dream-image of ourselves. Very rarely, we may become aware in the dream that we are dreaming, and have what the psychic researchers call a lucid dream. When this happens we can control with our wills the subsequent course of the dream.

Life can be likened to a long dream in which we mistake the mortal image of ourselves for our true Selves. And in a similar way, if we become aware that it is only a "dream," and move consciously into our true Selves beyond the dream, we become masters of that life-dream, instead of being its victims. Thus we attain liberation and freedom from its bondage.

The great truth about man's immortal identity has been taught before, of course, and every person can, through yoga paths, test and confirm it for himself, as did the ancient rishis, as do the modern yogis, seers and mystics. World scriptures show that it was taught by Krishna, the Buddha, and Jesus. But it was not emphasized so much as now.

In this age of sophistication it has been taught by spiritual leaders like Rama Krishna, Aurobindo and Ramana Maharshi to the disciples who gathered around them. And now, when communications have reached the electronic stage, it is being taught and emphasized by Satya Sai Baba to the multitudes.

Explanations, elucidations, living illustrations help us take a few steps towards the elusive goal of Self-identification, but so thick is the veil of *Maya* (illusion) around us that the sharp tools of yoga are essential for a break-through. All teachers, ancient or modern, even if they never use the word, yoga, use some of its tools. Every great master sharpens the tools for his own use, adapts them, and applies them in a unique way.

Sai Yoga is not quite the same as any other yoga ever taught. Yet in the main it can be called the *guru marga* (path), lying within the framework of the immemorial *bhakti* or devotional principles. This yoga asks for a one-pointed focus on the guru or spiritual preceptor, especially in the early stages. Diffusion of interest during the initial steps leads to confusion, while concentration and devotion towards the chosen leader, enables that leader to lift the pupil above the fog of mortal illusion.

Such exclusive direction of the disciple's attention and devotion towards the one chosen sadguru is surely what Lord Jesus meant when he said to his disciples: "No man cometh unto the Father (the Divine Principle) but by me" (the guru), and what Lord Krishna signified in many of his statements, including: "Those who worship and meditate on me with unswerving devotion I straightway deliver from the ocean of death-bound existence." When properly understood, as a principle of effective bhakti yoga, the doctrine is not narrow. It is like a man focusing his camera lens precisely on one object to the exclusion of others for better results.

Baba says, by way of analogy, that a fire on the end of an incense stick, for instance, will not set even dry wood alight. Whereas a forest fire will quickly consume even green or wet wood. Faith and understanding in the initial stages are like the glow on the end of the stick; they must be sheltered and protected. But when faith and spiritual understanding have reached the strength of a forest fire, they will absorb for their own purpose and progress the green wood of any diverse and seemingly contradictory teachings that are piled onto them.

"A devotee's heart must expand and his mind broaden." Baba says, "To have a narrow vision will prevent him spreading the Truth to the world." He says also that bhakti is the easiest and swiftest road to the goal in this Kali Age, and in this yoga each person should focus on the Divine Form his heart chooses, for there is only one supreme God, though His names and forms are many.

The Sai Path includes also the yoga of work done as worship, the yoga of wisdom through knowledge and discrimination, the yoga of self-enquiry, mind-control and meditation. These yogas are for preparing the soil and nurturing the plant. The real growth comes through the Divine Love and Grace that "droppeth as the gentle rain from heaven upon the earth beneath." Wherever the devotee may be, Sai Baba is there pouring his Grace into the spiritual buds that self-preparation and devotion have opened. "Only keep quiet and I will do the rest," he has often said.

Beyond the general principles that can be taught openly to many there is the individual, one-to-one relationship. This belongs and operates in the world beyond space and time, where the guru-disciple relationship really belongs. It is, of course, a help to experience Sai Baba's physical presence, but even so, many have found that a photograph, a packet of vibhuti, or just a word spoken by someone, is sufficient to trigger-off the devotion and the Sai Yoga process.

Indeed, some people have found it difficult to live physically close to Baba for long periods. The proximity will burn out the impurities that all of us have, and the "burning" is painful. Moreover, as Arjuna found with Krishna, the intimacy of living, day by day, close to an Avatar tends to obscure the Divine beneath the human aspects. "When you are away somewhere with him, and he pops into your room one morning to borrow your razor, it's hard to remember that he is God," one physically-close devotee put it.

Yet there must be the human side. To dive into the pool of physical matter to save us from drowning there, the Avatar needs must take a body. His body has to function according to the rules and requirements of physiology. It needs food, for instance, though, as Dr. S. Bhagavantam discovered, with the physicist's penchant for measuring, Baba does not consume enough calories to keep an ordinary man alive, let alone provide the energy for an Avatar's life-style. Still, Baba does eat.

From observation and enquiry, however, I am of the opinion that he does not sleep as we know sleep. He may go for a time into some altered state of consciousness to replenish his energies, but sleep does not overpower him as it overpowers us. The different states of consciousness required for his work on various planes, and for his rest, seem to be under the control of his will.

Those who follow the path of Sai Yoga are not encouraged to take the ochre robe. On the contrary, Baba encourages them to get married; he often finds them marriage partners, attends and blesses their weddings, and finds the right names for their children.

Reading minds and hearts as he does, Swami knows, I think, that few people are ready for the life of celibacy. Rather than dissipate their energies fighting the desires of the flesh, with all the psychological problems entailed, it is better to regulate the desires through marriage, better to live the life of a householder, the normal life of normal man.

Baba teaches that if there is devotion to God, life in the world can, itself, be used as an implement of Sai Yoga. The key to this lies in observing our motives. If the motive for our actions is for the good of mankind, for the glory of God, if we can remain detached from the results of our actions, if we can leave all to God's will, then the actions themselves become a yoga, helping us towards liberation. To the extent that our motives are self-centered, seeking gain or renown for ourselves, to that extent the actions bind us karmically to the earth.

Baba does not expect his devotees to reach this high ideal of pure, altruistic motivation immediately, but by striving towards it, by remembering, as he often says, that work is worship, they will be turning their daily lives into a course in yoga.

Will Sai Baba succeed in doing the great things he has come to do? Will he succeed in spiritualizing enough individuals to lead mankind in a new direction? Can he awaken enough people from the mortal dream of selfhood to their true identity — enough to spearhead a great change for the world? Ten good men could have saved the city of Sodom; how many will it take to save a world from destruction?

It is of the nature of Avatars to succeed in their mission. The Buddha turned Asia away from dark superstition, and raised its consciousness to higher levels. Jesus Christ brought a light that finally changed Western barbarism to the civilization of Christendom. Those two grand Avataric songs are still heard in the world, though growing somewhat faint with time.

But today the world may be a tougher proposition. The forces of ignorance, fear, hatred, violence are organized on a greater scale than they were when the Roman Empire was riding down the slippery trail to its doom, when a wave of barbarism engulfed the west, and a boy born in a manger at Bethlehem raised a timely torch of Truth. So, can a boy born in a humble home in remote Puttaparti turn back the greater tidal wave of darkness, and launch the kingdom of Divine Light on earth that Jesus prophesied and promised?

To the power of Divine Love nothing is impossible. One of India's greatest scholars and statesmen, Dr. R. R. Diwaker wrote at the time of Sai Baba's fiftieth birthday, "Once he was but a village urchin. Untaught, untutored, uncared for, he grew up in that little-known village, and grew from strength to strength, miracle to miracle, and today when we assemble from the four quarters of the globe to celebrate his fiftieth year, what do we find?" After outlining the wonders of the modern township of Prasanti Nilayam, "with great houses for thousands," that had grown up in the wilds, next door to Puttaparti, Dr. Diwaker writes of the mighty crowd, and of the variety of nationalities, vocations and religions represented: "Philosophers and politicians, legislators and educationalists, scientists and technologists . . . the ignorant as well as the learned, the rich as well as the poor, all have assembled in spite of inconveniences . . . in the name of Baba for the glorification of Satya, the Truth of Life . . .

"If Baba's capacity to weave the complex web of human hearts and minds from various countries and creeds, castes and communities, lineages and languages into a single Satya Sai spiritual family, is not to be termed a marvel and a living miracle, one would like to know what a marvel and a miracle is like."*

Jesus had only three years to strike the chord of a new age. Sai Baba has three lifetimes. He began his work quietly at the village of Shirdi in the latter half of last century. In 1918, when his fame was beginning to spread throughout India, he left his body, and returned to Incarnation eight years later at Puttaparti. Now his mission is gaining great momentum, but he does not expect to accomplish all his aims in this lifetime. After eventually leaving this present body, he says, he will return — again through the process of ordinary human birth — and continue his work under the name of Prema Sai.

Three successive births of an Avatar in a little over a century and a half! Are we then in the womb of a new age coming to birth? Considering all the conditions of today, it seems most likely. It seems to me that Sai Baba, with the helpers around him, in and out of the body, is composing a mighty Avataric symphony that will go echoing down the centuries ahead, changing the direction of history, raising humanity to wider mental horizons, beyond the blind, brutish struggle for survival that pertains today. If struggle there must be among men, to learn the lessons of earth's schoolhouse, it will be pitched on a higher level, where greater love and brotherhood provide the key-note.

Finally, I want to say that in these pages I have talked of only a few of the things I have experienced and heard, and that they, themselves, form but a tiny fraction of the marvels that take place around Sai Baba from day to day.

I said once that trying to speak about Baba is like trying to put the ocean into a jam jar. I still feel that way; and I have some idea of how St. John must have felt when he wrote, at the end of his Gospel: "Now there are many other things that Jesus did. If they were all written down one by one, I suppose that the whole world could not hold the books that would be written."

Your Reality is the Atma, a wave of the Paramatma. The one object of this human existence is to visualize that Reality, that Atma, that relationship between the wave and the sea. All other activities are trivial; you share them with birds and beasts. But this is the unique privilege of Man. He has clambered through all the levels of animality, all the steps on the ladder of evolution in order to inherit this high destiny. If all the years between birth and death are frittered away in seeking food and shelter, comfort and pleasure, as animals do, man is condemning himself to a further life-sentence.

SATYA SAI BABA

EPILOGUE

On a Thursday evening, late in October 1976, Iris and I attended one of Hilda Charlton's Sai Baba meetings in a great cathedral of New York. It was a supremely uplifting experience. When we arrived at about 6:30 p.m. some six or seven hundred people were there, singing the sacred songs of different religions as they sat on the floor around a flight of steps in the middle of the cathedral. On the top of the steps sat Hilda, and we were invited to join her there.

Then there were solos of sacred songs by young people, music, and group meditation; I gave a short talk about experiences with Sai Baba, and Hilda gave a moving address, chatty yet eloquent, on the subject of how to observe yourself and work on yourself. Her audience seemed to drink in every word eagerly.

Then came a healing session with the chanting of the sacred word, "Om." The air seemed to tingle with spiritual vibrations, and one felt that Powers from a higher region had made entrance.

Towards the end of the meeting, when Hilda was down among the people, bringing all her power to bear on the healing of individuals, a stranger walked up the steps and handed me a piece of paper. It was a short note, saying: "I have just heard that you are in New York. Would you please contact me." There was a phone number, and it was signed: "Jon Gilbert."

I could scarcely believe my eyes. That he was still alive seemed like the greatest miracle on that joy-filled evening. As soon as we got back to our hotel (about 11 p.m.) I phoned the number. Jon, himself, answered, his voice sounding positive and happy, very different from the flat, hopeless tones we had last heard in the garden in Bangalore.

Yes, he said, he had been kept alive by the Sai Power. Then he and his mother had gone back to see Swami just over two months ago and he was now cured. As Hilda was coming to the hotel for a farewell talk, and we were leaving New York at daybreak next morning, there was no opportunity to meet Jon, so he promised to write the details to us in a letter.

Three months later in Sydney we received his letter from Flushing, New York. Below are some extracts from it, revealing the great changes that had come to Jon's mind and body through the enigmatic, compassionate power of the shining figure in the orange robe:

"I was diagnosed as having Hodgkin's Disease cancer at the age of 22. Having been raised in a non-religious Jewish family, 'bad luck' was the only explanation available to me. I underwent radiation treatment, and later surgery.

"At this low point I felt the need to understand, philosophically and physiologically, what the heck was happening to me. I turned to eastern literature and found there a satisfying beauty and simplicity. Yet I still felt a deep thirst to know more of what life is about, and how I fitted into the scheme of things."

He describes in detail how he went to England to try acupuncture, how this was some help, but unable to cure him, and how the specialist, being a Theosophist, was able to nurture his spiritual enquiries.

He continues: "A homeopathic doctor I consulted in London suggested that my illness was spiritual in nature and, therefore, its cure should lie in that realm. He loaned me your book, *Sai Baba, Man of Miracles*, which I read with great skepticism. Yet I wanted very much to believe that such a Being could exist. Within a week of reading the book, I co-incidentally met two men, on separate occasions, who had just returned from Sai Baba's ashram. One, seeing the book, asked my opinion of Baba. I said that if he was, in fact, a Godman, I must see him immediately, since my condition was worsening. After hearing this man's personal experience with Baba, I booked my ticket the next day.

"In two weeks I was in Puttaparti, not knowing I would stay with Baba for eight months. At first I was amazed by the miracles — the vibhuti, photographs, rings, rosaries, and other things that he materializes. But I was upset because he did not pay immediate attention to me, since my 'big disease' was such a pressing matter. About a week later during darshan, he asked me how I was feeling. Before I could answer, he materialized vibhuti and told me to eat it. About every five weeks I got the same treatment.

"I had a lot of spare time to read his teachings in the published books. I discovered that questions I would have about health, every-day living and spiritual development would be answered within minutes of sitting down to read him. In one of his discourses he mentions that, since he knows everyone's past, he handles each differently; that his attention or inattention to an individual is meaningful and significant to their spiritual progress. Since I was receiving 'inattention,' I spent a great deal of time doing some serious introspection. I realized my illness was largely a result of my psychological negativity and unrest. Before meeting Baba my stark world-view perceived the negative things in life (war, poverty, disease) as outweighing the positive and good, such as love and peace. This attitude naturally filtered down into my personal life, making me a grumpy young man."

Jon then tells of an incident that took place in Bangalore soon after we had said goodbye to him there.

"The incident seemed to dramatize my negative outlook, and also point the way to its cure. As I was walking to a nearby clinic for a blood test, I noticed a crowd of people looking over a fence. I went to take a look, and saw a woman screaming hysterically and beating the ground; her infant son was lying naked and stiff next to a low, exposed water tank (in which he had obviously drowned). Death pervaded the atmosphere. Witnessing this brought my despairing attitudes to the surface. Here, I felt, is just one more example supporting my atheistic view of things. As I was about to walk away from the tragic scenario, the thought crossed my mind to close my eyes and talk to Sai Baba: 'O.K., Sai Baba,' I said, 'If you are who you say you are, let's see you save this kid's life!' I opened my eyes to a miracle. The child had started to breathe; the father quickly carried him to the clinic, where I was going. There, they drained the water from him. As he let out a healthy cry, my eyes were filled with healthy tears.

"After this incident, I realized that Baba was the 'living truth' my soul had been searching for. Feeling that I had enough to think about for a while, I asked Swami's permission to go home to New York. He gave it — and the cancer vanished.

"Nearly two years later, in August 1976, the symptoms showed up again. I felt I should see Baba before having any other treatment. My mother came with me on this three-weeks trip. Baba gave us an interview and confirmed that my cancer was largely due to my worrying, anxious, restless mind. He said I would be O.K. in three months.

"On introspection, back in New York, I saw that I had only been giving lip service to the two key spiritual principles — surrender and faith

— and not really practicing them in my life.

"I now have renewed faith that Swami is guiding us all along the best (not necessarily the *easiest*) course for our spiritual development, and that life, itself, seems to be the best possible testing ground. By the way, I'm no longer grumpy.

"Jai Sai Ram, Jon Gilbert."

Jon's letter seems to give the burden and refrain of what I have been trying to say throughout the book on the subject of Sai Baba's Divine healing. There must be an inner cure before a true outer cure is possible. To Jon came gradually the inner transformation, the surrender of his lower doubting self to the higher Self of Love and Faith, as represented and embodied by Sai Baba. If he can maintain that realization of Truth, that new positive attitude, I am sure that the disease can never again penetrate the bulwarks of his defenses.

SANSKRIT TERMS

AVATAR (or AVATARA): This word of Sanskrit origin is defined by the *Concise Oxford Dictionary* as, "a descent of deity to earth in incarnate form."

> According to theosophical thought, there is an *ascent* before the *descent*; the Avatar, himself, in remote ages climbed the evolutionary ladder to humanity and beyond, finally reaching union with the Godhead. His ascent was along the Bhakti Path, says Dr. Annie Besant, and after merging with the Divine Ground, he must "keep the center that he has built, even in the life of Ishvara (God), so that he may be able to draw the circumference once again around that center, in order that he may come forth as a manifestation of Ishvara, one with Him in knowledge, one with Him in power, the very Supreme Himself in earthly life."

> Bishop C. W. Leadbeater, the great seer, has this to say: "When the human kingdom is traversed, and man stands on the threshold of his superhuman life, a liberated spirit, seven paths open before him for his choosing. On one of these he may enter into the blissful omniscience and omnipotence of Nirvana, with activities far beyond our knowledge, to become, perchance, in some future world, an Avatar, a Divine Incarnation."

> If, as many Hindus think, the *descent* is by one of the highest Gods of Form, such as Vishnu or Siva, there was still, according to their own scriptures, an

earlier *ascent*. In the *Yoga Vasishtha*, Dr. A. Besant points out, there is "a clear statement that the Deities, as Mahadeva, Vishnu and Brahma, have all climbed upward to the mighty posts They hold."

Concerning the number of Avatars, the *Srimad Bhagavata* says: "Countless are the descents of the Lord. Of these some are major, like Rama and Krishna, but most are minor *amsas* (rays) from His supreme radiance."

The minor Avatars are great spiritual Teachers; the major are, in the words of Vivekananda, "The Teachers of all Teachers, the highest manifestation of God through man. We cannot see God except through them. We cannot help worshipping them; and, indeed, they are the only ones whom we are bound to worship."

The descending Divinity is not limited to taking only one Form at a time. When Vishnu assumed a body as Rama, the major Avatar, for instance, rays of his Divine Splendor were incarnated in Rama's three brothers, who were thus born as minor Avatars. And it should not be assumed that Avatars belong to remote times only. In letter number 13 of *The Mahatma Letters to A. P. Sinnett* Mahatma Morya wrote (sometime between 1881 and 1884): "Verily we have as yet some Avatars left to us on earth."

Perhaps, during every century, mankind is helped by one or more minor Avatars, but the time intervals between the major ones are measured by ages rather than centuries. In the *Bhagavad Gita* Krishna (God) says: "When goodness grows weak, when evil increases, I make myself a body. In every age I come back to deliver the holy, to destroy the sin of the sinner, to establish righteousness." Writes Theosophist, Bhagavan Das: "When the forces of evil have reached the end of their appointed time, come the history-making Avatars."

It would be quite wrong to think that such Great Ones should be easy to recognize. History and story show that very few of their contemporaries recognized, for instance, Lord Krishna, Lord Buddha or the Lord Christ as Avatars.

In the *Srimad Bhagavatam* the saintly Suta states: "Difficult indeed is it for the ignorant to understand the Avatar's glory and power. Only those, who with love and devotion, worship and meditate at the blessed Feet of a Divine Incarnation can realize the Truth."

ARATI: The waving of lights accompanied by a special song at the end of the bhajans.

ATMAN (or ATMA): The spiritual Self, the true identity of a human being. *Paramatman*, another name for Brahman, the Absolute or Supreme Reality.

AMRITA: Nectar of the gods, an ambrosial liquid sometimes materialized by Sai Baba.

AHIMSA: Non-injury, avoidance of violence, harmlessness.

AKASHA: Space. Ether as the subtlest form of matter from which all elements are made, and into which all are ultimately resolved. It permeates all grosser matter. Sometimes used synonymously with the ASTRAL LIGHT in which, it is said, all thoughts and actions on the physical and astral planes are recorded. These are called the *Akashic Records*.

BHAKTI: The yoga path in which single-minded devotion to God, in one's chosen Form, is given the main emphasis. The practice and development of Divine Love within the devotee is the means of liberation or salvation. A follower of Bhakti yoga is called a bhakta.

BHAJAN: Sacred song. The singing of songs in praise of God during group worship. Usually a leader sings a line or verse, which is then sung in chorus by the group.

DARSHAN: The word includes the seeing of holy persons, places and objects, all of which will bring great blessings to the viewer. "The saints purify you at sight," says the *Mahabharata*. People travel great distances just for the blessing of a sight of Sai Baba. If he looks into their eyes, the spiritual benefits are multiplied, they believe.

DHARMA: Righteousness; it signifies the inner law or principle of religion; it can also be used to mean duty and virtue. The *Sanathana Dharma* means the eternal spiritual verities, which have their fullest statement in the Hindu scriptures.

DASARA: Great Hindu Festival celebrating the victory of the

Goddess Durga over the demons, symbolizing the conquest of evil by the beneficent forces of Light.

GURU: Teacher, one who dispels darkness or ignorance. There are various classifications of Gurus. He who teaches about God, or *Sat*, is sometimes called a Sadguru. A *Paramguru* is one who looks after the entire welfare, secular and spiritual, of his disciple.

JNANA: The yoga path in which emphasis is laid on knowledge and discrimination, leading to wisdom, and the awareness of one's identity with the Divine. A *jnani* is one who follows this path. The word is also used to denote one who has reached awareness of his Divine identity.

JAPAM (or JAPA): The repetition of a name of God, either aloud, or silently. For this a 108-bead rosary called a *japamala* is often used.

JI: A syllable added to a word to denote respect, *e. g.* Swamiji, Babaji.

KARMA: The idea of karma is related to the idea of destiny, except that instead of being imposed by some unknown force, karma is created by ourselves through our past actions, either in this life or in former lives. According to this concept, all action has long-term moral as well as physical and mental effects. The long-term effects of our actions is our karma. The word also sometimes refers to the actions themselves as well as to their consequences that rebound on the doer.

LEELA (LILA): Divine play or sport, carrying the overtones of joy and spontaneity. The word is used to mean Divine miracles. But the whole of creation, being regarded as an inexplicable miracle, is sometimes called the Lord's leela.

MOKSHA: Liberation or final emancipation of the soul from bondage of the world, which is the goal of spiritual practice. *Mukti* has the same meaning.

MAYA: The Cosmic Illusion on account of which the One appears as the many. Also means the power of creation. Used to denote attachment and ignorance.

MARGA: Path, road, way, course.

MAHIMA: Superhuman power, miracle.

MANTRA: Sacred words or verse repeated during meditation.

NAGA: Name of fabulous serpents with human faces.

NAGAR-SANKEERTAN (SANKIRTAN): Bhajan singing by a group walking through the streets, usually in the early hours as dawn breaks.

OM (AUM): Sacred word of the Vedas, symbol of God and Brahman, the creative sound.

SHAKTI: The creative Divine Power; a name of the Divine Mother; the feminine aspect of a God, representing His power and energy.

SADHANA: Spiritual exercises and disciplines of all kinds, including meditation, self-observation, devotional practices, and repetition of the Name of God.

SAMSKARAS: The tendencies inherent from a previous birth.

SATSANG: Intercourse with, or being in the society of, good, spiritual people.

SIDDHI: Personal perfection entailing the acquisition of supernormal powers; the yogic powers acquired.

SIVA: One of the Triune Godhead of Hindu scriptures, the others being Vishnu and Brahma. The name is sometimes used for Mahadeva or Ishvara, the supreme manifested God.

SADHU: A holy man, generally used with reference to a monk.

SANYASI: A Hindu ascetic; one who has adopted the monastic, celibate life.

VIBHUTI: Some meanings given in the Sanskrit dictionary are: manifestation of might, power, magnificence, prosperity, wealth. It is the name given to the holy ash materialized by Sai Baba, but he says that it also means the power used to produce the ash. Used as a symbol, sacred ash signifies the destruction of material forms that hold back our progress towards the wealth of the Spirit.

UPADESA (UPADESH): Spiritual instruction.

PROPER NAMES

ARYAVARTA: Land of the Aryans, ancient name for India.

ARJUNA: One of the five Pandava brothers who were close friends of Krishna in the epic, *Ramayana*, and other ancient literature of India.

BRINDAVAN: Sai Baba's residence at Whitefield, named after the place where Krishna lived as a youth.

BHAGAVAD GITA: Meaning the "Song of God," this renowned scripture of India is part of the great epic *Mahabharata*. It contains the spiritual teachings given by Lord Krishna to Arjuna, and meant for all mankind.

BRAHMA SUTRAS: Sometimes called the *Vedanta-sutras*, this is a treatise written in aphorisms, called Sutras, meaning clues. It attempts to systematize the teachings of the *Upanishads*. Tradition ascribes the authorship to the great seer Vyasa who wrote the *Mahabharata*.

NARADA: The ancient rishi or seer who wrote the classic of bhakti yoga, called *Narada Bhakti Sutras*.

PUTTAPARTI: The remote village where Sai Baba was born, some hundred miles north of the city of Bangalore, but in the State of Andhra Pradesh.

PRASANTI NILAYAM: Meaning a place of great peace, this is the name of the ashram established by Sai Baba a few hundred yards from Puttaparti. It is now a township, with its own post office, situated in the Anantapur district in

	the State of Andhra Pradesh. Sai Baba spends most of his time here.
PATANJALI:	The name of the ancient sage who wrote the basic guide to raja yoga, known as *Patanjali's Yoga Sutras*.
UPANISHADS:	This word means sitting down near the Teacher, and implies an esoteric doctrine given only to those students who have been prepared for it. The *Upanishads* are part of the *Vedas*.
VEDAS:	The ancient scriptures of the Hindu religion. They are regarded as revelations to the great seers, owing their authority to no individual. There are four *Vedas*: the *Rig-Veda*, the *Yajur-Veda*, the *Soma-Veda* and the *Arthava-Veda*.
VEDANTA:	The word means the end, goal or gist of the *Vedas*. It is a system of spiritual philosophy based on the *Upanishads* and the *Brahma Sutras*.
WHITEFIELD:	A township about thirteen miles from the city of Bangalore.

REFERENCE NOTES

page 5:   Once when Baba was at Mysore city for the Deepavali Festival, his devotees back at Puttaparti saw a cobra coiled around the portrait of Baba which had been placed on a temporary shrine on the steps leading to the front door of the old Mandir. A pair of lamps burned day and night before the portrait. The cobra remained there several hours while the devotees sang bhajans, did puja to it, and placed bowls of milk before it; they regarded it as a vision of Naga and a darshan granted to them by Sai Baba. Finally, "the cobra slid down, and, within a yard or two, became invisible."

This kind of phenomena was also known to the devotees of Sai Baba during his former life at Shirdi.

See *Sathyam, Sivam, Sundaram* Vol. 1, pp. 72-73 by N. Kasturi, M. A. B. L.

page 18: See: *J. Krishnamurti, The Years of Awakening*, by Mary Lutyens (John Murray, 1975).

page 70: See: N. Kasturi, *Sathyam, Sivam, Sundaram*, Vol. 1, p. 56.

page 83: See: *J. Krishnamurti, The Years of Awakening*, by Mary Lutyens (John Murray, 1975), ch. 4.

page 89: Arnold Schulman, *Baba*, Viking Press, Inc. U.S.A., and MacMillan London Limited.

page 93: See: Howard Murphet, *Sai Baba, Man of Miracles* (Frederick Muller) Ch. 12, p. 127 *et. seq.*

page 96: See: Howard Murphet, *Sai Baba, Man of Miracles* (Frederick Muller).

page 143: From the Sanskrit *avasthos*, consciousness, and the Greek *logos, avasthology* means the science of consciousness.

page 165: See: Howard Murphet, *Sai Baba, Man of Miracles* (Frederick Muller, 1971) p. 184.

page 167: Vol. 71, Jan. 1977.

page 195: Mary Lutyens, *J. Krishnamurti, The Years of Awakening* (John Murray, London 1975).

page 199: Douglas and Marybeth Mahr have started a record company to promote contemporary spiritual music which they hope will help foster an awareness of the brotherhood of man.

page 209: *Sanathana Sarathi*, March, 1976.